# COMPUTING SKILLS FOR ECONOMISTS

*Economics students frequently receive limited formal instruction in the software used by professional economists. This text provides students with an excellent introduction to the "tools of the trade" for conducting analysis and producing articles and reports. The section on spreadsheets, in particular, introduces students to a number of useful techniques that they are unlikely to have learned from other classes. Economics faculty concerned about their students' computer literacy will want to take a close look at this text.*

Tod S. Porter, Professor and Chair,
Department of Economics, Youngstown State University

*A unique book, essential to any economist's toolkit. From the level of the absolute beginner, and in a very user-friendly style, it takes the reader step by step through the entire range of computing skills essential to the study of economics. The book answers innumerable questions and saves many hours otherwise typically squandered on "trial and error" methods of mastering software. Almost any economics student, whatever their level, will learn something new from this book.*

Geoff Renshaw,
Lecturer in Economics, University of Warwick

*This book is impressive for the comprehensiveness and clarity of its explanations of mainly Windows applications of personal computer research tools for economists. Its accessibility to those with diverse computer literacy will raise the bar of the skills instructors can reasonably expect of their students without sacrificing valuable class time or having to prepare elaborate handouts to level the playing field. Its extensive examples will teach students a good deal of economics as well as enriching their research abilities.*

Arnie Katz,
Economics Professor Emeritus, University of Pittsburgh

*A goldmine of skills for every aspiring economist. Something for everyone.*

Ron Shone,
Senior Lecturer in Economics, University of Stirling

# COMPUTING SKILLS FOR ECONOMISTS

by

## Guy Judge

*University of Portsmouth*

JOHN WILEY & SONS, LTD

Chichester · New York · Brisbane · Singapore · Toronto

Copyright © 2000 by John Wiley & Sons, Ltd
Baffins Lane, Chichester,
West Sussex PO19 1UD, England

*National*        01243 779777
*International*   (+44) 1243 779777
e-mail (for orders and customer service enquiries): cs-books@wiley.co.uk
Visit our Home Page    on http://www.wiley.co.uk
or http://www.wiley.com

*Trademarks*
Products and services that are referred to in this book may be either trademarks or registered trademarks of their respective owners. The Publishers and the Author make no claim to these trademarks.

*Other Wiley Editorial Offices*
New York, Weinheim, Brisbane, Singapore, Toronto

***Library of Congress Cataloging-in-Publication Data***

Judge, Guy.
    Computing skills for economists / Guy Judge.
        p. cm.
    Includes bibliographical references and index.
    ISBN 0-471-98806-5 (alk. paper)
    1. Economics–Data processing. 2. Economics–Computer programs. I. Title.

HB143.5.J83 2000
330'.0285–dc21

99-089746

***British Library Cataloguing in Publication Data***
A catalogue record for this book is available from the British Library

ISBN 0-471-98806-5 (pbk)    ✓

Typeset in 11/13pt Garamond by The Midlands Book Typesetting Company, Leicestershire
Printed and bound in Great Britain by Antony Rowe, Chippenham
This book is printed on acid-free paper responsibly manufactured from sustainable forestry, in which at least two trees are planted for each one used for paper production.

# Contents

# Acknowledgements

In writing this book I have spent many hours working at the computer in my office in the university and with my laptop at home. Writing a book can be a lonely task. However, a great many people have given me help and encouragement along the way, and I should like to take this opportunity to express my thanks to them.

The most important debt that I owe is to past and present members of the CALECO Research Group and other colleagues of mine in the Department of Economics at the University of Portsmouth. Over the years Barry Andrew, Matt Ayres, Louisa Coglan, Pat Cooper, Pauline Crichton, Steve Drinkwater, Dave Fysh, Shabbar Jaffry, Richard Harris, Lester Hunt, Simon Mardle, Barry Murphy, Sean Pascoe, Martin Snell, Andy Thorpe, Eddy Waller and Richard Welford have all contributed to building up the Group's shared stock of knowledge and expertise. As a Group we have worked closely with the members of the Institute for Learning and Research Technology at the University of Bristol, especially on CHEER and the annual CALECO Conferences. I appreciate the help given to me by all the staff in Bristol, particularly Chris Mitchell, Ros O'Leary and Martin Poulter and, earlier on, Mike Emslie and Phil Hobbs. I have also learned a lot from those with whom I have come into contact while working on the WinEcon project, especially Ziggy McDonald, Simon Price and Jean Soper. Debra Hiom and Nicky Ferguson as they have developed SOSIG, Thomas Krichel as he has energetically driven forward WoPEc and other NetEc projects, and Jurgen Doornik as he has created Ox and the recent versions of PcGive, have also contributed greatly to my thinking.

For several years I have been fortunate enough to be able to attend the CAI Sessions at the annual Allied Social Sciences Association meetings in America. Wittingly or unwittingly the following have all influenced my perception of what computing skills are needed by economists: Betty Blecha, Jim Clark, Bill Goffe, Michael Lovell, Bob Parks, Tod Porter, Teresa Riley, Kim Sosin, Richard Wood and Bill Yohe.

Finally I should like to thank all those people at John Wiley & Sons who have enabled me to convert the content of my files into the book you now hold. I am particularly grateful to my Publishing Editor, Steve Hardman, and to his Assistant, See Hanson. They arranged for a number of economists to read through draft chapters of the book, asking them to point out errors and to suggest improvements. Gerald Harbour, Bill Goffe, Ray O'Brien, Tod Porter, Geoff Renshaw, Colin Roberts, Ron Shone and Steve Trotter are amongst those I must thank for the care that they took in undertaking this task. Gary Koop, whose excellent *Analysis of Economic Data* may be regarded as a companion book to this one, also provided encouragement and helpful feedback. I alone, of course, accept responsibility for any errors that remain.

Guy Judge
Portsmouth, November 1999

# Preface

## Who is this book for?

This book is primarily aimed at undergraduate students of economics and allied subjects (such as finance and economic history) who are just beginning their studies. However, it may be of use to other economists who have gone beyond their initial training in the subject but who feel that they could benefit from refreshing or updating their computing skills; postgraduate students, lecturers and researchers in economics and professional economists.

The book is intended to be either a textbook for an introductory course in computing for economists, or a guide for those individual economists who are attempting to develop their computing skills on their own through self-directed study. The book is not a substitute for those subject-free introductions to computing software packages such as the Wiley "Getting Started with" series edited by Babette Krinstadt and David Sachs or the "Computing for Dummies" set of books. Rather it is a book written specifically for economists who will be using computers and related technology in their work. As such there is a focus on the tools and resources that are particularly relevant to economists, with examples of their use in economics and ideas and suggestions of how to apply and exploit them in applications in economics. I have occasionally been struck by the fact that students (and indeed some staff) who have acquired basic computing expertise in the use of a particular software tool (such as a spreadsheet) are nevertheless not aware of some of the ways in which such packages can be useful to economists. This book attempts to bridge the gap between basic IT literacy and the use of hardware, software and other resources in learning and doing economics.

Such a book could not at the same time be reasonably brief and readable and also be all-encompassing and encyclopedic. Indeed I do not claim to have a full and complete knowledge of all areas of the use of computers in economics. Writing this book and putting on courses on computing for economists has helped me develop my knowledge and skills, but I do not know the ins and outs of all the rival spreadsheets, word-processing packages and statistics or econometrics packages. In any case computers and the associated communications and information technology are constantly being upgraded, sometimes smoothly but occasionally with big steps forward in power, user-friendliness and cost. What I have tried to do with this book is to provide a reasonably up-to-date introduction, covering the kind of topics that would be of interest and value to most economists, and at the same time giving a basis for readers to extend and update their own skills in the future.

## Web site

With the aid of the publishers, John Wiley & Sons, I have set up a supporting web site to provide supplementary material, information on new developments and a route by which you can advise me (and through me other readers) of further ideas and suggestions which you might have for developing the range of computing skills for economists. You can find it at http://www.wiley.co.uk/judge. In between updates of the book's official web site you can also visit my own home page for the book at http://www.pbs.port.ac.uk/~judge/skills/ or send e-mail to me at Guy.Judge@port.ac.uk.

## Coverage

Today's undergraduate students of economics are likely to make considerable use of computers while studying for their degrees. They will probably use modern business software tools to prepare essays and other documents and to analyze quantitative information (word processing and spreadsheet packages). They may be asked to make seminar presentations using OHP (overhead projector) slides or perhaps even to project their displays directly from a computer. They will expect to be able to make use of the Internet for electronic mail and for accessing information on the World Wide Web. Perhaps some lecturers will keep in touch with them via e-mail or make use of the web to provide an on-line notice board for course announcements. They might go even further and use the web to provide full course notes or even deliver parts of their courses interactively on the web. Perhaps they will use computer based learning software programs such as WinEcon to support student learning on introductory economics courses. Increasingly students will buy their own computers to use at home so that they do not have to rely on those available to them in university laboratories.

As students move into their second and third years they will probably be asked to familiarize themselves with more specialized software packages, so that they can undertake practical exercises in statistics, econometrics and optimization. Students specializing in more quantitative courses may be asked to use programming tools or languages to develop their own routines and procedures rather than just relying on "canned" software.

Course managers will emphasize to students that many of the skills in computing and IT which they will develop during their degree programs will be valuable to them after graduation, whether they pursue a career as an economist or not. Many of the skills that students acquire during their training as economists are "transferable" in that they are applicable in a variety of situations. This is especially true of economists' computing skills.

Exactly how computing and IT knowledge is conveyed to students on the various economics degree programs around the world seems to vary considerably. In some institutions students are given an IT awareness course early in their studies, perhaps by members of the Computing Centre or a university-wide IT training group. No specific effort may be made to link the training to economic applications, but the material will be tailored to the hardware and software provision at the university in question. After that students may be expected to make use of word processors in preparing their essays and assignments and perhaps other relevant software for quantitative work or for seminar presentations. But there may not always be a place on the curriculum where they are shown explicitly how to use the software in economics. For example, students may not be shown how to use the equation editor in their word-processing software – something which will be necessary for economics students to know about. This could be either because of shortage of time on the course, or because economists are taught together with students from other disciplines where this skill is irrelevant, or because the instructor does not realize that this skill is one required by economists.

Economics students will probably be shown how to use a statistics and/or an econometrics software package as part of courses in these subjects. But the development of their overall IT skills may tend to be rather piecemeal and haphazard, depending more on their own enthusiasm and what they pick up from other students that they live and work with rather than on any carefully planned course structure.

Some universities have developed a more structured approach to the use and development of computing skills beyond the basic introduction. Here at Portsmouth, for example, we provide a sequence of compulsory courses for students covering much of the material found in this book.

## Different software packages and versions of them

A problem for a writer of any book like this is how to deal with the fact that the actual computing software (and hardware) available at different universities can vary quite considerably. For example, some universities have adopted the Microsoft products Word and Excel as their standard word-processing and spreadsheet packages while others use WordPerfect and Quattro Pro. When it comes to econometrics software there is even greater variation in the software used. Students may be asked to work with EViews, TSP, RATS, Microfit, PcGive, or any one of several other excellent packages that are available. A further problem is that at any one time a number of versions of these packages may be in use at different institutions. Not every university can afford to update its computer laboratories immediately a new version of the package becomes available. Lecturers may also be reluctant to allow software updates in the middle of an academic year because of the disruption to teaching programs and handouts that have been produced for an earlier version of the package. You might find that although you have bought the same program for your PC that is available on the university laboratories, yours is a later version.

In this book, as far as standard office software is concerned, I have linked my discussion to Microsoft Office products, but in a way that I hope will permit users of substitute packages to recognize how to modify the instructions given so that they become applicable to their circumstances. I have also not necessarily used the latest versions of the products in my illustrations. In some cases this was because I did not have them myself, but I also discovered that the expert reviewers appointed by the publishers to read through my manuscript were sometimes in the same situation. In any case, one of the skills that you will need to develop as an economist working with computers is the ability to move between software packages and between different versions of the same package. I try to give some guidance on this in the book and there is extra help available on the web site. Please e-mail me with comments on your own experiences of using different software so that I can feed back information to other readers via the web site.

## Why did I write this book?

I wrote this book because my colleagues and I could find no suitable text that we could use on our courses; we had to develop our own course materials. As with an earlier book of mine (Judge, 1990) it seemed likely to me that other lecturers who wished to provide more guidance for their students would be pleased to have a book of this type available to recommend to students and to use with them. It seemed to us at Portsmouth that students should not just be taught the basic computer skills and then left to fend for themselves, but that specific guidance should be given on how to use and develop these skills in applications in economics. Economists with computing skills should teach these courses, rather than IT specialists; people who are fully aware of what skills would be needed by students of economics and who have sufficient computing skills themselves to be able to provide the right kind of guidance and advice. The argument is very similar to that used to justify introductory courses in mathematics and statistics for economists being taught by quantitative economists, rather than specialist mathematicians. Such people would have a better appreciation of the kind of applications for which the skills would be useful and would be able to motivate students of economics by integrating into their courses examples and applications along the way. That is not to say that there isn't also a place for more advanced courses in computing or mathematics, taught by specialists in those areas, for economists who might wish to become experts in computational or mathematical economics. Some readers of this book may indeed go on to become experts in those areas. This though is an introductory book.

# CHAPTER 1

# Introduction: tools, tasks, resources and skills

## Objectives

The objectives of this chapter are to:

- give an overview of the use of computers by economists
- provide an introduction to the book and its contents, structure and approach
- provide some essential preliminary information and to identify some key concepts
- distinguish between tools, tasks, skills and resources

## 1.1 Economists, computers and IT in today's world

Economists, like everyone else in today's world, are highly dependent upon computers and communications and information technology in the work that they do. Whereas a generation ago it was only the econometricians and applied quantitative economists who would use computers to do their "number crunching" for them, today even the most nonquantitative economist will make use of computing technology, probably every working day. A knowledge of the use of computers and the associated communications and information technology has become an indispensable part of the training of every economist.

What kind of tasks will economists undertake and what kind of computing tools and resources will they use? In their research or professional consultancy economists will use word processing software to write their articles and reports. In most cases they will use standard office software such as Microsoft Word or Corel WordPerfect, but if their documents contain many mathematical expressions and equations they might prefer to work with a more specialist tool such as Scientific Workplace. They might maintain a database of articles and books relevant to their research through which they can quickly search and into which they can add comments and annotations. To do this they might make use of a specialist bibliographic database tool such as ProCite, or they might just use standard database management software such as Paradox or Microsoft Access. Alternatively they might prefer simply to create a plain text file which they can use with a basic accessory such as Notepad.

Most economists will probably use a spreadsheet package such as Microsoft Excel or Quattro Pro for data analysis and for creating simple tables, graphs and charts. They might go further creating models, which can be analyzed by exploiting the software's "what-if" capabilities or even their optimizing routines. Some will prefer to use more dedicated mathematics, statistics and econometrics software to analyze data and models through estimation and testing, optimization and simulation. Most applied economists will probably use "canned" econometrics software where the routines for accomplishing particular tasks have been pre-programmed and can be activated by a mouse click on an icon or a selection from a menu. However, some might want to use procedures which are not available in the standard software packages. If they have the expertise they could write a program themselves using a computer programming language such as C++. Increasingly they would be more likely to use one of the specialist languages that have been developed to enable people to work with matrices, such as Matlab, Gauss or Ox.

Most economists will use e-mail to keep in touch with colleagues and associates right across the globe, perhaps sending them the latest drafts of joint papers as e-mail file attachments. They will probably subscribe to a number of electronic mail discussion lists to keep up with new developments in particular areas. They might keep track of new books, articles and working papers in their area by searching relevant sites on the web or by subscribing to a bibliographical news service, which will deliver results by e-mail. They will probably download data from data archives and other on-line information sources. When looking for relevant information on the World Wide Web they might simply use one or more of the web search tools on offer (such as Alta Vista, Excite or HotBot), or they may be able to target the information more precisely by going through a *subject gateway* such as SOSIG (Social Science Information Gateway) or via Bill Goffe's "Resources for Economists" web site. The latter approach, whilst it may not produce so many "hits", will tend to find material which is both relevant and of verified quality.

For their teaching economists will produce reading lists, course notes and problem sheets for their students. Rather than just using a word processor and then printing the documents for duplication and distribution at lectures, lecturers might put their files on the World Wide Web for students to view or download. They might even develop interactive web-based material for students to use in their learning. Data files for use in practical exercises may be made available in electronic form and placed on the local network or web server for students to access. Class lists and student assessed work marks may be kept in spreadsheets, or entered into a university-wide information system. Lecture overheads may be prepared and printed onto acetates for display using an overhead projector. Or a set of slides may be maintained in electronic form for direct display from the computer in the lecture, perhaps with a chance to view them again later on the course web site.

As a student and trainee economist you must expect to learn to use the tools that professional and academic economists use. You will be expected to use word processing software yourself to prepare your essays and reports. You may be asked to make a presentation to the class and you might find it helpful to make use of a package such as PowerPoint which has been designed to help people prepare such presentations. You will probably use a spreadsheet such as Excel to analyze data and models, perhaps moving on later to more dedicated statistics, econometrics and optimization software. You will be encouraged to search electronic databanks and bibliographical databases both on CD-ROM and on the web to obtain statistical data and up-to-date references. You might be able to read some key articles on-line. You will be able to keep in touch with your lecturers and your fellow students by e-mail, perhaps participating in e-mail discussion lists or creating your own web site. You might use computer-based learning software such as WinEcon on the local network, or on-line material on the web to assist you in your learning of the subject. You might use electronic quizzes to test your knowledge of course material. You could even be required to take some of your examinations making use of the computer.

Unless you opt to take courses in mathematical economics or econometrics you may not have to work with some of the more specialized software which has been developed for work in these areas. In fact you will find that today's standard office software will enable you to undertake quite a number of the tasks for which dedicated software was previously required. For example, you can use a spreadsheet to obtain a basic set of regression results or solve a linear programming problem. However, these tools are limited when you wish to work in a more sophisticated way with such models. As your experience with computing in economics grows, you will come to realize that certain tasks can be performed in a variety of different ways using a number of different software tools. Which tools you choose to use for them will depend partly upon your familiarity with the software (and your access to it), partly on the depth of your knowledge about the problems you are working on, but also on how much detail and sophistication you require in a particular case. Most of you will probably be introduced to one of the standard econometrics packages such as EViews, Microfit, PcGive or TSP.

One thing is for sure. Computers themselves and the software that runs on them are developing all the time. New versions of packages extend the range of applications for which they can be used. They become easier to use (and misuse!). What an economist needs is not just training in a particular package or set of packages but an understanding of what tasks he or she is trying to undertake and an appreciation of how the computer can help with such tasks. A skilled user can quickly adapt to a new version of a software package, or from one package to a similar one produced by a rival developer.

Much of the time you don't need to know exactly how the hardware or a software package works, only how to make it work. It is a bit like driving a car. We don't all need to be mechanics. But a bit of background knowledge about the different parts of a car and their basic functions can be valuable, particularly if something goes wrong!

The list of situations for which IT tools are now available for the professional and trainee economist may seem daunting for the newcomer. Thankfully, one aspect of the rapid rate of progress in all things computing in the last twenty years or so has been the extent and quality of the "help" systems (about which we say more later). For the moment, the three most important things to learn about a piece of computer software are, in order, (a) how to get it started, (b) how to close it down in an orderly fashion and (c) how to use its help system.

## 1.2   The contents, structure and approach of this book

This book has been written to help you to become familiar with the various computing tools and resources which are available to you as an economist, and to assist you in the development of your computing skills, whether or not you are following a formal course on computing for economists. Each chapter has a clear set of objectives, some expository material to convey to you essential concepts and ideas and some practicals for you to work through to help you to develop your skills. "Find out" boxes are used to alert you to things that you will need to find out (such as "What word processing software do I have access to?" and "What version of the software am I using?"). Additional text boxes are used to provide further information on a topic without disturbing the flow of the main exposition. At the end of each chapter there are also suggestions for exercises, further activities or mini-projects which you can pursue independently to reinforce the skills developed within the chapter and to find out more about the tools and resources covered. You may be referred to the web site which has been created to accompany this book for yet further information, exercises and ideas.

The book is structured so that the first three chapters cover the basic material likely to be needed by all students of economics. These chapters provide an introduction to computers and computer networks and to the essential software tools that you will work with as an economist. The next section of this chapter goes over some essential preliminary information and key concepts concerning hardware and software, operating systems and networks while the following two chapters show how economists can begin to use standard office software in their work. Chapters 4 to 6 cover more applications of computers in economics, looking at further uses of spreadsheets and the Internet, and the use of statistics and econometrics packages. Chapter 7 looks briefly at more advanced computing skills for economists and considers how things might develop in the future.

The material of these chapters is likely to be related to that found on an IT induction course at your university but with two important differences. First, since

I cannot know the particular selection of hardware and software which is available to you at your university there are likely to be some differences between what is described here and what you find at your place of study. Although there are many common features across universities there are also substantial differences in the set-up between universities. Even if two universities both use Windows and mainly other Microsoft products, there may be differences between the institutions in the versions which have been installed or the way in which they have been configured (for example, some spreadsheet "add-ins" may not have been loaded when the software was installed on the network). So although I have attempted to provide an introduction which identifies the main things you need to know about, there will undoubtedly be some details about the local set-up that you will have to fill in for yourself. The second way in which the material of these chapters may differ from handouts provided for local induction courses is that, because it is addressed explicitly to economists as users, it is likely to contain more specific advice on how to use these tools and resources in your work as an economist. As a computer-using economist myself I am more aware of the kind of tasks you will need to undertake than an IT specialist with no background in economics.

## 1.3   Preliminary information and key concepts

### Hardware

The computer set-up that you have can vary in a number of ways. If you are working in a university computer lab the computer in front of you is probably connected to a local *network*, and in turn to the *Internet*. If you are working independently at home you probably have a *stand-alone* machine. You may also be able to link up to the Internet using your telephone line if you have a *modem* through which you can connect to a *service provider* such as AOL, Demon or Freeserve. Being linked to a local network and the Internet can provide you with a great many advantages, but there will be costs as well as benefits.

Let's start though with stand-alone machines. You might have a standard *desktop* PC, or a portable *notebook* or *laptop* machine. A standard desktop PC set-up will consist of a main *system unit*, a screen or *monitor*, a *keyboard* and a *mouse*, and probably some kind of *printer*. Inside the main part of the computer will be the *microprocessor* itself, together with a variety of *memory*, *graphics*, *sound* and *video cards* (the last two of which will be needed to run various *multimedia* applications) and the *hard disk* (also known as the hard drive or C drive) where you can store your programs and documents.

The microprocessor or "chip" at the heart of your system will determine the speed at which your computer can operate. The clock speed of the microprocessor will be measured in megahertz (MHz) – millions of cycles per second. A typical modern PC will run at somewhere between 450 and 600 MHz, but there are still PCs on the market with slower speeds. As a rule of thumb the faster the clock speed, the faster the computer will do its work, but there will be other factors that can affect this too, such as how much memory you have, how much space there is left on your hard disk and the way in which your computer is attached to a network.

The computer's current memory (also known as RAM – short for random access memory) is where the computer does its work (although it may also pass information to and from the hard disk, which is why you can run into problems when the hard disk fills up even if you don't try to save your files there). RAM is usually measured in megabytes (MB). Computers which are being advertised for sale as I write this book can have anything between 32 and 128 MB of RAM, although a typical PC might have 64 MB. Computers which were on sale at the beginning of the 1990s often only had 640 K RAM (1 K = 1 kilobyte, 1 MB = 1000 K). Modern software requires much more memory to run, and broadly speaking the more you have the better. It is unlikely that you will be able to run big multimedia applications unless you have at least 64 MB of memory. You might also have difficulty in running several big applications together – one of the big advantages of the Windows operating system (see below) – unless you have plenty of memory.

When you switch off your computer all the information in the current memory will be lost (although most of today's computers have built-in systems to recover your work if your system is switched off unexpectedly, say by a power cut). The hard disk or C drive is the built-in part of the computer where you can store your programs and files. Here the memory will be measured in gigabytes (1 GB = 1000 MB) and a typical amount of hard disk "space" might be in the region of 6 to 8 GB. As software packages have grown in size they have required increasingly more storage space on the hard drive. Fortunately the price of both current memory and hard disk space has come down dramatically over the same period. You can also install additional RAM and hard disk drives (or replace the old ones with bigger new ones) to upgrade your computer.

Your computer is also likely to have a *floppy disk drive*, which will enable you to save files onto a portable 3.5 inch diskette so that you can take your work from machine to

## Files

When you store information on your computer (that is on one of the drives associated with it) it will be in the form of a *file*. Files can be created by you whenever you save information using a software package such as a word processor or a spreadsheet. These files will be stored inside *folders* (sometimes called directories) that you can create so that you can keep together a group of files which relate to a common topic or project. The programs themselves are also stored as files. So your hard disk will contain a variety of files: some program files which you use to *run* the software, and files that have been created *using* the software. When you use a program it can call up information stored in other files, or even launch another program.

machine. Files are the electronic versions of the documents and other items that you create using the computer. If you don't save them the information will be lost when you switch off the computer! A much smaller amount of information can be stored on a floppy disk than on the hard disk; a standard floppy disk has just over 1.4 MB of storage space on it. However, with the right software you can compress or "zip" files so that they take up less space.

Nearly all today's PCs will also have a CD-ROM drive from which you can load information stored on a CD. Huge amounts of information can be stored on a CD, maybe 500 times as much as you can get on a floppy disk, and this provides the potential for multimedia applications with sound and video clips being taken from the CD-ROM drive and played back to you on the computer. (If you have the right hardware and software on your computer you might also be able to play standard audio CDs.) When you buy new software you may find that it is only available on a CD and has to be installed from there. With the right equipment you can now record onto a CD from your computer, taking the ROM out of CD-ROM (ROM means "read only memory") although at the time of writing most systems do not have CD recording (i.e. "writing") capabilities.

### The monitor

There are a few things you should know about computer monitors before you begin. PC monitors work in conjunction with the graphics card in your computer so what you see on screen will depend upon how good that is as well as the monitor quality itself. The screen is divided up into small squares called *pixels* (picture elements). The minimum for a modern monitor is 640 × 480, although many will have 800 × 600. Each pixel can be defined from a finite number of colors; the minimum is 256 colors, but some systems will be able to call upon many millions of different colors. Some modern software will have been designed to work with high resolution monitors and may not look so good on a lower resolution screen.

Another factor which can affect how good things look on screen is the *refresh rate*, i.e. the frequency with which the graphics card sends updates of the images to the monitor. To avoid flicker this would need to be at least 70 Hz (70 cycles per second).

### Networks

If your computer is in a university lab it will probably be connected to a network. This means that the software programs that you use will not be stored on the hard disk of the machine that you are using, but on a special computer which is connected to the network, called the *server*. This is usually a big, fast computer under the control of the computer technicians. It is more efficient for them to install the software on the server, and then have people working at each machine connected to the network call it up from their own machines when they need it, than to install the software on each computer separately. On a network the technicians can install new software (or new versions of existing software) on the server and be sure that every user will now have access to the same version. They can monitor use of the software and ensure that the terms and conditions of software licenses are adhered to.

Another advantage of being linked to a network is that you will probably also have an allocation of space on the network drive (at Portsmouth this is called the N drive) where you can store files. Whichever computer on the network that you sit and work at you will always be able to call up files that you have saved on the network drive. In order to make sure that the computer system can distinguish between different users, when you use a computer on a network you will have to log-in. You will be asked to give your user name and password. These will be unique to you and will mean that any files that you save on the network will be stored in the file space allocated to you and will be private and secure.

### Find out

If you will be working in a university lab you will need to find out the *user name* (or code number) you will have been given before you can use the system. You will also be given an initial *password* (although you may be able to change that once you are on the system). Find out this information as soon as possible.

### Important

Make sure that you log-out properly whenever you finish a network session. If you do not, another user may be able to gain access to your files. *Never* tell anyone else your password. If the computer system is misused by someone operating under your user name it will be assumed that it is you.

Computers in some university labs do not have their own hard disks (C drives) so you will only be able to save your files on the network drive or onto a floppy disk (on the A drive). If you are working on a lab machine that does have a C drive and you accidentally save a file there, as soon as you realize what you have done you should copy it on to the A or network drive or you won't be able to work with it again unless you sit at that particular computer. You should also delete it from the C drive to avoid clogging up that drive with unwanted files. Some networks have procedures which automatically remove such unwanted files once a day so you might find your file has gone the next time you work at the same computer.

**Tip**

It is a good idea to keep backup copies of files, just in case something happens to your floppy disk. You could lose it, knock coffee over it, or it could become accidentally corrupted in some other way. On a stand-alone machine of your own you could save your file to both the A drive and the C drive (or even save the file on to two separate floppy disks). On a machine connected to a network you could save your file both to the A drive and to the network drive.

*Sharing files*

Sometimes a lecturer will want all the students on a course to have access to a file. Or you may be asked to work together with other students in a group on a mini-project so that you will all need access to a file or collection of files. Usually on a network there will be a drive to which all users can have access. For example, at Portsmouth it is the L drive. You may find that for some folders (or directories) on the drive you have read only rights (you can download files which are stored there but you cannot save your own files into those folders). For other folders you may have the right to save files there too. Obviously for group work you would need joint file space of this type.

*Printers*

Although on some occasions you will work on the computer with no need for "hard copy" printed output, most of the time it will be necessary to print material to take away with you. In a lab it is unlikely that each computer will have its own dedicated printer. More likely there will be a number of printers connected to the network and probably located in a different room or building. When you send your output to the printer it will join a queue to be printed in turn.

**Find out**

If you will be working in a university lab, find out the location of the printer(s) that are connected to the network. In some universities you will have to collect printed output from a reception point rather than taking it from a printer directly. Find out what the printing arrangements are at your university.

If you are lucky enough to have your own computer and printer you will be able to have virtually instantaneous printed output. However, you should always carefully check your documents before printing. Most software allows you to preview your output on screen so that you can see exactly what it will look like when printed. You may feel that it is helpful to have a printed version of the material to check through even when you know that the document is not finished – it is a lot easier to read printed text on paper than on screen, and you can highlight errors and changes that will need to be made when you go back to the computer.

The best quality printed output comes from laser printers, but ink-jet printers now also produce very acceptable printed output quality (although they are much slower than laser printers). Particularly for graphs and charts you may wish to work with color printers.

*Other peripherals*

Your computer may be connected to a *modem* to enable you to send and receive messages via the telecommunications system. It might possibly be an internal modem which goes into one of the slots inside the computer. More likely it will be an external modem, connected up to your PC via appropriate cables. In both cases you will connect up to the outside world via an ordinary telephone point. You will, in addition, need suitable software to operate the modem and an account with a *service provider*.

My laptop has a built-in drive for CD-ROMs, but no internal floppy disk drive. Consequently I have to use an external floppy disk drive which I can attach to my computer through an appropriate connection. For other computer users it may be the other way round, with an internal floppy drive and an external CD ROM drive.

## DVD disks, Zip drives and Jaz drives

Some new computer systems may be connected to a *DVD player*. DVD stands for digital versatile disk, and it is a form of disk which can hold even more information than a CD. DVD technology has been developed as an alternative to the video tape as a format for prerecorded movies, but it also offers huge potential for multimedia applications. DVD technology is still in its infancy, but already some multimedia reference works such as Encarta Reference Suite have been published in this format.

*Zip drives* and *Jaz drives* effectively allow you to have removable and portable hard disks. The cartridges for Zip drives currently give you up to 250 MB of portable disk space, while the newer Jaz drives provide up to a gigabyte of storage space. This is very useful for people who need to work at more than one site, say at the office and at home, or for people who must travel from site to site to make presentations or discuss spreadsheet models.

*Note*: don't confuse a Zip drive with zipped files. Zipped files are files that have been saved in a compressed form using a software utility such as Winzip so that they occupy less space on your floppy or hard disk. They will need to be "unzipped" before they can be used with the relevant software application.

Modern desktop computers will probably have both a floppy disk drive (A) and a CD-ROM drive (probably drive D).

There may be other hardware peripherals connected to your university network which you can make use of, such as a *scanner*. This can be used to create electronic versions of graphical images presented to it on paper. You might also find that the system has *optical character reader* software which allows you to interpret printed text which is scanned in, turning it into a standard electronic format which can then be manipulated in the usual way (edited, formatted etc.).

## Software

Now that you have had a briefing on the computer *hardware* that you will be working with (the physical pieces of the system that you can see and touch) it is time to turn our attention to the *software* that runs on it – the programs which give the instructions to the computer to make it undertake the tasks you have for it. Software can be categorized in a number of ways. An obvious category to distinguish is what is often called *office software* or *standard business applications software*. This category covers such things as word processors, spreadsheets, databases, web browsers and e-mail software. Quite often these days you will find that such software has been bundled together in one integrated suite such as Microsoft Office, Lotus Smart Suite or Corel WordPerfect. We will look in detail at this kind of software in the following chapters, focusing particularly on uses that you as an economist would have for it. Other types of software are aimed at more specialist markets and we look in particular at statistics and econometrics software. First, however, we must consider a type of software without which none of these other programs could run, *operating system software*.

### *Operating systems*

Modern computers are not only more powerful than those of earlier generations – the laptop I am using to write this book has more memory and a faster processor than the mainframe computer I shared with the rest of the university when I was a student at the end of the 1960s – but they also use operating systems and software which are much more "user-friendly". The operating system on my laptop computer is Windows 95. This is a program from the Microsoft Corporation that runs on PCs (personal computers) to provide an overall environment for you to work in, and to manage the flow of information between different parts of the computer system. Every computer must have an operating system in place and functioning properly before you can do anything else on it. If you are working with an IBM or IBM-compatible PC you will almost certainly be using Windows 98 or some other version of the Windows software (you might even have the newer Windows 2000 operating system). Other computers such as those manufactured by Apple make use of a different but quite similar operating system. The operating system enables you to operate the

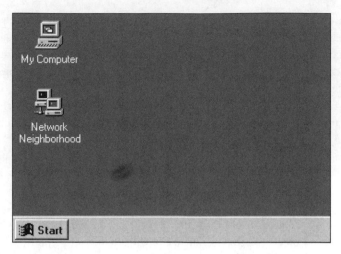

**Fig. 1.1**   A basic Windows 95 desktop.

hardware and software tools available to you and helps you manage the programs
and documents on your computer. Earlier operating systems such as DOS (Disk
Operating System) required you to type in commands or instructions to get things
done. By contrast today's operating systems have what is known as a *graphical user
interface* which provides a more visual front end to the tools that are available to you.
When you start up your computer you will see a representation of a *desktop*, with
small images called *icons* which you can click on with the mouse to run the associated
software or to open a document. Figure 1.1 shows a rather basic Windows 95 desktop
with the taskbar at the bottom on which you see the Start button and with My Computer
and Network Neighborhood icons. Most desktops are likely to have rather more
icons than this, through which users will be able directly to go to the software
applications that are available to them.

## The desktop metaphor

Computing specialists like to make use of metaphors to describe the tools with
which they work. So the initial area that you begin to work in when you start up
your computer or log-in to the network is called the *desktop*. Although it doesn't
look like any desktop I have ever seen, the metaphor is supposed to make you
think of it as the place where you sit down to work.

*Key features of the Windows environment*

Working with a graphical user interface like Windows offers several major benefits to
users. The first two stem directly from its graphical (rather than text oriented) nature.

## Pointing and clicking to get the computer to do things

Windows, and the software programs that run under it, make substantial use of *icons* (small pictorial representations of programs or program instructions) which you use the mouse to point at, then click on to get things done. For example, in the program I am using as I write this book (Microsoft Word) there is a small picture of a printer just under the menu bar at the top of the screen. If I want to print the contents of this document I can use the mouse to point at this icon, and then just click on it to get the computer to send the document to the printer. And when I started up my computer today, in order to get the Word program to run in the first place all I did was to point at the small Word icon on the desktop and click on the mouse. If you are unsure what an icon does you can usually just point the mouse at it (without clicking) and the computer will tell you what the icon is for. Sometimes you first have to click on a Help button – signified by a question mark – and then point at the icon to find out what it does. Many people find this way of working with the computer to be both intuitive and quick and easy to use. However, there are other ways you can get the computer to do things. Usually the software will include *drop-down menus* which will offer a number of options for you to choose from. This is a bit closer to the old way of issuing instructions, but instead of having to type them in (and remember what keywords you need to use), you simply select the command from the menu by using the mouse to "point and click" on it. You can also use various "hot-key" combinations to get the computer to do what you want it to do. For example, in many programs if you simultaneously press the Control and P keys the computer will print the current document. (The Control key has Ctrl shown on it.)

## WYSIWYG (what you see is what you get)

Because what appears on the screen is an image, even when you are working with just text you can see it on the screen exactly as it will be when it is printed. For example, if I want my section headings to be in a larger size font than the rest of the text I can select the relevant text and then choose the size and style of the font that I want to use. I will see it on screen exactly as it will look when printed. (You select a section of text by pointing at it with the mouse and then sweeping over it while pressing down on the left mouse button.)

If you decide to include in your document a chart, or some other graphic image, you can insert it at the place where you want it and you will see it on screen exactly how it will be printed. You can also use the mouse to increase or decrease the size of the image on the page if you wish. This way of working marked a substantial step ahead compared with earlier systems where you could not see what the contents of the document would look like and work on the document at the same time.

## Keeping several windows open at once

Another big benefit of the Windows system is the fact that you can keep open several windows at once, running a number of different programs together, possibly moving information between them. (You might also have several different windows within the same program.) Only one window at a time will be the *active* one (the one that the mouse is pointed at), but you can easily switch back and forth as you need to just by using the mouse to point at the window you want or selecting it from the *taskbar* at the bottom of the screen. You can alter the size of a window so that you can see several windows on the screen at once, maximize it so that it fills the whole screen, or minimize it so that it is temporarily taken off the screen (although it remains open until you close it or shut down the program associated with it).

You can *cut and paste* material between windows using the mouse to select the bits you want. You can also have *dynamic links* between windows so that, for example, a table or a chart in one document can be related to values in another file which is linked to it. If you change any of the values in this second file, the table or chart in the first one will be automatically updated.

### Running programs

There are a variety of ways to get a program to run. Which one you use will depend partly on the circumstances of your set-up, but it may also be influenced by what you have been doing previously. For example, you may already have been working on a document which has been saved on the A, C or network drive. If you have a Windows 95 or later operating system you can use Windows Explorer (more on this below) to look at the folders and files available to you. First select the appropriate Directory, and then the Folder and lastly the File you want to work with. Each time just use the mouse to point and click (once) to move along the *path* to the file you want. Then, if you double click on the file the computer can automatically load up the program that is needed to work with the file, opening the file at the same time. The reason for this is that file names come in two parts. The first part is the name that you give to the file. This should be something that is relevant to the work and that you will remember and recognize again. Examples might be EXERCISE1, CV, Microeconomics Essay etc. Older operating systems limited you to a maximum of eight characters (letters or numbers) for file names, but with Windows 95 and Windows 98 you are no longer restricted in this way. You can even include spaces in your file names, as the third example above illustrates. When you save a file in a particular program the computer will automatically add a three letter file extension to the file name which identifies the program used to create it. For example, Word files are given the extension .DOC (or .doc), Excel files will have the extension .XLS (or .xls) and PowerPoint files will have the extension .PPT (or .ppt). Because of this extension the computer will know what program to use to open the file when you double click on the file name.

If someone has sent you a file as an e-mail attachment you could also open it straight away by clicking on the "View" button in the e-mail software. From the filename extension the computer would identify the appropriate package to use, run the program and open the file.

**Tip**

Because of possible problems with computer *viruses* you are advised always first to save any files that are sent to you as file attachments so that you can check them for viruses before you open them.

Some other ways of running software are described below. The more experienced you become the more familiar you will be with all these different ways of working.

1. *From the Start Menu (or its equivalent).* Windows 95 has a Start Menu which can be activated by pointing at the Start button on the left hand end of the taskbar (which will be at the bottom of your screen). When you click on it a pop-up menu will appear with various options that you can select. If you point at *Programs* a further list of programs that are available to you will open up. Point at the one you want and double click on it. Alternatively you can click on "Run" from the Start menu, use the "Browse" button to move through the folders until you find the program you are looking for, and double click on it. The path to the file will appear in the Run window and when you click *OK* the program will run.

2. *Double clicking a desktop icon.* It may be that a shortcut route to the software has been set up using a desktop icon. You can just point at the icon and double click the mouse and the software will be run. The icon activates a command to run the program, telling it exactly where to find the program (it gives the full path to the drive and folder where the program is stored). By the way, you can usually distinguish program files from other files as they tend to have the file extension .exe.

3. *From an office bar on the desktop.* Some commonly used programs, such as those contained in the Microsoft Office suite, create a special toolbar when they are installed that will be shown on screen at all times. Whether you are looking at the desktop or whether you are already running an application this office toolbar will be visible to you at the top of the screen and you can run one of the programs in the suite just by double clicking on its icon on the toolbar.

4. *Network Application Launcher.* If the software you wish to use is on a network you may find that there is a link on your desktop to an Application Launcher folder. First double click on the Application Launcher icon to go to that folder. Then look for the icon for the software you need and double click on it to launch the software.

*Help*

Modern software is usually fairly intuitive to use. Windows software tends to stick to a common set of menu headings such as **F**ile, **E**dit, **V**iew etc., and it is usually obvious what will happen if you select one of the options available to you. If you need to find out more you can, of course, always read the manual (many people seem to treat this as the last resort and an admission of failure). Despite the developments in computing to which we have already referred, the written word can still be a useful source of help for the new user. Whilst the official manual might be a rather turgid read, it is now possible to purchase "third party" instruction books about particular pieces of software in which the style of presentation often includes a fictitious example through which the reader is guided as to how to perform the relevant tasks. Course tutors or instructors whose courses rely on the use of a computer may include recommendations for such publications on their reading lists. More conveniently you can call up the *help* system which is built-in to most programs. You can either search for a topic if you can guess the keyword the information will be stored under, or you can browse through the material until you find what you are looking for. Help systems usually contain *hypertext* links. This means that some parts of the text, identified by being underlined or in a different color or font, will be hot links to material elsewhere (either somewhere else in the same file or even somewhere in another file). Such hypertext links are a feature of modern computing software and constitute another way in which computers have become so much easier to work with. Many packages also contain examples and demos illustrating how to accomplish different tasks. Usually these will be found via the Help option in the main menu. There might also be a Tutorial program you can run before you begin to work with the software. Increasingly software also includes "Wizards" – interactive guides to help you through a task.

If you can't find how to do something you can always ask someone else who you think might know. This might be a fellow student, your course tutor or instructor, or someone else who is an experienced user of the software in question. For many specialized software packages there will be a mailing list where users exchange questions, answers, tips and ideas. However, if you are a new user of the software you should resist the temptation to send simple questions to the list which will have been dealt with time and time again. If you do so you will only antagonize most list members. Try to find out if there is a *Frequently Asked Questions* page on the web, usually abbreviated to FAQs, or an archive of mail list postings through which you can search.

## Defaults and dialog boxes

Many programs have default settings which you can choose to work with, or if you prefer you can change the settings to suit your requirements. For example, when I started typing this document into Word the selected *font* (text style) was Times New Roman, size 10, with text left justified (aligned so that every line starts at the same point on the left hand side of the page). The margins were set at 2.5 cm and each page was set up to fit A4 size paper. All of these settings were perfectly suitable for me so I did not need to change them. Many software users will not even be aware that such settings can be changed. They will just start the program and begin working.

At some stage when you are working with a program you may be faced with a *dialog box* where you will need to select appropriate options. Sometimes you must choose only one from a list of mutually exclusive alternatives. Sometimes you can select as many as you wish from a menu of features available to you. In the latter case there will most likely be a small square next to each of the choices available. As you click on an option it will be indicated by a tick or check sign (✔) or perhaps a small cross (✗). Clicking again on an option will deselect it. In the case of mutually exclusive options the choice might be made by working your way down a list until you come to the option you want to choose (e.g. the text font such as Times New Roman or Arial). The option you want is selected by clicking the mouse whilst the pointer is over the word on the screen. Another way of accomplishing this is by using *radio buttons*. In this case a small circle will be seen adjacent to each available option. The option which is "switched on" will be shown by a dot (•) inside the circle. Selecting any other option will cause the dot to be removed from the circle next to the original option and placed in the circle next to the selected option. When the options are quantitative in nature (for example text font size) the choice could be indicated by using a little "spinner" – clicking on the up arrow will cause the value of the setting to be increased, clicking on the down arrow will cause the value of the setting to be decreased.

Some dialog boxes will have the appearance of a number of cards in a stack with a "*tab*" at the top of each card. Clicking on the tab at the top will take you to the card with the options relating to a particular group of properties. In some cases it will be possible to preview the effect your choice will have – an example will be displayed in a small pane within the tab. For example, if you want to put a box around a block of text and then shade in the box you can see how dark a 5% or 10% setting would make it.

### Exiting programs

When you have finished working with a software application, make sure that you have saved your work and then exit the program (usually by selecting File and then Exit from the main menu). When you have finished working at the computer, shut it down properly (click on the Start button and select Shut Down) or log-out of the network.

> **Tip**
>
> Save your work at regular intervals, just in case the program hangs up or the network crashes. In fact it is a good idea to save your document as soon as you begin to work on it, selecting an appropriate file name and directory location at that stage. Then all you will have to do later is click File Save and the most recent version of your file will overwrite what you had there before. (On some systems a periodic automatic file save procedure may have been set up, but don't rely on this.)

*Ctrl-Alt-Del:*   Sometimes a piece of software will seize up and just not respond to any mouse clicks or keyboard input (I find this happens more often on networked than stand-alone PCs). To escape and close down the offending software program hold down simultaneously the Ctrl-Alt-Del keys. Follow the instructions and you should be able to quit the program without having to close down all other programs or switch off the computer. Occasionally things are so bad that you will have to do this, either by pressing Ctrl-Alt-Del again or by pressing the Restart switch on the computer. If you have been saving your files frequently you won't have to redo too much work.

## *Windows Explorer and File Management*

You can use Windows Explorer (or the equivalent File Manager that goes with other operating systems) to take a look at the files and folders on the various disks which are accessible to you, to create new files or folders, or to move or copy them from one place to another. As we have already noted, you can also open files and run programs from Windows Explorer.

Begin Windows Explorer either from the Start button, or from a special Windows Explorer icon if there is one on the Desktop. A window will open rather like the

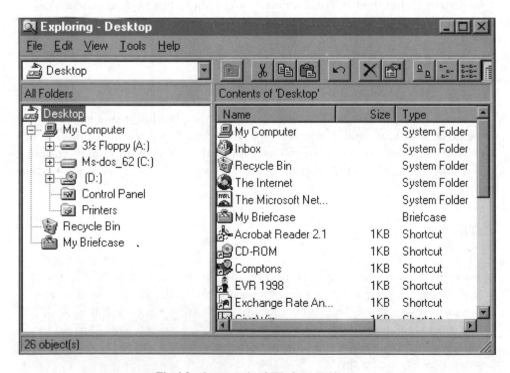

**Fig. 1.2**   Screen grab of Windows Explorer.

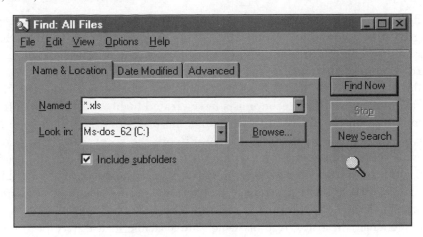

**Fig. 1.3**    Finding files.

one in Figure 1.2, with information in the left hand pane showing All Folders and drives that are accessible to you, and in the right hand pane the contents of whichever folder is currently selected in the left hand pane. Along the top are the menu options **F**ile, **E**dit, **V**iew, **T**ools, **H**elp. Underneath that are icons which can be used to move up a level, cut, copy, paste or undo etc. If you point the mouse at each of them you can see what they do. If you experiment by pointing and clicking on the last four of these icons you will see that you can change the form in which this information is displayed. To appreciate fully what you can do with Windows Explorer you will need to consult a book on Windows 95 (such as Russakov and Bacon, 1997) or you can experiment a little by seeing what options are available to you in the menu. One useful command under **T**ools is **F**ind, which can help you track down a file or folder if you can remember its name but not exactly where it is stored. Try putting \*.xls into the **N**amed box (see Figure 1.3). The \* in the name is the "wildcard" character and means that you are asking for the computer to find all files with the extension .xls (which indicates that the files are Excel files). If you have any Excel files in the directory that is indicated (shown in the **L**ook in box) the computer will find them for you.

## 1.4    Tools, tasks, skills and resources

Earlier in this chapter I have referred to a variety of tools, tasks, skills and resources. It might be worthwhile clarifying the distinctions between each of these a little more explicitly. The *tools*, both hardware and software, are the products that are available to you to work with. Some software and even some hardware products have been created for use only in very specific circumstances, to be used by highly skilled specialists. On the hardware side, special measurement devices have been created in some of the physical sciences to monitor the state of an experiment, feeding back to a computer readings in a digital form which can be immediately processed. For example, probes working on the moon, or at other locations which are hard or impossible to get to, can analyze the mineral components of a sample of material as it is encountered. Such specific hardware tools are unlikely to be of any direct interest to us, but economists have created highly *content specific* software programs that can only be used for the single purpose for which they have been designed. An example of this might be WinEcon, the software system that has been created by members of the Economics Consortium to help in the teaching and learning of introductory economics. Even here, however, it is possible to customize WinEcon, that is to tailor it for use with specific groups of students, so it is not really a single use product.

More generally the software tools which are available to use have been created with a wide range of applications in mind, that is they are *content free*. For example, a spreadsheet program such as Excel can be used to analyze and display quantitative information from any number of subject areas and types of application. Although the first spreadsheet programs were designed to make it easier to manipulate accounting information arranged in rows and columns, people quickly realized that the tool that had been created could be used for many other types of task. We shall look at some of these that are of interest to economists in Chapter 4.

By a *task* I simply mean something that you want to get done. It may be necessary to use a computer to do it – it may not. For example, if I wish to fit a simple least squares regression line through a small scatter of observations on two variables (e.g. on aggregate UK consumers' expenditure and income in the 1990s) I could do this without using a computer. If I had a pencil, a sheet of paper and a small pocket calculator, provided that I knew the formulae by which to calculate the slope and intercept estimates, I could complete this task relatively easily. Indeed I have done so on many occasions. You might even have a calculator which has a button on it which enables you to complete the task without the need to know what the formulae are. These days, however, I would be more likely to undertake such a task on a computer using a spreadsheet package such as Excel. There are several reasons for this. First, I can enter the data into the spreadsheet and carefully check that all the values are correct before instructing the computer to calculate the slope and intercept estimates. On a calculator I couldn't really do that. Secondly, I can save the data file for further analysis. If I was able to collect some more observations on these variables I could then add them into the file. Before that I might even be able to avoid having to type in the numbers if the series are already available to me in electronic form. I can just read them in from a file, or copy and paste them from another window. I can use the computer to produce a plot of the scatter diagram with the fitted regression line drawn in to give a visual representation of the fitted line rather than just an algebraic description of it. And of course I can print out the results to take away with me, say to a macroeconomics seminar where we might be discussing the marginal propensity to consume.

The task described above does not require specialized econometrics software – a simple spreadsheet will do. But if I really wanted seriously to study what has happened to UK consumers' expenditure over the years I would need to use more specialized econometric software. Such a software tool would enable me to pay attention to some of the concepts and techniques that econometricians say we should look out for in such a case, calling upon specialized routines which have been built into such programs for that purpose. Chapter 5 looks at both the tools and the types of tasks they would be used for.

By *resources* I mean all the information and services which can be called upon when undertaking a task of some kind. For example, in obtaining the data for the consumers' expenditure exercise I might go to the on-line ONS Time Series Databank which is held on a computer at Manchester University as part of the MIMAS service. (MIMAS – Manchester InforMation and Associated Services. This service was formerly known as MIDAS.) This can be accessed via the World Wide Web, although you need to register first so that you are able to provide your user name and password when you use the service. Conducting a similar exercise using US data would be easier. You could go to the NBER web site and download the data you need from the latest Economic Report to the President.

You might also want to check out any recent studies of consumption before you begin your own work. Various resources would be available to you to assist you with that task, both on the web and published on CD-ROM and perhaps available to you in your library. We shall look in detail at such resources in Chapter 6.

The *skills* you will develop as you work through this book include not only the facility that you have in working with each of the hardware and software tools but also the expertise which helps you select the right tool (or set of tools) for the task in hand. They include too the ability to adapt to new versions of tools that you have worked with before. They might even extend to a more imaginative and creative level as you stretch the use of the tools in new directions or for new types of applications. The more you work with these tools and resources, and the greater the variety of tasks that you use them to perform, the more you will develop your skills. Who knows, you might be one of those people who go on to create new tools or resources for the rest of us to work with!

## Summary

This chapter has provided an initial glimpse of some of the ways in which economists make use of computers in their work. It also gave an overview of the material in the rest of the book, together with an indication of the approach that would be taken. Some essential concepts were identified and distinctions were made between hardware, software and operating systems and between tools, tasks, resources and skills. In the next chapter we start to look at how standard office software can help economists in their everyday work.

**Find out**

1. Which of the following drives can you access?
   A, C and D. Any others?
   (Hint: use Windows Explorer or the equivalent File Manager on your system.)
2. Which of the following packages are available to you to work with (and which versions)?
   Microsoft Word (WordPerfect); Excel (Quattro Pro); Access (Paradox); Netscape Communicator (Navigator) (Internet Explorer).
   (Hint: click the Start button and then **P**rograms – or its equivalent if you have a different file management system. Note: some of these programs may be available within a software suite. Look also on the desktop or in the Application Launcher to see if there is an icon for these programs.)
3. Are there any files on the C drive with the extension .exe? What does this mean?
   (Hint: with Windows use the **F**ind button either from **T**ools in Windows Explorer or directly from the Start button.)
4. Find out how to resize, maximize and minimize windows.
   (Hint: practice on the Control Panel window pointing at one of the edges until a little double-headed arrow appears. Holding down the left mouse button, drag the edge in or out to reduce/increase the size of the window. Experiment by changing the options available under **V**iew in the menu. Try clicking each of the three icons at the top right of the Control Panel window. Select the ✕ icon last as this will close down the window.)
5. Find out what the screen settings are for the monitor which comes with your PC.
   (Hint: Use Start, **S**ettings, **C**ontrol Panel, click on the Display icon and then the **S**ettings tab.)
6. Find out more about the computer system you are using.
   (Hint: Use Start, **S**ettings, **C**ontrol Panel, and double click on the System icon.)

**Further activities**

1. If you are using Windows 95, or a later version of Windows, click the Start button at the bottom left hand corner of the desktop and then select **H**elp. Take the Ten Minute Tour to using Windows.
2. Now use the **H**elp system to find out more about using windows. Select the index tab and type the word "window" in the box. Click **D**isplay and then select "The Basics". Browse through the material making a few notes on key points.
3. Find out how to create new folders and files in Windows Explorer. Find out how to copy, move and delete files and folders and practice with a few

"dummy" files and folders. Notice that when you delete a file it goes first to the Recycle Bin, so if you accidentally delete a file you should be able to recover it.

(You should have found out how to do these things in the previous two activities, but if you still don't know what to do, go to Windows Explorer and select Help.)

4.  Find out how to use the Notepad accessory to write and edit text files. (Hint: Click on the **F**ind tab in **H**elp and type 'notepad' in the box.)

5.  Use the **H**elp system to find out about other things that look interesting. Copy and paste material from the **H**elp system into Notepad so that you can print it out or retain it for further reference. Share any useful points that you find with friends on your course.

## Appendix. Skills for file and disk management tasks

At various points in this chapter (most notably at the end of section 1.3, where there was a brief introduction to Windows Explorer) reference has been made to the need to manage your files, folders and disks. Experience has shown that this is an area where beginning students can face problems, mislaying files and then thinking that they have been permanently lost, or even accidentally over-writing or deleting them. This appendix provides a number of suggestions that should help you develop your skills in this area. It can be skipped by readers who are experienced computer users, but who want to refer to other parts of the book where computing applications that are more specific to economists are covered.

### File names

Every computer file has a name which generally consists of two parts, separated by a dot or period (.). The part after the dot is called the file extension and this usually indicates the kind of file with which you are dealing. For example, the extension .doc indicates that you have a Word document, while .xls indicates that you have an Excel worksheet file. These extensions are usually added by the relevant software when you save the file. To work with these files you will need a copy of the software program that goes with them (or a read only version that will let you examine the contents of the file but won't let you change it). Files with the extension .exe are executable files and these are programs that can run on their own.

The first part of the file name is for you to choose. With some software or operating systems you may be limited in the number and set of characters that you can use here. For example, you may be restricted to a maximum of eight characters and be unable to use spaces, or characters such as ? and * in the name. Recent versions of Windows and other Microsoft products have allowed users to work with longer file names, and even allow spaces within the names. You will need to check whether a particular software package and operating system that you are using will allow this.

Try to use file names that help you to remember what is in them. So, for example, if you use your word processing software to create a curriculum vitae (CV) or résumé it would be sensible to call the file CV.DOC or RESUME.DOC. Windows and most software applications that run under it do not distinguish between upper and lower case letters, so if you save a file as CV.DOC it may show up in Windows Explorer as cv.doc. However, if you are working on a big computer that uses the operating system called UNIX you will have to be careful to distiguish between upper and lower case letters as they are regarded as different characters under UNIX.

If you have a series of related files you might want to give them similar names, but use a number to distinguish one from another. For example, when preparing your dissertation you might save each chapter separately with names like DISS1.DOC, DISS2.DOC, etc. If you want a space between two parts of a name but the software won't allow it, you can use the underscore (_) symbol instead, e.g. DISS_1.DOC etc.

Earlier in the chapter I encouraged you to get into the habit of keeping backup files of your work in case of accidental damage to files or disk. So you might save a file both on the C drive and on the A drive (on a floppy). Although these two files might have the same name, and have identical contents, they are of course two separate files. So if you amend the contents of one file you will have to change the contents of the other file too (or overwrite the original file by copying the revised file on top of the original file). But only do this when you are sure that the revised file is exactly as you want it. If you are not yet happy that the revised file is just as you want it, you might want to retain a copy of the original file until you are sure. In this situation give a slightly different name to the revised file (e.g. CV_V2.DOC). Again this provides a logical name to help you recognize which is the original version and which is the revised version (although you can also use Windows Explorer to examine the properties of the file, including the date the file was created).

**Renaming files**

If you decide that you want to change the name of a file you can do this within Windows Explorer by highlighting the file and right-clicking on the mouse. Then you can choose Rename from the list of options. (Properties is also on this list if you want to check when a file was created, modified or last accessed). If you **D**elete a file using Windows Explorer it will not immediately be destroyed but moved to the Recycle Bin, so if you change your mind and you want it back you can get it from there. If you save a different file with the same name and in the same location (drive and folder) then you won't be able to get back the contents of the original file. However, most software applications and tools like Windows Explorer will warn you if you are going to overwrite a file with the same name. If you are in any doubt you should cancel the operation and save your new file with a different name.

## Deleting files

Periodically it is a good idea to delete unwanted files that might be clogging up your hard disk or network space – this includes files in the Recycle Bin. Check carefully first though that all the files you dispose of are really no longer needed. If you are in doubt copy a file onto a floppy disk so that you can get it back again if you later realize that you need it.

## Folders

Try to keep your files organized neatly in appropriately named folders where you can find them. For example, in writing this book I set up a separate folder on my computer's hard disk for each chapter so that I could save the Word document corresponding to the chapter and all the other related files for the chapter (data files, graphics files etc.) in a logical structure. You can create new folders using Windows Explorer.

## Copying and moving files or folders

With Windows Explorer it is easy to copy or move files or folders from one location to another. To copy the file or folder just select it and then choose **E**dit and then **C**opy from the menu in Windows Explorer. Go to the location where you wish to place the copy and click on **P**aste. A copy of the file or folder will then be created. If you just want to move the file the procedure is similar except that you use Cu**t** rather than **C**opy at the first stage. If you realize immediately after one of these actions that you have made a mistake, you can undo the move (**E**dit **U**ndo Move). In fact, cutting, copying and pasting files and folders works in just the same way as cutting, copying and pasting selected parts of a document or file within a word processing or other applications package.

## Using DOS

The Disk Operating System which preceded Windows (DOS or sometimes MS-DOS) issues instructions via commands that are typed in at the keyboard at a command line prompt rather than by clicking with a mouse to select an option from a menu. Sometimes it can be quicker to work with files this way, but you will have to know the commands to use. To get to a DOS window you will have to select the MS DOS Prompt option from the Start Menu (or perhaps there will be a DOS icon on your desktop).

You will then see a black DOS window (it might occupy the entire screen depending on the set-up) with a blinking cursor following a letter and folder name to indicate the current drive and folder (or directory as they are called with DOS).

For example, you might get

```
C:\WINDOWS>
```

If this isn't the directory (or folder) where you want to work you must use the change directory (cd) command to move to the one you want. So, for example, if you want to go to the basic *root* directory (the top-level directory on the C drive) you should type cd\ and then press the ***Enter*** key. The prompt will change to C:\>

To move to a lower level directory you can either type in the whole path in one, for example, cd\book\ch1, or you can first go to the route directory and then choose the subdirectory to move to. So at the C:\> prompt I could type cd\book. Then when I have the prompt C:\book> I can go to the subdirectory ch1 by typing cd ch1 and then pressing the ***Enter*** key (notice this time there is a space but no "\" – "backslash").

To switch to a different drive just type the letter of its name, followed by a colon (:) and press the ***Enter*** key. For example, to switch to the A drive type A: and press ***Enter***.

It is beyond the scope of this appendix to deal with all the DOS commands but those listed in Table 1.1 may be useful. Notice that you can use the "wildcard" feature (*) to work on several files at once.

**Table 1.1**   Some DOS commands.

| Command | What it does |
| --- | --- |
| DIR | Lists all the files in the current directory |
| DIR/W | Lists all the files in the current directory in compact form (if there are a lot of files in the directory the list will scroll off screen) |
| DIR/P | Lists all the files in the current directory, pausing at the end of each screen – press any key to carry on |
| DIR *.doc | Lists all the files in the current directory with the extension .doc |
| ERASE filename | Erases (or deletes) the named file |
| ERASE *.doc | Erases all files in the current directory with the extension .doc |
| COPY *.* A:\ | Copies all the files in the current directory to the floppy disk |

*Warning*. If you use DOS to erase a file it will be deleted then and there (it will not be put in the Recycle Bin) so *be very careful* when you use this approach.

## Tip

To avoid accidentally deleting files on your floppy disk you can "write protect" them by moving the small slot on the bottom right hand corner of the disk. It is a good idea to put a sticky label on your floppy disks with some indication of what files are on the disk (to remind you if you forget and to save you having to list them all). You should also write your name on the label to increase the chances of getting the disk back if you accidentally leave it somewhere.

To return to Windows from DOS type exit and press the ***Enter*** key.

# CHAPTER 2

# Beginning to work with computers in economics

## Objectives

The objectives of this chapter are to introduce the reader to the main standard types of office software packages and to provide some simple applications for economists.

Types of software packages covered are:

- word processing software
- spreadsheets
- e-mail software
- web browsers
- presentation software
- database software

## 2.1 Beginning to work with a word processor

Every computer user will want to make use of word processing software to produce text documents for printing. As a student of economics you may well be asked to word process the essays that you write for some of the courses that you are taking. Or you might need to produce an OHP slide with a list of headings or points that you want to make in a seminar presentation. At some stage you might want to produce a CV or résumé, or type letters of application for jobs or postgraduate courses. You might want to handle a bigger task, such as your dissertation.

As a student of economics you will probably find that some of your word processed documents will need to contain mathematical symbols or equations and graphs or charts. We will consider such refinements in the next chapter. Here we look only at standard text-based documents.

It is simple enough to begin typing text in your word processing software. Whether you are using a version of MS Word, Corel WordPerfect or some other word processing software you can just start the program and begin typing.

If you make a mistake it is easy to correct or even erase text. You just select the section of text that you wish to change (drag the mouse over it while holding down the left mouse button) and either begin typing the replacement text or, to delete the selected text, just press the delete key on the keyboard.

If you change something, but then you immediately decide that you want to change back to the original, you can use the <u>U</u>ndo Typing option in the <u>E</u>dit menu. If you want to move a block of text to somewhere else in the document you can just select it and then use <u>E</u>dit followed by <u>C</u>ut. Move to where you want the text to be and select <u>E</u>dit and then <u>P</u>aste. You can centre, or align blocks of text to the left or right margins (sometimes called left or right justification) or indent text.

When you use a word processor you will be able to *format* the text so that when it is printed it looks the way that you want it. You can change the font type, size and style for selected blocks of text. For example, depending on the printer drivers

## Fonts

Times New Roman is a serif typeface. Small fine lines are used to produce "tails" to finish off each letter. This is good for long stretches of text at small font sizes since it is easy to read.

**Arial is a sans-serif typeface. It looks better at larger point sizes and is good for headings.**

```
Courier is like the old typewriter typeface. It uses
fixed spaces for each letter (unlike Times New Roman and
Arial, which have proportional fonts so less space is
used for letters like i and l than for w or m).
```

Some older software relied on a fixed number of characters per line to create tabular output. Should you find yourself viewing output from such packages on a monitor you will find a non-proportional font such as Courier will re-establish these tables.

Depending on your printer and printer driver there will be other fonts available for you to use.

available to you it may be possible for you to select many alternative font types. *Printer drivers* are special program files that allow your software to use the printer's features – the software may have to be configured so that it recognizes the printer and printer driver that you are using. The default text type will probably be Times New Roman, but you might prefer to work with a *sans-serif* font such as Arial. For the kind of concentrated blocks of text that you get in essays Times New Roman is to be preferred, but for titles and other short headline blocks of text you may like to use Arial.

You can change the *size* of the font in a block of text from something quite small (8 point) up to something much larger (72 point). (There are 72 points to an inch, so 10 point is approximately 0.14 inches.) The sizes available to you will depend on the printer and the selected font. If the size you select is not available on the current printer, your word processing software will choose the closest available size.

You can also change the *style* of the text from the default "Regular" look, making it **bold**, *italic* (***or both***) or <u>underlining</u> sections of text. In Word you can do this either by selecting F**o**rmat and then **F**ont from the menu or, if it is showing, by selecting what you want from the Formatting toolbar. (Use **V**iew and then **T**oolbars and check Formatting if this is not showing and you want it to be.)

---

**Find out**

Before you go any further check to see whether your word-processing software has any built-in tutorial material. For example, in Word 6, under the Help command in the menu, you will find a "Quick Preview" tutorial that you can run. There are also some Examples and Demos. Either now, or later when you have time, work through these to discover some features of the software that space restrictions prevent me from covering here.

---

## Practical 2.1  Your first word processed document

When a lecturer or instructor is faced with a new group of students it can take him or her a little while to get to know them all. By completing this practical you will not only produce your first word processed document, but you will also provide your lecturer with some details about who you are and what you know about that will help your lecturer get to know you.

Run your word processing software and create a short document which begins with your name (make sure this is in bold and in a bigger font size than the rest of the document). Then add further information about who you are under each of the following subheadings (which should be underlined):

<u>Degree or pathway</u> [put the name of the degree for which you are registered, e.g. BA Economics, BA Business Economics etc.]

<u>Home town or city</u> [or country and town if you are not from the UK]

<u>Knowledge of computing</u> [previous experience of working with word processors, spreadsheets etc.]

<u>Other courses I am taking</u> [e.g. Maths for Economists, Politics, Economic History – whatever other units or modules you are taking]

<u>How I hope studying economics will help me in the future</u> [what you expect to learn from the course and how you think it will assist you in your future career]

<u>My three main hobbies or interests</u> [list three hobbies or interests that you have that might help the lecturer to remember you; e.g. perhaps you play a sport or support a football team, or you like a particular band or type of music, or you like reading science fiction or playing computer games]

If you are using Word, investigate the following items from the **T**ools menu to see what they do: **S**pelling, **W**ord Count. You can use **F**ind in the **E**dit menu to find a word in your document. Try it out to find the word "knowledge".

Now select the word "knowledge" in your document and then choose **T**hesaurus from the **T**ools menu. What suggestions, if any, does your word processor have as synonyms for this word? (If you are using a different package find where the equivalent tools are and use them on your document.)

When you are happy with your document, preview it to see what it looks like (in Word use **F**ile, Print Pre**v**iew). Then **S**ave it on to a floppy disk (or onto the network drive) and **P**rint out a copy to give to your lecturer.

> **Tip**
>
> It is a good idea to save your files regularly as you are working on them – don't wait until you have finished perfecting them. That way if the system crashes or you suddenly have to leave the lab because of a fire alarm you won't lose the work that you have already done.

Use Windows Explorer (or its equivalent) and look on your disk to see the size of the file in kilobytes, the type of file (it should say Microsoft Word 6 or whatever other version/program you have used) and the date and time when you last modified it.

## 2.2 Beginning to work with a spreadsheet

You can use a spreadsheet program (such as Microsoft Excel, Quattro Pro or Lotus 1-2-3) for all kinds of applications involving quantitative information. Here you will simply enter a small amount of data and text, add in some formulae to calculate some expressions based on the original values, and then construct a chart to display this information graphically. In the next chapter we will see how this type of program can be used for conducting "what-if" type exercises by changing one of the original values and observing how both the formulae and the charts are automatically adjusted to reflect this revised information. The whole of Chapter 4 will be devoted to further spreadsheet applications in economics, illustrating just some of the huge range of data analysis, model analysis and problem-solving tasks for which this type of software can be used.

When you start up a spreadsheet program such as Excel or Quattro Pro you will initially be faced with a screen something like the one shown in Figure 2.1.

The exact screen that you see may look slightly different, depending upon the package and version number you are using, and the way that it may have been configured on your system. However, whatever the differences, it will have the following common features. At the top of the screen will be a *menu bar* with the main commands that are available to you (**F**ile, **E**dit, **V**iew, **I**nsert etc.), followed by one or more *toolbars* containing icons (buttons) that you can click on to perform many of the commands that are available in the program.

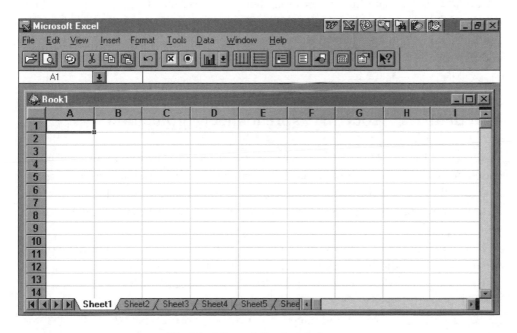

**Fig. 2.1** Microsoft Excel ready for use.

Underneath the menu and toolbars you will see the *worksheet* area, which consists of a number of columns, labelled A, B, C etc., and rows, labelled 1, 2, 3, etc. Columns run vertically down the worksheet, rows run horizontally across the width of the worksheet.

This area is where spreadsheet information (in the form of *numbers, formulae* or *text*) can be entered and manipulated. At the intersection of each row and column is a *cell*, which will be identified by a name consisting of its column letter followed by its row number. Thus the top left hand cell will be A1 and in Figure 2.1 you can see as far down and across as cell I14. A single worksheet contains up to 256 columns and over 16 000 rows, although you can only see a small part of this on screen at any one time. You can scroll down or across the worksheet to move to other parts of it, either by using the arrow keys on the keyboard or by pointing the mouse at the vertical or horizontal scroll bars on the edge of the worksheet. Column headings after Z continue with AA, AB, etc., all the way up to IV. Notice that the *active cell* (the one you use your mouse or the arrow keys to point at) will be shown in the *name box* just underneath the menu and toolbars.

Modern spreadsheets allow you to work with many worksheets within the same *workbook*. You begin on Sheet 1 but you can move to another sheet by clicking on its tab at the bottom of the worksheet area. A new workbook will contain 16 separate worksheets, but you can add more if you need them, up to a maximum number of 256. In our first example we will keep to just one worksheet but in later chapters we will see how you might make use of some of the other worksheets. Excel labels the different worksheets within a workbook Sheet 1, Sheet 2 etc., Quattro Pro calls them sheets A, B, C etc., so each cell in a workbook can be identified first by a reference to the sheet that it is in and then labels for the column and row position; e.g. A:A1 is the address for the top left cell in sheet A.

## Practical 2.2   Your first spreadsheet application

In this practical you will enter into a worksheet some information about consumers' expenditure on alcoholic drink in the UK (text and numbers, in the form of a table). You will then be asked to enter some formulae to calculate row and column totals. Finally you will use the spreadsheet commands to create a chart to illustrate the data in your table.

Run your spreadsheet software (from the Start button or by clicking the icon on the desktop or in the Network Applications Launcher folder).

Beginning in cell A1 type the text: `UK Consumers' Expenditure on Alcoholic Drink in 1997`. Then in cell A2 type: `in £ million at current prices`. Now go to row 4 and in cells B4, C4, D4 and E4 type: `Q1, Q2, Q3` and `Q4`.

Add row labels for your table as follows:

Cell  Entry
A5    BEER
A6    WINE etc.
A7    SPIRITS

and then enter the values, as shown in Figure 2.2.

These figures show consumers' expenditure on the three sub-categories of alcoholic drink which are distinguished in the Office for National Statistics figures for each of the quarters in 1997. ("Wine etc." includes fortified wines, cider and perry). As we are looking only at one year's figures we can use the series expressed at current prices (constant prices series will have been adjusted for inflation by dividing by a suitable price deflator and will be most relevant when we are looking at data covering a number of different years). The information shown here was obtained from the ONS Time Series Databank which is held on the MIMAS computer at Manchester University. In Chapter 6 we will see how to access this and other sources of on-line data.

Now let's develop this worksheet. Go to cell A9 and type: TOTAL. Then go to cell B9 and type: =+B5+B6+B7 (as you are doing this you will see the formula displayed in the formula box to the right of the cell name box). Press the *Enter* key and you will see that the number 6424 appears in the cell within the worksheet. If you make this cell again the active cell (using the arrow keys or by clicking the mouse on it) you will see that the formula is still shown in the formula box while the result of the formula is displayed in the worksheet itself.

If by any chance you have entered the formula incorrectly you can either simply go to the cell and overwrite the formula with what should be there, or click on the formula box and edit it there until it shows the right formula. Then when you press the *Enter* key the result of the amended formula will be shown in the worksheet.

| | A | B | C | D | E | F |
|---|---|---|---|---|---|---|
| | **EX2_2.XLS** | | | | | |
| **1** | UK Consumers' Expenditure on Alcoholic Drink in 1997 | | | | | |
| **2** | in £ million at current prices | | | | | |
| **3** | | | | | | |
| **4** | | Q1 | Q2 | Q3 | Q4 | |
| **5** | BEER | 3702 | 4165 | 4141 | 3903 | |
| **6** | WINE etc. | 1609 | 1861 | 1841 | 2252 | |
| **7** | SPIRITS | 1113 | 1340 | 1345 | 1961 | |
| **8** | | | | | | |

**Fig 2.2**  Information for Practical 2.2.

If you were now to enter similar formulae in cells C9 to E9 you would be able to calculate the total Consumer's Expenditure on Alcoholic Drink for each of the other quarters in 1997. However, rather than entering each formula separately you can use a facility that is available within spreadsheets to *copy* formulae from one cell to another, whenever the structure of the formula is the same.

With cell B9 as the active cell click on **E**dit and then **C**opy in the menu. Then go to cell C9 and drag the mouse over cells C9 to E9 so that they are selected (there will be a grey border shown around them). Now choose **E**dit and then **P**aste from the menu. Appropriate row totals will be displayed in these cells. If you point the mouse at each of them in turn you will see suitable formulae displayed in the formula box, i.e. formulae which add the values in rows 5, 6 and 7 but with the column adjusted appropriately.

There is an alternative method of copying formulae which just involves dragging outwards from the cell holding the formula. Point the mouse at the bottom right hand corner of cell B9. As you so do the cursor should change shape from an empty cross to a filled-in cross shape. If you hold down the left hand mouse button and drag the mouse across into cells C9 to E9 the formula will be copied into these cells (again adjusting for the relative column positions).

To get the year totals for each category we will make use of the spreadsheet's built-in functions. If you are working with Excel version 5, go to cell G5 and then use the mouse to click on the formula box. A small button with $f_x$ should appear. Click on it (if it was there already just click on it). The *Function Wizard* (Step 1 of 2) dialog box should open up (Figure 2.3). (Later versions of Excel use the built-in *Office Assistant* to guide you through the steps. If you are using Quattro Pro you can use the *Sum* icon button Σ, or for more options select **I**nsert **F**unction from the menu.)

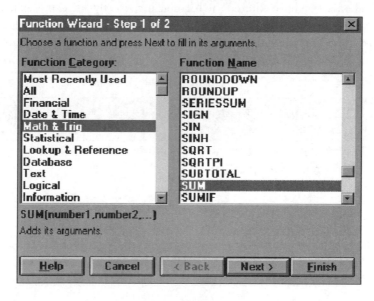

**Fig. 2.3**   The Function Wizard (Step 1) window.

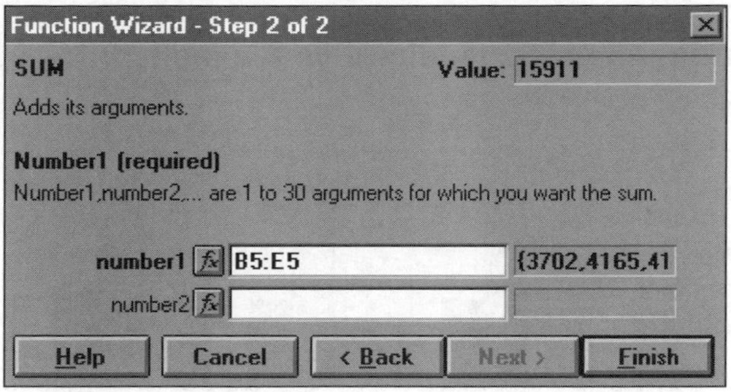

**Fig. 2.4** The Function Wizard (Step 2) window.

In the left hand pane click on Math & Trig and then in the right hand pane scroll down until you find SUM and click on that. The Function Wizard (Step 2 of 2) will open (see Figure 2.4). In the entry box next to number 1 enter B5:E5 (or just copy and paste these cells from the worksheet itself). As you do so you will see a list of the values in these cells appearing next to the number 1 box and the result of the application of the formula will be shown next to the word *Value* at the top right hand corner of the window. Click the **F**inish button and you will return to the worksheet. Press ***Enter*** and cell G5 will display the figure for the total expenditure on beer in 1997 (in £ million of course). Copy this formula and paste it into cells G6, G7 and G9.

As this practical illustrates, you can construct your own formulae using the usual algebraic operators (+ for plus, – for minus, * for multiply and / for divide) or you can utilize one of the many built-in functions. When you have time return to the Function Wizard and explore some of the other formulae that are available. As well as the Math & Trig formulae many of those listed under Financial and Statistical are likely to be particularly useful to economists.

Finally in this practical, you will use the spreadsheet to construct a chart showing the information in a visual form. If you are working with Excel 5 use the mouse to select cells A4 to E7 (i.e. those containing the original table of values without the row and column totals). Then from the menu click **I**nsert, followed by **C**hart and the **O**n This Sheet. A floating version of the chart icon should appear. Drag it down with the mouse to an empty part of the worksheet, say somewhere around cell A12. Click on the mouse. The first of a number of *Chart Wizard* windows should appear (Step 1 of 5). If the correct cell range doesn't appear in this window you should correct it at this stage. Click Next and you will move to Step 2 where you will be offered a selection of chart types. Pick the one labeled **C**olumn and click Next (this gives you a set of clustered columns which allows you to compare values across categories). In Step 3 you select a F**o**rmat to use – choose option 1 and click Next. Step 4 should show you a chart similar to that in Figure 2.5 (without the titles). Click Next and move on to Step 5 where you can give the chart a title. (It is good practice to provide a title and to label the axes in your chart properly.)

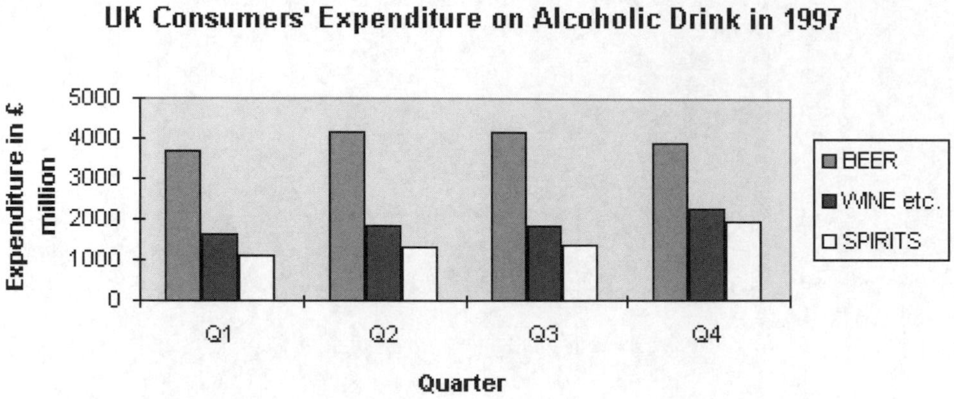

## UK Consumers' Expenditure on Alcoholic Drink in 1997

**Fig. 2.5**   Clustered column chart displaying the alcohol expenditure data.

As with the construction of formulae, there are various ways of constructing charts in spreadsheets. With your spreadsheet you may have to go about things in a slightly different way to that described above to achieve the same effect. You may be able just to click on a Chart Type icon button on the toolbar (it looks like a small bar chart). Again the floating chart icon should appear. You can then work through the rest of the steps as outlined above. In Excel 97 instead of first selecting a place in the worksheet to put the chart and then working through the various steps as described above, the chart is created first and then you choose whether to put it on a new sheet or drag and drop it at a particular place on the current sheet. You may also have to turn off horizontal grid lines if you don't want them.

Suppose having created the chart you decide that it should have had a title. This is no problem; you can always go back and edit a chart, adding additional information or changing various features as you wish. Select the chart by pointing and clicking at it. Small markers around the edge of the chart will be shown. Then double click the mouse and a further set of markers will appear. Now click the right hand mouse button and a list of options will be presented. To add a title just click on Chart Title and then **OK** and you will be able to add in a suitable title for your chart.

> ### Tip
>
> It is worth noting that you can often go straight to a list of relevant options for a Windows object (such as an axis or graph title) just by selecting the object and then clicking on the right mouse button.

At this stage you should save your spreadsheet file so that you can work with it again. Just choose **F**ile and **S**ave from the menu and save the file either on your floppy disk (drive A) or on your part of the network drive.

**Find out**

Before going on you may want to experiment with other aspects of Excel (or any other spreadsheet that you are using). Try searching through the topics in the **H**elp menu or running through any Examples and Demos. Take a look too at some of the other built-in functions and chart types that are available.

You might also like to experiment with formatting the information in the table on your worksheet. In Excel 5, for example, select cells A4 to G9 and then click on F**o**rmat and then **A**utoFormat. From the Sample pane you can see what effects you can produce from the options on offer. If you see one you like click on OK to choose it.

## 2.3   Beginning to work with e-mail software

Electronic mail (*e-mail*) is a way of communicating electronically with people in your own organization, or elsewhere across the world via the Internet. Messages can be sent to individuals or to groups of people. Similarly you can receive messages which have been sent to you individually, or to a group of people on a list to which you belong.

You can keep in touch with friends at other universities, or your parents if they have access to e-mail. If you are fortunate enough to be able to make a "round-the-world" expedition between college and work, e-mail can provide an effective means of communication with loved ones back home. As you journey from city to city you could use a "cyber-café" or similar facility to connect to your e-mail site and send messages to those back home who have e-mail facilities. They can reply to your e-mail address, which you can then log-in to whenever and wherever convenient.

Your lecturers may want to contact you via e-mail. For example, they could send a message to the whole class to let you all know about a change in the lecture program. Or perhaps they might communicate with you individually, asking why you were absent from a particular class. Conversely you could send a message to your lecturer asking for clarification on a point that was made in a lecture or for help on an assignment. You can join e-mail discussion lists, sending and receiving messages on a particular topic or area of interest.

Early e-mail systems were quite restrictive in what they could do and how they operated. You could only send plain (ASCII) text and software commands had to be issued by using combinations of control keys. Today's e-mail software will usually have a friendly user interface, easy editing, built-in help and many other additional useful features such as the ability to attach files to messages that you send, to check when messages that you send have been read, or to filter out "junk" e-mail messages. At Portsmouth we use Pegasus Mail but you might be using some other popular system such as Microsoft's Outlook Express or a version of Eudora. Most modern systems will have a similar range of features. Some of the newest systems even allow you to send audio and video messages. Of course this won't be very much use unless the recipients of your messages have the hardware and software to deal with them.

---

### ASCII text

ASCII is the acronym for *American Standard Code for Information Interchange*. Each character on the keyboard has been assigned an ASCII code so that information can be sent between computers in binary digital form. For example, the ASCII code for the letter A is 0100 0001. Files that consist only of characters covered by the ASCII code can be read on any computer without the need for additional software. Such files cannot include special fonts or additional formatting that you use your word processing software to add.

---

In this section we shall look only at simple text e-mail messages sent from one person to another. In the next chapter we shall look at the use of mail discussion lists and other e-mail refinements such as file attachments.

## E-mail addresses

Before you can send an e-mail message to anyone you have to know his or her e-mail address. They might have given it to you, or if you are an experienced computer user you might have tracked it down using one of the Internet tools which can be used for this purpose. An e-mail address will contain all the information necessary to get the message to the recipient, wherever they are in the world (provided that they have an e-mail account).

Each e-mail address consists of two main parts as shown below. First comes the *user name* and then the *domain*. They are separated by an @ symbol (pronounced "at").

```
[User name]@[domain]
```

For example, my e-mail address here at the University of Portsmouth in the UK is as follows:

```
Guy.Judge@port.ac.uk
```

Guy.Judge is my user name on the Portsmouth system. User names will often be the person's actual name or their name and initial (for example, on an older system that we had here my user name was judgeg). Notice there will be no spaces in a user name. Different parts of a person's name might be separated by a full stop ("dot" or period). Student user names are often strings of letters and characters referring to the degree course, year of entry etc., so your university e-mail user name might be something like eco99007.

The domain name is also likely to have several parts, connected by "dots". Here mine has just three parts. "port" is short for Portsmouth. E-mail addresses at other universities might have similar shortenings (e.g. "bris" for Bristol and "ox" for Oxford).

Sometimes this part of the address will be preceded by another word which denotes the name that has been given to the e-mail server computer at the institution. For example, my old address used to be `judgeg@pbs.port.ac.uk`. Here 'pbs' was used to direct mail to the mail server in the Portsmouth Business School.

The other parts of an e-mail address provide information about the kind of institution and the country that it is to go to. Here "ac" is short for academic. In the US and some other countries this will be "edu", short for education. If you are sending a message to a company (or an e-mail system run by a service provider) you would have "co" (in the UK) or "com" in other parts of the world. Government departments would have "gov" while there would be "org" for other organizations.

The "uk" tells you that I am in the UK. Other country codes include "fr" for France, "es" for Spain and "de" for Germany. E-mail addresses in the US usually omit the country code. If you see an e-mail address without a country code it will probably be somewhere in the US, or on a system operated by a service provider that is based in the US.

Finally, note that if you are sending an e-mail to someone in your own institution you may be able to use only the user name.

## Practical 2.3   Your first e-mail message

In this practical you will compose and send your first e-mail – to me! This way not only will you be able to practice how to send e-mail, but I will get some direct feedback from the readers of my book.

Run your e-mail software (by clicking on the icon on the desktop or from the Start button). Once it is loaded up you should see both a menu bar with the various command names along the top (**F**ile, **E**dit, **A**ddresses etc.) and a toolbar (or button panel) with icons that you can click on to operate the most commonly used parts of the program.

To begin the process of sending a new message either click on the Send mail button or select File from the menu followed by New message (you could also use the appropriate hot-key combination). If you are using Pegasus, a message editing window as shown in Figure 2.6 will appear (you should get something similar with other e-mail systems).

Enter my e-mail address in the To: box (i.e. `Guy.Judge@port.ac.uk`). In the Subject box enter: `My First E-Mail message`.

Now type me a brief message in the main message box, telling me who you are, where you are studying and maybe the three hobbies or interests that you told your lecturer about in Practical 2.1. Keep it reasonably brief – I don't want your full life history!

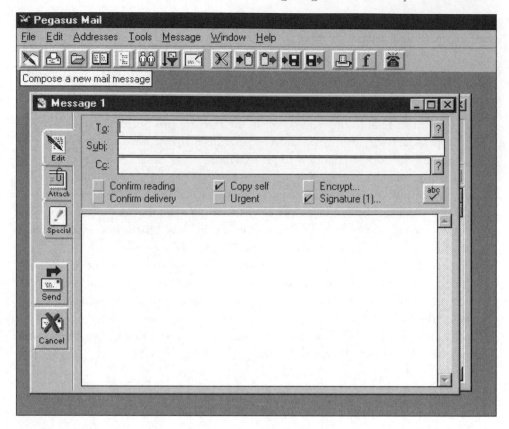

**Fig. 2.6**   The Pegasus Mail Message Editing window.

Check through your message for typing errors and correct any that you find. Then send the message to me (in Pegasus you do this by clicking the Send button towards the bottom left of the message window, or by pressing the Ctrl+Enter keys). You will have sent your first e-mail message. I am looking forward to receiving it. I shall certainly reply to it, although this may not happen immediately.

### Find out

Find out the e-mail address of one of your fellow students and send him (her) an e-mail message. If you receive a message from a fellow student you can *reply* to it just by clicking on the Reply button. You will have the option of including the original message in your reply. It is often helpful to include all or part of the message you are replying to in order to give a context to your message (see the section below on "E-mail guidelines and Netiquette").

Type your response and then click "Send" to send it.

**Find out**

Find out the e-mail address of your lecturer. Send a brief e-mail to let him/her know (a) that you are working through the exercises and practicals in this book, and (b) that if your course tutor wishes to do so you may be contacted via e-mail at that address. Don't forget to include something suitable in the subject line.

**Find out**

Find out more about your e-mail system by clicking on **H**elp in the main menu. If there is an introductory tutorial, work through it. Find out how to attach a *personal name* to your e-mail address (particularly helpful if your user name is just a jumble of letters and numbers) and how to add an automatic *signature* to the bottom of every message.

Find out how to keep a *copy* of any messages that you send, and how to ensure that a copy of a message that is sent to one person will also be received by someone else (for information only) (Hint: investigate what the cc: – short for carbon copy – line is in the message box. Find out also what bcc: means.)

Find out how to *forward* a message that has been sent to you to someone else.

Find out how to *print* out a message that you have received. Find out how to *delete* messages that you don't need any more and how to organize messages you want to keep in *folders*.

## E-mail guidelines and Netiquette

Before you send very many e-mail messages you should consider some of the "dos and don'ts" of e-mail. Just because it is so easy to send an e-mail message doesn't mean that you shouldn't think carefully about a message before you send it. Try to keep within the bounds of Internet etiquette (or "Netiquette" as it is sometimes called).

First, always remember that the point of electronic mail is communication. Don't send an e-mail until you have checked your message. Have you said everything that you want to? Have your corrected any typos, spelling mistakes or other errors? Never send an e-mail when you are angry or upset. You may regret it afterwards.

Don't type your messages all in upper case letters – it is regarded as rude and the equivalent of shouting. However, you might want to use capital letters for certain words to give them emphasis since most e-mail software won't allow you to use bold or italic fonts to do this. It can be difficult to judge the tone of someone's comment from a written message. People sometimes use the "smiley face" shown by :-) when they are intending to be funny.

E-mail messages come in a variety of types and sizes, from short and rather informal messages to a friend, through to longer and more formal messages perhaps to people you haven't met in person. Except for those short messages to your friends you are advised to keep your messages polite and business-like. Since the recipient can quite easily print the e-mail message it is quite possible for the e-mail to achieve the same status as the conventional printed word, so you should be as thoughtful as you would have been in preparing a letter. Use correct grammar and spelling and try to keep your messages as brief and to the point as possible. Although a number of e-mail abbreviations have grown up over the years (such as IMHO for "In My Humble Opinion" or BTW for "By The Way") try not to overuse these, especially when you are communicating with someone who might not know what they mean.

Always use the *subject line*. All mailers will list new messages so that you can see not only who they are from but also what the subject of the message is. Busy users might choose to scan the subject lines so that they can pick out the messages with the highest priority.

If you are replying to a message, include parts of the original message in your reply (use some kind of visual indication to distinguish the text of the original message from your replies – the > symbol is often used for this purpose). Or you might briefly summarize a point to which you wish to respond (e.g. Guy Judge said that it is a good idea to use correct grammar and spelling).

Do not abuse the power of e-mail. Avoid all kinds of sexist and racist language and be sensitive to people's cultures and beliefs. Remember messages can be traced back to you and your system administrator may remove people from the system who do not respect other users.

### Bounced mail and e-mail headers

If you enter an e-mail address incorrectly (you mistype it or the name is not quite right in some other way) the mail system will return ("bounce") the message back to you. Take a careful look at the e-mail address you sent your message to (it will be included as a message *header* in the returned mail) to see if you can spot the error.

## 2.4    Beginning to work with a web browser

The World Wide Web links together literally millions of web sites belonging to universities, government departments, companies and other organizations as well as the "home pages" of many individuals. With an Internet connection and a web browser (the software that enables you to connect up to sites on the web) you will have the possibility of accessing all kinds of material which has been placed on the web.

The quality and reliability of the material on the web varies enormously. Because the web is open to anyone with a server and an Internet connection (or space on someone else's server) all kinds of strange, weird and wonderful (and even not so wonderful) material is to be found there. It can be fun just browsing through such material. But from the point of view of the work that you have to do as an economist you will want to be more directed in the way that you use the web. There are certain key sites that you ought to know about because they give you access to economic data and other relevant information. You can use *search tools* to try to track down web sites with material on specific topics or you can use *subject gateways* to point you in the direction of material of guaranteed quality.

In later chapters we will return to the issues of how to track down relevant material on the web and how to assess the quality of material that you do find. In this introductory session we will simply direct you to a number of key sites for economists.

As with other software products there are several alternative web browsers that are available for you to use (and different versions of each of them could be installed on your network). At the time of writing the two best known web browsers are Netscape Communicator (Navigator) and Microsoft Internet Explorer. By now you should have found out which of these is available to you on your system. Run the browser software either by clicking on its icon or going through the Start button.

When the software is run it will look for the web page that has been designated as the home page location. If you are in a university lab this might be the university's main home page, or one for your department. If you have your own computer you will be able to change this if you wish (perhaps eventually to a home page that you have constructed yourself). Later on when you have time, come back and explore this initial home page clicking on any *hyperlinks* that are apparent when you move the mouse over the document to see where they take you. You can always use the browser's Back button to return you to the page whence you came.

As with the other software you have been using, you will see at the top of the screen a main menu bar and underneath it a toolbar or button panel that you can click on to operate the most commonly used parts of the program. Within the toolbar you should see the *Location box*. This contains the address on the web of the page that you are looking at. A web address like this is often called a *URL* or *Uniform Resource Locator*. It will be unique to the page that you are viewing and if you enter a valid URL into the Location box and then press **Enter** you will be taken to the page associated with it (that is you will be able to view that page on your screen).

Rather like e-mail addresses, URLs have a standard type of structure and you can often tell quite a lot about a site from studying its URL.

The URL for the main site at the University of Portsmouth is `http://www.port.ac.uk`. You can try it if you like. The http: stands for "Hypertext Transfer Protocol", which tells the browser that you are looking for a standard web page document. Other protocols can be handled using web browsers, the most common of which is FTP (File Transfer Protocol). We will return to this later.

The // acts as a separator (rather like the @ in an e-mail address). The rest of the URL tells your browser which server (or "host" computer to look on) and where in the directory structure on that computer to find the file which it needs. The www element of the address is the server name. Although it is conventional for organizations to name their web servers www, it is not essential (indeed some that we shall look at very shortly do not follow this convention). The rest of the Portsmouth web server address tells us where on the Internet we can find the server and the kind of institution that it is.

The URL for the main web page of an organization is usually fairly short and simple. For example, `http://www.wiley.co.uk/` is the URL for the home page of the UK division of John Wiley & Sons, Ltd.

Longer URLs will be needed to take you to specific pages within folders on a server. For example, I have a web page for a course on introductory econometrics that I teach at Portsmouth which has the following URL:

`http://www.pbs.port.ac.uk/~judge/econ255/index.htm`

The material is not on the main university web server but on the one in the Portsmouth Business School (hence `pbs.port`). Each member of staff has a designated folder which is indicated by the ~ (tilde) sign followed by their surname. Within mine I have set up separate folders for each of my courses – econ255 is the official university name for the econometrics course. Each of the / (slash or sometimes forward slash) signs in the URL indicates that the computer should look at a subdirectory within a directory. Finally index.htm is the main file in the econ 255 directory or folder (it is conventional for main home page files to be called "index"). The htm indicates that the file is a "hypertext markup language" file (more on this in Chapter 5). (Actually you can leave out the index.htm if you like. The computer will assume that you want to use the index file in the directory.) Sometimes on UNIX machines the file extension is html.

## Practical 2.4   Your first time browsing the web

It is now time to look at a few useful sites. In fact I suggest you begin by connecting to the special web site that has been set up for this book by the publishers, John Wiley & Sons. Enter the following URL in the location box and press the **_Enter_** key.

`http://www.wiley.co.uk/judge`

The publishers have set up some special pages on this site so that I can provide you with supplementary material that there is not space for in the book. There I can let you know about software updates and new web sites that have been set up since the book went to press, and provide feedback to you on ideas and suggestions that have come from other readers. As the Wiley web site won't be continuously updated, I have included a link from it to a web page of my own at Portsmouth that will have the very latest news on it. You can either go there from the Wiley site, or directly using the URL:

```
http://www.pbs.port.ac.uk/~judge/skills/
```

*Bookmarks*

Rather than having to remember the URLs for sites that you want to visit again you can store them as Bookmarks. Internet Explorer calls them "Favorites". Click on the **B**ookmark button or select it from the menu in your browser. Then select **A**dd Bookmark. The URL for the web page that is currently being viewed will be added to the list of bookmarks. If you want to come back to this page all you will then have to do is select **B**ookmark and then **G**o to Bookmarks. Then you can locate the page you want to go to by simply double clicking on its bookmark. Of course this assumes that you will be using the same computer again. If you always work in a lab but not usually on the same machine you could save the Bookmarks file onto a floppy disk to take away with you. Alternatively you could use Notepad to keep a small text file on a floppy disk, copying and pasting URLs between the Notepad file and the Location box in the browser. Using this approach you could annotate the file, including additional text to add comments about the different web sites that you have visited. Another alternative is to store the URLs in a Word file, since recent versions of this package enable the browser to be activated directly from within Word as you click on a URL.

*Some key sites for economists*

There are many useful sites on the web for economists. The following is just a short list of sites that I would like you to visit now. Others will be mentioned in the next two chapters and I have set up links to many more from the book's web site.

Go to each of the web sites in the list below. Explore each one for a few minutes. Remember you can use the Back button to go back to a previous web page. You can also use **G**o on the browser's menu to go directly to any of the sites previously visited during the current session.

Establish a small text file containing the URLs for each of these sites and a few words describing your reaction to what can be found at the site.

*Short list of key web sites*

**1.** *CTI Economics at the University of Bristol*
   ```
   http://www.ilrt.bristol.ac.uk/ctiecon/
   ```
   Look in particular at the CHEER site
   ```
   http://www.ilrt.bristol.ac.uk/ctiecon/cheer.htm
   ```

2. *SOSIG (Social Science Information Gateway)*
   `http://sosig.ac.uk/`
   Look in particular at the section called Economics on the Internet – A SOSIG Subject Guide
   `http://sosig.ac.uk/subject-guides/economics.html`
   Note that if you are in the US you can go to the *mirror* site at
   `http://scout18.cs.wisc.edu/sosig_mirror/`
3. *Biz/ed Business and Economics Information Gateway*
   `http://www.bized.ac.uk/`
4. *Resources for Economists on the Internet*
   If you are in the US go to
   `http://econwpa.wustl.edu/EconFAQ/EconFAQ.html`
   If you are in the UK go to
   `http://netec.mcc.ac.uk/~adnetec/EconFAQ/EconFAQ.html`
5. *WebEC*
   The original site is in Finland at
   `http://www.helsinki.fi/WebEc/`
   In the UK go to
   `http://netec.mcc.ac.uk/WebEc.html`
   In the US go to
   `http://netec.wustl.edu/WebEc.html`

If you feel that you have done enough hard work for one day, I give you permission to go to one of the following "fun" sites. But don't stay too long. It's easy to waste time on the web!

*A few fun sites*

1. *Pasi Kuoppamaki's Economist Jokes page*
   `http://netec.mcc.ac.uk/JokEc.html`
   Mirrored in the US at
   `http://netec.wustl.edu/JokEc.html`
2. *The Dilbert Zone*
   `http://www.unitedmedia.com/comics/dilbert/`
3. *Randy Glasbergen's cartoon site*
   `http://www.norwich.net/~randyg/toon.html`

## Mirrors

Popular web sites are often mirrored on servers in other countries in order to reduce unnecessary use of international phone lines. Many European economics web sites are mirrored in the US on the server at Washington University, St Louis run by Bob Parks. In the UK you can often find important overseas economics sites mirrored on the MIMAS server at Manchester University.

> **Tip**
>
> URLs have a tendency to become outdated fairly rapidly. Sometimes when information is revised it is also organized in a slightly different way on the server. So if you click on a link (or enter a URL that you have found) and the browser can't find the exact location requested, try truncating (shortening) the URL to just the main home page URL for the site. You may find that you are then able to track down the information you want.

## 2.5 Beginning to work with presentation software

You may be asked at some point on your course to give a brief prepared talk about some topic or other to the rest of the students in your class. You might decide to produce a list of headings and key points to help you provide a structure and a focus for the talk. These could then either be printed and distributed as a handout, or turned into OHP slides. If the facilities are available you might even be able to project your slides straight from the computer in electronic form.

Of course you could just use an ordinary word processing package to help you prepare your handout or slides. If your OHP slides are created in this way remember to limit the amount of text that you put on any one page so that it can be seen when it is displayed on screen. You should choose a suitable font type (sans-serif styles like Arial look good for this kind of application) and use a sufficiently large size (at least 30 point) so that they can be read at the back of the room where you will be giving the talk. It is not a good idea to display on screen slides of continuous prose which have been written up in essay form. It will be hard for your audience to read and you will also be tempted simply to read through it for your presentation. To make your talk more dynamic it is better to work just with headings and key points on screen and then to talk around them. You can look at the heading on screen to remind you what the next point is, but then turn to face your audience as you say what needs to be said about it.

A number of specialized software packages are now available specifically to assist in the preparation and delivery of talks or presentations of this type. The Microsoft product is called PowerPoint, but other packages such as Corel Presentation are also popular. Packages like this can help you to make an effective presentation by providing a suitable *template* into which you place your information. You can ensure that each screen has a common design, perhaps with a small header or footer with a page number or other identifying information contained in it. For electronic presentations you can select different *build effects* (gradually adding information to each screen rather than displaying it all at once) and alternative *transitions* (the way that the next screen is brought in to replace the current screen).

As you build up your slide presentation you can usually view it in several different forms. For example, you may want to look at the detail of just one particular slide that you are working on, or you may wish to take an outline view which enables you to preview all the slides on screen at once (so that you can cross-check them for consistency of style, progression of ideas etc.).

You should always begin with a title slide, giving as a bare minimum the title of your talk and your name. You might want to add the date and some other information, such as the title of the course that the talk has been prepared for. Later, after graduation, if you are making a presentation on behalf of a department or an organization, you may want to include its title or its logo. It is very easy to incorporate graphics images or clipart into presentation files, either to brighten up their appearance or to convey information in the form of graphs and charts. Quite often the points on a slide will take the form of a list. These can be numbered or highlighted through the use of bullets (•) or other symbols.

If some of the information that you want to use in a presentation already exists in another file (say in a table as part of a word processed document or as a spreadsheet chart) you will be able to copy and paste it into the presentation document. You may also be able to link the documents together dynamically so that the presentation file will be automatically updated if you change the information in your word processed document or spreadsheet. We will return to this point in the next chapter. In the practical in this chapter we will begin with a free-standing presentation file.

**Fig. 2.7**   Illustration of the use of PowerPoint Version 4.0a showing the Slide View.

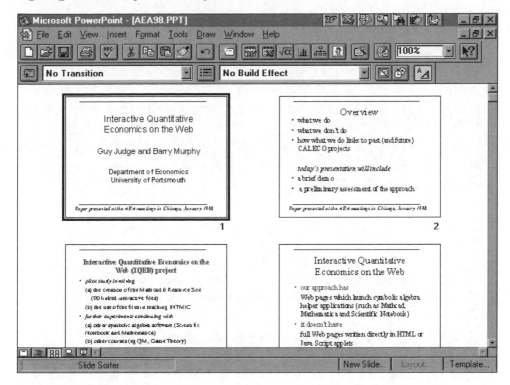

**Fig. 2.8** Illustration of the use of PowerPoint Version 4.0a showing the Slide Sorter View.

Figures 2.7 and 2.8 illustrate the use of PowerPoint version 4.0a as it was used to create a slide show for a presentation with the title "Interactive Quantitative Economics on the Web" that I gave on behalf of Barry Murphy and myself at the January 1998 meetings of the American Economic Association in Chicago. Figure 2.7 shows the program in "slide view" with the initial title slide on screen. I chose a simple white background for the slides with two horizontal lines drawn across the screen and a standard footer containing the words "Paper presented at the AEA meetings in Chicago, January 1998" displayed on every screen. This was accomplished by setting up a *Master* slide for the file with this format. Figure 2.8 shows the slide sorter view of the presentation (you can use this to change the order of the slides in the presentation if you so wish). Slide 2 gave a brief overview of the talk and this was followed by further slides looking at specific points in detail.

At the bottom left of the screen you may be able to see the different buttons that you can click on to switch between the different views such as Slide View screen, the Slide Sorter Screen etc. Clicking on the last button will run through the Slide Show. In other packages (such as Corel Presentation) the buttons for switching between the different views may have slightly different names or be shown elsewhere on the screen, but similar buttons will be available for you to use.

Start up the presentation software that is available to you. See if there are some example slide shows that you can look at (try **F**ile **O**pen and then select any file from the list on offer). Investigate the different views that the software can give you, e.g. Outline, Sorter, Slide Show (or Play). View the slide show.

### Find out

Find out if the package has an interactive tutorial guide (perhaps stored under **H**elp in the main menu). If so run through it. Investigate some of the other options stored under **H**elp.

### Tip

If you like the look of a particular slide show that you have seen you can save the file under a different name and then replace the content with your own, editing it to keep the look and feel of the original.

### Tip

Always rehearse your presentation before you have to give it. Make a note of how long each slide takes. Then, if necessary, you can revise your presentation to fit the time that you have been allocated.

## Practical 2.5   Preparing your first presentation

In this practical you will prepare a short presentation about some key international economic agencies: the World Bank, the IMF, the World Trade Organization and the OECD. There will be an introductory slide showing the title of the talk and your name, followed by an overview slide that lists all the organizations covered in the talk. Then will come four slides, each one displaying some basic information about the organization concerned. Finally, there will be a summing up slide to be viewed as you end your talk.

Use your presentation software to produce a slide show containing seven slides. Some basic information that you can put on each slide is listed below, but you must decide how much of it actually appears on the slide and how much you keep back for your accompanying spoken remarks – *remember it must be possible for your audience to be able to read the information that you display so don't include too much.* When you have finished don't forget to check through each slide to make sure that the information is all correct. Then save the file on your floppy disk or in your space on the network drive.

Contents of your first presentation

Slide 1    Title: Some key international economic agencies
           Author: your name
           Date: put the date here

Slide 2    Overview
           • World Bank
           • IMF
           • World Trade Organization
           • OECD

Slide 3    World Bank
           • Headquarters: Washington DC
           • Established: 1946 (following the Bretton Woods agreement in 1944)
           • Membership: over 180 countries
           • Purpose: to lend money to the governments of developing countries for specific development projects and to economies in transition

Slide 4    IMF
           • Headquarters: Washington DC
           • Established: 1946 (following the Bretton Woods agreement in 1944)
           • Membership: over 180 countries
           • Purpose: to maintain a stable system of buying and selling currencies on the international market and to ensure smooth trade relations

Slide 5    World Trade Organization
           • Headquarters: Geneva
           • Established: 1995 (following Uruguay Round negotiations, 1986–1994)
           • Membership: 134 countries (as of 10 February 1999)
           • Purpose: to administer WTO trade agreements, to act as forum for trade negotiations, to arbitrate in trade disputes, to monitor national trade policies and to provide technical assistance and training for developing countries

Slide 6    OECD (Organization for Economic Co-operation and Development)
           • Headquarters: Paris
           • Established: 1961
           • Membership: 29 countries (mainly richer economies – OECD countries produce over two thirds of world output) but membership is limited only by a country's commitment to a market economy and a pluralistic democracy
           • Purpose: to monitor economic trends and evolving patterns in trade, environment, agriculture, technology and taxation; to undertake research and to debate and establish policy priorities on these matters

Slide 7    Conclusion
            Various international economic organizations with different roles.
            For more information visit the organizations' web sites at
            •  `www.worldbank.org`
            •  `www.imf.org`
            •  `www.wto.org`
            •  `www.oecd.org`

**Find out**

Find out more about each of these organizations by visiting their web sites
(URLs shown above).

## 2.6   Beginning to work with database software

A *database* is a collection of information with some kind of underlying structure, and
in this context it is understood to be stored in electronic form.

For example, the personnel department of a firm might have a database covering
all employees, recording their names, National Insurance numbers, job grade, normal
weekly or monthly pay, date of appointment etc. A database such as this can naturally
be thought of in tabular form with each column relating to a *field* in the database (each
field holding a variable such as employee's name, National Insurance number etc.)
and each row relating to a *record* (in this case all the information relating to a particular
employee). Notice that some fields hold purely textual information while others may
hold quantitative information.

Another example of a database might be one that you have constructed in
conjunction with a survey that you are undertaking of manufacturing firms in your
local area. Each record would relate to a particular firm with some fields holding
textual information (name of firm, address, telephone number etc.) while others
would hold numerical information of various kinds. Some numerical variables might
be purely categorical (for example, a Standard Industrial Classification code to identify
the industrial group that the firm belongs to, or a code such as 1 or 0 to record
whether or not the company's head office is in the UK) while others might be more
genuinely quantitative (number of employees, annual turnover etc.). Some of the
information in the database might have been collected by you trawling through
directories or extracted from other databases. Some might have been obtained directly
from the firm in their responses to your survey questionnaire.

Information in this form could easily be held in a spreadsheet. As we have seen,
worksheets in such packages consist of cells organized into rows and columns and as
such they provide a natural framework for database information. Indeed many
economic databases will be held as spreadsheet files. However, often more specialist

statistics, econometrics or qualitative analysis software would be needed to process data held in this form (see Chapter 5).

When we refer to database software we mean software that is designed not only to store information of this type, but also to *retrieve* information from the database in order to answer questions or *queries* that may be posed about the information in the database. For example, the personnel department might want to find the records of all those employees who are 50 years old or older (perhaps to offer them an early retirement package). Or you might want to discover how many of the firms over a certain size (measured, say, by the number of employees) have a Staff Development and Training program. You might want to sort the information, ranking it alphabetically in terms of one of the text fields, or quantitatively according to the values of one of the numerical variables.

Database software will typically be able to display the information you request when you make your query in the form of a report that you can then print out. You may be able to save your queries so that you can recall them again at a later point.

With most databases it will be important that the information contained in them is kept up to date. There may be new records to add or existing records may need to be edited. User-friendly database software will help by providing an on-screen form that you can use to enter or amend information that is to be held in the database.

The design of the database too is something that you will need to think about. Database software will require you to be very specific about the number and types of fields you want to have in the database. With older packages it could be very difficult, perhaps even impossible, to change this structure once it had been set up. Modern database software is much more flexible and will probably have a wizard or assistant to help you through the initial stages of setting up the framework or structure for the database and will allow you to add new fields later if you find that you need them.

The database software that is included in the Microsoft Office suite is called Access. Its equivalent in the Corel suite is Paradox. When you are ready, run the program by clicking on its icon or from the Start menu.

## Find out

Find out whether your database program has a built-in tutorial that provides an introduction to the software. If it does, spend some time working through it to get a feel for the main features of the software. Microsoft Access 2, which comes as part of Microsoft Office version 4.3, features a number of cue cards which help you work with the program, including a set to give you a quick overview of the software. Information of this type in other software may be found beginning with **H**elp in the main menu or by clicking on the **H**elp icon (which might look like a question mark).

# Practical 2.6   Creating your first database

In this practical you will use the database software available to you to create a simple bibliographical database. You will be provided with some information on 12 books and asked to create a database with 10 fields as specified below. This is obviously only a small database. If this were likely to be as far as it would ever extend it would be hardly worth using database software. You could simply produce a short list of the titles and other information on paper that you could quickly scan whenever you wanted to find information from it. But you may feel that it is worth keeping such a bibliographic database yourself, covering all the books that you discover which are of help to you in your work with computers. Or you might want to create an all-encompassing references database covering other subjects too and also including journal articles, newspaper cuttings, web pages etc. If so you would have to include some extra fields to identify the type of resource (book, article, web site etc.) and the subject areas (general economics, macroeconomics, microeconomics, economic history etc.). You might also wish to include a field that records the date on which you became aware of the resource.

The reason that your first database has been kept to such a small size is that we wish to focus on issues to do with its structure and the way that you can work with it rather than becoming distracted by the volume of information at this stage.

In the database which is being constructed in this practical you should have a field for each of the following (data type in parentheses):

- reference number (number)
- the author's name (text – allow enough characters to cover full names of more than one author)
- the title of the book (text – allow up to 80 characters)
- the year of publication (text or date – the date data type may require day and month, which would be superfluous in this case)
- the name of the publisher (text)
- the place of publication (text)
- the number of pages in the book (number)
- the ISBN number (text)
- the price of the book (currency)
- comments (text – somewhere you can add in some extra comments about the book)

The full information that you need is given in the box below.

| | |
|---|---|
| Book | 1 |
| Author | Bacon, Lynn Marie |
| Title | Getting Started with Microsoft PowerPoint 7.0 for Windows 95 |
| Year | 1997 |
| Publisher | John Wiley & Sons |
| Place of publication | New York |
| Pages | 217 |
| ISBN | 0-471-15870-4 |
| Price | £9.99 |
| Comments | Part of Wiley's Getting Started with Windows 95 series |

| | |
|---|---|
| Book | 2 |
| Author | Kronstadt, Babette |
| Title | Getting Started with Microsoft Excel 7.0 for Windows 95 |
| Year | 1997 |
| Publisher | John Wiley & Sons |
| Place of publication | New York |
| Pages | 193 |
| ISBN | 0-471-15871-2 |
| Price | £9.99 |
| Comments | Part of Wiley's Getting Started with Windows 95 series |

| | |
|---|---|
| Book | 3 |
| Author | Russakoff, Sylvia |
| Title | Getting Started with Microsoft Word 7.0 for Windows 95 |
| Year | 1997 |
| Publisher | John Wiley & Sons |
| Place of publication | New York |
| Pages | 187 |
| ISBN | 0-471-15868-2 |
| Price | £9.99 |
| Comments | Part of Wiley's Getting Started with Windows 95 series |

| | |
|---|---|
| Book | 4 |
| Author | Russakoff, Sylvia and Bacon, Lynn Marie |
| Title | Getting Started with Windows 95 |
| Year | 1997 |
| Publisher | John Wiley & Sons |
| Place of publication | New York |
| Pages | 176 |
| ISBN | 0-471-15943-3 |
| Price | £9.99 |
| Comments | Part of Wiley's Getting Started with Windows 95 series |

| | |
|---|---|
| Book | 5 |
| Author | Gaylord, Henry |
| Title | Getting Started with Microsoft Access 7.0 for Windows 95 |
| Year | 1997 |
| Publisher | John Wiley & Sons |
| Place of publication | New York |
| Pages | 242 |
| ISBN | 0-471-15869-0 |
| Price | £9.99 |
| Comments | Part of Wiley's Getting Started with Windows 95 series |

| | |
|---|---|
| Book | 6 |
| Author | McKnights, Lee W and Bailey, Joseph P (eds) |
| Title | Internet Economics |
| Year | 1997 |
| Publisher | MIT Press |
| Place of publication | Cambridge MA |
| Pages | 544 |
| ISBN | 0-262-13336-9 |
| Price | £14.95 |
| Comments | Papers presented at the MIT workshop on Internet Economics, March 1995 |

| | |
|---|---|
| Book | 7 |
| Author | Judge, Guy |
| Title | Quantitative Analysis for Economics and Business Using Lotus 1-2-3 |
| Year | 1990 |
| Publisher | Harvester-Wheatsheaf |
| Place of publication | Hemel Hempstead |
| Pages | 204 |
| ISBN | 0-7450-0513-6 |
| Price | |
| Comments | Relates to pre-Windows (DOS) versions of Lotus 1-2-3 Now out of print but available in some libraries |

| | |
|---|---|
| Book | 8 |
| Author | Soper, Jean |
| Title | Mathematics for Economics and Business: An Interactive Introduction |
| Year | 1999 |
| Publisher | Blackwell Publishers Ltd |
| Place of publication | Oxford |
| Pages | 294 |
| ISBN | 0-631-20781-3 |
| Price | £18.99 |
| Comments | Includes the MathEcon software on CD-ROM |

| | |
|---|---|
| Book | 9 |
| Author | Soper, Jean and Lee, Martin |
| Title | Statistics with Lotus 1-2-3 |
| Year | 1987 |
| Publisher | Chartwell-Bratt |
| Place of publication | Bromley |
| Pages | 208 |
| ISBN | 0-86238-131-2 |
| Price | |
| Comments | Relates to pre-Windows (DOS) versions of Lotus 1-2-3 Now out of print but available in some libraries |

| | |
|---|---|
| Book | 10 |
| Author | Whigham, David |
| Title | Quantitative Business Models Using Excel |
| Year | 1998 |
| Publisher | Oxford University Press |
| Place of publication | Oxford |
| Pages | 476 |
| ISBN | 0-19-877545-8 |
| Price | £22.99 |
| Comments | Includes diskette containing example files |

| | |
|---|---|
| Book | 11 |
| Author | Stein, Stuart |
| Title | Learning, Teaching and Researching on the Internet |
| Year | 1999 |
| Publisher | Longman |
| Place of publication | Harlow |
| Pages | 352 |
| ISBN | 0-582-31935-8 |
| Price | £14.99 |
| Comments | Includes a chapter on Resources for Economists |

| | |
|---|---|
| Book | 12 |
| Author | Cooke, Alison |
| Title | A Guide to Finding Quality Information on the Internet |
| Year | 1999 |
| Publisher | Library Association Publishing |
| Place of publication | London |
| Pages | 169 |
| ISBN | 1-85604-267-7 |
| Price | £29.95 |
| Comments | Includes a section on how to evaluate the quality of web resources |

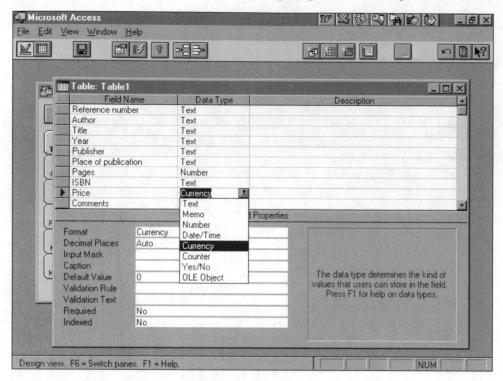

**Fig. 2.9** Setting up the fields in Access with Table Design.

Notice that some fields for some records may be empty – the information is not known. It can be added later if is obtained.

Figure 2.9 shows the initial stage of setting up the *fields* and *data types* for the database in Microsoft Access. (*Data type* refers to the format of the data held in a particular field, e.g. text, number, date, etc.) Whereas spreadsheets structure information in rows and columns, databases hold information in records and fields. A full set of information for an individual or a case is a record. Any one piece of that information will be stored in a separate field. In most cases you can use the default settings, but for some fields you will have to change the data type or the size of the field. It is fairly straightforward to do. As you can see in Access if you don't want the data type to be text, you simply run down the list of available types until you get to the one you require. Once the structure of the database table is complete you can save the file using a suitable name. In this case call it BOOKS. The program will add the appropriate file extension. In Access it will be .mdb.

Next you must enter the data. For this you need to select the *Datasheet View*. Enter the relevant information for each record into each row of the table. Don't worry if you find that a field is of the wrong type or isn't big enough. You can simply go back to the Design view and change the setting.

Figure 2.10 shows how the screen looks as you enter the data into the table in Access version 2. At this point remember to save the table. You can come back to it

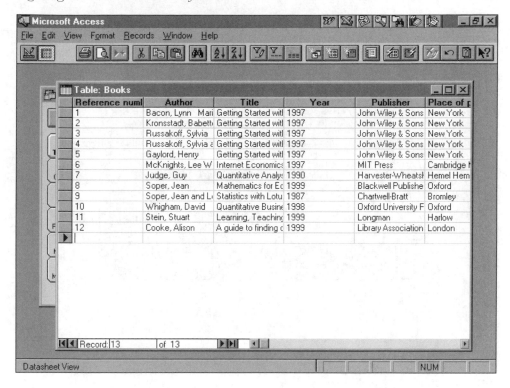

**Fig. 2.10** Entering the data into the table using Access.

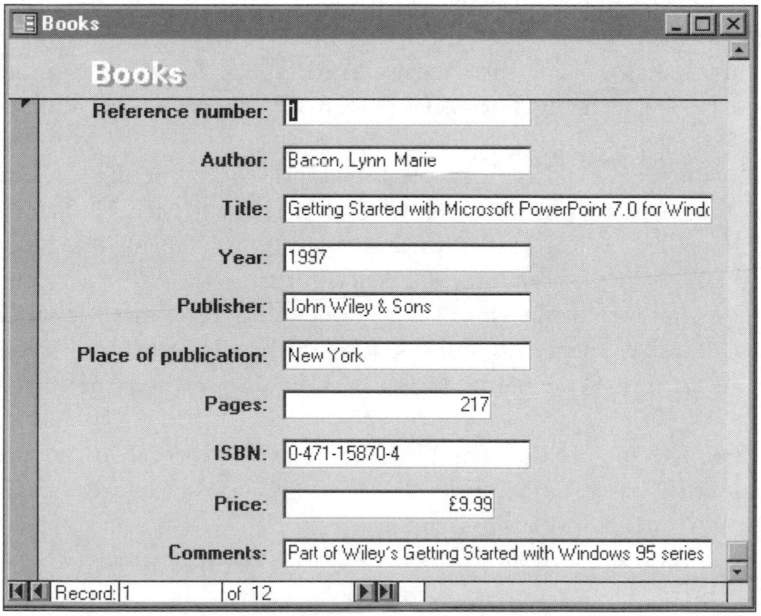

**Fig. 2.11** Form view of the first record in the database.

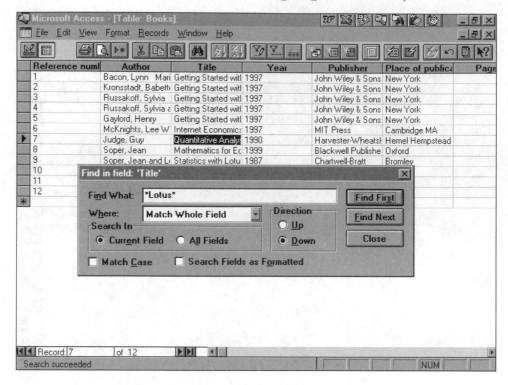

**Fig. 2.12**   Searching an Access database for a text string.

at any time to add additional records, or new fields, or to edit the information in the database. As well as viewing the database in its tabular form you can look at each record, one by one, using the Form View. Figure 2.11 shows a Form View of the first record in the database.

You can search the database for records that include a particular text string as part of one of the fields. Highlight the field and select **E**dit and then **F**ind from the main menu. Then enter the text string; for example, if you highlight the Title field and search for "*Lotus*" the computer will take you first to record 7 and then to record 9 since these both include the word Lotus in the title. Notice that you would have to use the "wildcard" character * before and after the word Lotus as this word could be anywhere in the title. See Figure 2.12 for an illustration of how the screen looks in Access.

Something else you can do from the Table View is to sort records in ascending or descending order based on any field. To try it out click on the Year field and then select **R**ecords, **Q**uick Sort and **A**scending.

A more complex query might involve asking for all records which satisfy a particular criterion – for example, you might want to find all the books which have the year of publication as 1998 or later. Experienced database users will probably frame their queries using something called SQL (Structured Query

## Wildcard characters

When you search a document for a particular word or phrase, it may be helpful to include what are called *wildcard* characters. This will allow you to find all occurrences of a text string that is contained with a word or phrase. The ? (question mark) character allows a single character in the word or phrase to be unspecified while the * (asterisk) character can be used to represent a group of characters that can take any form. The # (hash) character can be used to represent any digit.

So, for example:
- wh* finds what, white, and why
- *at finds cat, bat, and what
- 1#3 finds 103, 113, 123

Language), which is the standard language for working with databases. Unless you want to become a database expert you will not need to learn the commands as you will be able to make use of a software wizard or assistant to generate these commands automatically. For example, in Microsoft Access 2 you can use the Archive Wizard to create a new table which contains only those records for which the field year is $\geq$ 1998 (Figure 2.13).

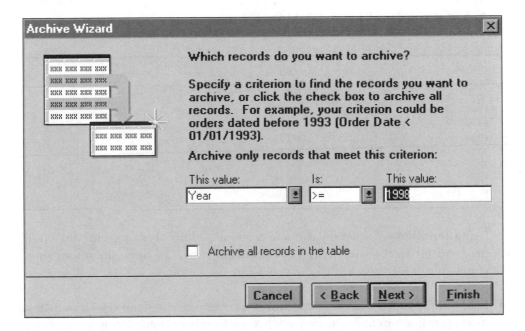

**Fig. 2.13** Using the Archive Wizard in Access to specify a criterion for a query.

# Summary

In this chapter you have been introduced to the main standard types of office software packages that are in use today, and you have been able to experience their practical application for simple tasks which economists need to undertake. Some further exercises and mini-projects for you to work on are outlined below to help you consolidate the skills that you have begun to acquire. The material in the next chapter will help you develop these skills a little further.

# Exercises and mini-projects

1. Produce a short word processed document (no more than 1000 words) containing a discussion of the essential issues of concern to modern economists. (Hint: refer to your economics textbook or WinEcon software.)

   Make sure that you use the software's spell checker before you Save and Print the document. Remember to include a list of the references that you have used in preparing the document. Beware of plagiarism. Do not copy material from other sources, but express the ideas in your own words. If you do want to quote something from another author make sure that you show clearly where the quote comes from.

2. The following table shows GDP (in US$ millions) and population (in thousands) for the seven major OECD countries in 1997 (source: World Development Indicators 1998, CD-ROM, World Bank).

| Country | GDP | Population |
|---|---|---|
| Canada | 609 778 | 30 270 |
| France | 1 391 712 | 58 579 |
| Germany | 2 097 225 | 82 076 |
| Italy | 1 145 558 | 57 424 |
| Japan | 4 190 264 | 126 084 |
| United Kingdom | 1 288 252 | 58 920 |
| United States | 7 834 036 | 267 575 |

   Using a spreadsheet, enter the data and create an additional column showing GDP per head for each country. Create a spreadsheet chart to show the information graphically.

3. Find out the e-mail address of a friend at another university and send him (her) a message telling him how you are and what you have been doing. Reply to a message if someone sends one to you.

**4.** Return to the key economics web sites listed in section 2.4 and the notes that you made about what can be found at each of them. Prepare a brief presentation about them using PowerPoint, Corel Presentation or whatever software package is available to you.

**5.** Expand your Books database to include all the other texts that have been recommended to you on your courses. Add additional fields to help identify the course they are used on and to give library catalog numbers for those books on the list that are in your university library. Don't forget to add additional comments about the books in your Comment field.

# CHAPTER 3

# Building on the basics: skills development

## Objective

The objective of this chapter is to extend the reader's skills in working with standard office software for economics related tasks. Skills covered are:

- the incorporation of graphics images, symbols and equations into word processed documents and presentations
- other word processing skills, particularly those required when working with long documents
- the use of spreadsheets for building and analyzing simple models in economics
- further e-mail skills including sending file attachments by e-mail and the use of e-mail discussion lists and awareness services

## 3.1 Incorporating graphics, symbols and equations

As we noted in the previous chapter, on many occasions when an economist produces a report or a paper there will be a need for it to include graphs, charts or other graphic images and perhaps also symbols and equations. This section provides some guidance on how this can be achieved and Practical 3.1 provides an application for you to practice the required techniques.

## Different types of graphic images

The graphic images that you may want to incorporate into your document can be created in a variety of ways. For example, you might have used a spreadsheet package such as Excel to produce a chart (as you did in Practical 2.2). Similarly, if you are working with a more specialized statistics or econometrics package (see Chapter 5) you may use this to produce graphs that you wish to include in a written report.

Economists often use diagrams to convey the essence of a model, sketching the lines or curves which show the relationships between the variables in the model. So another possibility is that you might use drawing or painting software tools to create diagrams to put into your document.

Scanners can be used to create digital versions of an image. For example, an economic historian may have access to a document which provides evidence to support a particular argument that he/she wishes to advance. This can be scanned in to produce another form of graphical image that can then be incorporated into a document. (Scanners with optical character reading facilities can recreate the basic text of a document. So, for example, if one only had a table of data in printed form – say as a photocopy – it would be possible to scan the sheet and the computer would be able to create an editable electronic file from it.)

A digital camera provides yet another way that an image in electronic form can be created. Perhaps a writer may wish to include a picture of a person, a building or a piece of equipment. Even without a digital camera a similar effect could be achieved by taking a picture using an ordinary camera and then scanning in the photograph.

Or an author might simply wish to incorporate a graphic that has been created by someone else, for example a company logo or a bit of clipart to give a visual clue to what is to be covered in a particular section.

In writing this book I have occasionally wished to show you what should appear on the computer screen at a particular stage when you are using a certain piece of software. This can be accomplished by making use of the "screen grab" or capture facility that is available in the computer's operating system which places a temporary copy of the image onto the clipboard. You can then either simply paste it into your word processed document or use a suitable graphics accessory program such as *Paint* to save the image for later use.

## Different graphics file types

As you work with different software programs you will come across a variety of types of graphics file types which may differ enormously in size (i.e. the number of bytes or kilobytes needed to store them) and their resolution (i.e. the detail of the picture that you can see on screen or on paper). Some of the most common types are briefly described in the text box below. More detailed information can be found on the book's web site. You can usually tell an image's file type by looking at the extension

## Grabbing the contents of a screen or window

To place an image of what is currently shown on the computer screen onto the clipboard you just press the PrintScreen [PrtScrn] key. A bitmapped image of what you can see on screen will then be placed on the clipboard. You can save it by running the Paint accessory and selecting **E**dit and then **P**aste from the menu to view it in the Paint utility. (To open Paint go to the Start button at the bottom left of the screen and choose **P**rograms, Accessories and then Paint.) If you are told that "The image in the clipboard is larger than the bitmap" and asked "Would you like the bitmap enlarged?" just click on the **Y**es button. You can then select **F**ile and then Save **A**s to save the file as a 256 colour bitmap image.

If you want to "grab" only what is in the current window (rather than the whole screen) the steps are just the same except that you hold down the Alt key at the same time as you press the PrintScreen key.

used in the file name. When you use Windows Explorer to look at a list of files in a particular folder you might also be able to see at a glance the type of file you have by recognizing its characteristic icon.

A number of other general points are worth noting here. First, some file types are related more or less exclusively to one particular software application or group of applications (e.g. the .GWG graphs created by GiveWin and PcGive) and can only be viewed and edited using that software. However, quite often it will be possible to take graphics files created in one package and view them in another (if the latter software incorporates the relevant graphics filter). There are even programs that have been created to allow you to open a file of one graphics type and then save it in a different format (for example, the program LVIEW is very useful in this regard – it is worth checking whether it is available to you on your local system). A second complication is that different versions of a piece of software may produce different file types, or different versions of the same file type. Usually (but not always) a later version of a software application will be compatible with graphics files created using earlier versions of the software. There may be options to save graphics files in color or monochrome and at various degrees of resolution. Black and white and/or lower resolution files will be smaller, but you won't be able to go back up a level in quality if you save in a lower end format. Next, note that some graphics (vector graphics) can be separated into their component parts so that each element or *object* can be edited separately. Other graphics images (e.g. bitmapped images) can only be treated as a single entity. Finally, some graphics file types (e.g. JPEG files) have been developed primarily for use with the World Wide Web. Thus they have been designed mainly for on-screen display (rather than printing) and for rapid transfer across the Internet.

**Some standard graphics file types**

BMP  Microsoft Windows bitmap files. This is the format that you get if you use PrintScreen to "grab" the contents of a screen and place it on the clipboard. BMP files tend to be rather large in size.

EPS   Encapsulated PostScript. Special PostScript format with a header describing the width and height of the image and how it is to be displayed on the page.

GIF   Graphics Interchange Format. Format created by CompuServe. Often used for icons and images accessed from the World Wide Web. Limited to 256 colors.

JPEG  Joint Photographic Experts Group, an independent group that has created a format to enable image files to be heavily compressed without too much loss of quality; for use on the World Wide Web. Especially good for scanned pictures or images created with a digital camera.

WMF  Windows Metafiles. If you copy and paste into Word for Windows a graphic created using another application it will be in the form of a Windows Metafile.

**Note**

The basic distinction between bitmap images and vector images is as follows. Bitmap images are based on pixels – small areas of the screen – so the quality of the image that you see will be highly dependent on the monitor and its settings. Vector images are mathematical constructs and are therefore independent of the resolution capabilities of a computer monitor.

Whether you have created the image yourself, or simply taken it from another source, you may find that you wish to manipulate it in some way before or after it is finally placed in your document. Examples of what I mean are: editing (e.g. changing the appearance of a line on a graph to show it as a dotted rather than a solid line), annotating the image (adding explanatory text or labels), resizing the image (making it bigger or smaller) and cropping the image (slicing off unwanted parts of the image).

**Find out**

At some point you should review the information which is available in your word processing software's **H**elp system about creating and importing graphic images. View any Examples and Demos that are on offer on the topic.

# Practical 3.1   Including a graphics image in a word processed document

In this practical you will produce a short word processed document which incorporates in it a graphics image. The graphical image that we shall include, first by **C**opying and **P**asting, is the chart that you created using your spreadsheet software in Practical 2.2.

First run your spreadsheet software and open the file that you saved at the end of Practical 2.2. Select the chart that you created by clicking on it (it should look like my Figure 2.5). From the menu select **E**dit and then **C**opy. This will put a bitmapped copy of this image onto the clipboard.

Now run your word processing software and begin a new document. Type some text such as

```
An example of a word processed document containing a graph.
```

Make sure that the mouse cursor is positioned after this text. Now select **E**dit and then **P**aste from the menu. The graphics image will then be copied straight from the clipboard into your document. Type some more text underneath it such as `Figure 2.5`.

If you wish you can resize the graphics image to make it bigger or smaller. Using the mouse click onto the bottom right hand corner of the image and either drag it outwards (to make the image bigger) or inwards (to make the image smaller). The relative dimensions of the image will be preserved. If you were to stretch or squeeze the image by clicking onto one of the handles on the side of the image you would change the size of only one dimension of the image (there may be occasions when you want to do this).

When you are ready save your word processed document. The file will include in it the spreadsheet chart. You can of course delete a graphic at any time by selecting it and then pressing the delete key. Do that now so that you can practice a different method of bringing graphics images into a document.

Now suppose that the image that you wish to include in your word processed document is in a file, rather than on the clipboard. You need to use a slightly different approach. Make sure that you are at the position in the document where you want the

## Positioning images and wrapping text around a frame

You can position a graphics image by placing it in a frame. You can think of a frame as an invisible container for the item that you want to position. Then, you can move the frame anywhere that you want it by dragging and dropping it using the mouse. If you wish, you can wrap text around the frame. To find out more about this, look up either "frame" or "wrap" in your word processor's Help system.

### Saving images from the clipboard using Paint

If you have copied an image to the clipboard and you want to save it as a separate bitmapped file for later use (rather than pasting it in to a document there and then) you can use the Microsoft Accessory program called Paint. To open Paint go to the Start button at the bottom left of the screen and choose **P**rograms, Accessories and then Paint. Click on **E**dit and then **P**aste. A copy of the spreadsheet chart should appear in the window. You can save the image as a bitmap by choosing **F**ile and then Save **A**s. Enter a suitable name for the image and then save it to an appropriate drive (either your A drive or the network drive – only use the C drive if it is your own computer rather than a lab machine). Once the file is saved you can close both the Paint program and the spreadsheet software.

image and select **I**nsert from the menu. If you are using Word you can then select **P**icture (in WordPerfect you would need to choose **G**raphics and then **F**ile). A dialog box will open and you can select the file that you wish to insert and then click ***OK*** (you may have to change folders or directories). If the **P**icture Preview option has been selected you will be able to view the contents of the file before it is inserted. This can be particularly helpful if you have a number of graphics files and you can't remember the file name that you need, although you can recognize the picture when you see it. It is also possible to set up a dynamic link between your word processed document and the file that is used to generate the graphics image. This would mean that if the data used to create the graphics image were changed at some point (say to incorporate more recent data) the image in the word processed document would be automatically updated when the document was next opened.

## Incorporating symbols and equations into word processed documents

As you may already know, economists make extensive use of mathematical symbols and equations in their work. Sometimes it is just a matter of using a few special symbols such as $\geq$, $\leq$, $\neq$, $\approx$ or $\pm$. Or it may be that they wish to use a Greek letter such as $\alpha$, $\beta$, $\Pi$, $\Sigma$ or $\sigma$. To include individual symbols (as I have here) just select **I**nsert and then **S**ymbol from the menu. A symbols palette as shown in Figure 3.1 should open and you can click on the symbol you need and then click again on the **I**nsert button to copy the symbol into your document. (Note: the Font in this box should be set at Symbol. If it is not, just work your way down the list until you find it.)

Try to create in a document of your own each of the symbols that I used in the previous paragraph.

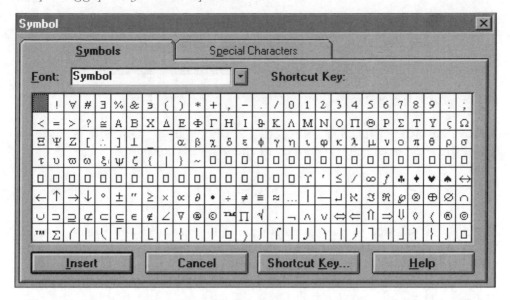

**Fig. 3.1**   Microsoft Word Symbols palette.

Alternatively with Greek letters you can enter the Roman (normal English looking) version of the characters as you are typing and then go back and select any letters whose appearance you want to modify and just change the font to Symbol afterwards. For example, if you want to have $\Pi = TR - TC$ just type $P = TR - TC$ and then change the font for P to Symbol. Try it for yourself.

For superscripts (powers) or subscripts you can type in the characters you need as normal and then use F**o**rmat **F**ont selecting the Effect you require (click next to it on the Font tab and then click ***OK***). For example, to create $y = 3x^2$ you first type $y = 3x2$. Then you paste over the 2 to select that character and then use the F**o**rmat **F**ont Effects sequence of choices. If the next character in your document is not also a superscript you will have to make sure that the Effect toggle is switched off before you get to it.

Subscripts work the same way. For example, try creating the expression $x_1^2$ by first typing x12 and then formatting the 1 and 2 respectively as subscript and superscript. Note: You may wish to put these buttons on the toolbar if you are going to use subscripts and superscripts frequently in your work. Check the Help system in your package to find out how to do this.

For longer expressions and equations you need to use the *Equation Editor*. (Note: The standard installation of Microsoft Office does not install the equation editor by default. Users must check whether this has been installed and if not install it themselves, or seek guidance from their lecturer or a computer technician.) In Word select **I**nsert and then **O**bject; then choose Microsoft Equation 2.0 from the list (unless you have a later version available). You should see something similar to what is shown in Figure 3.2.

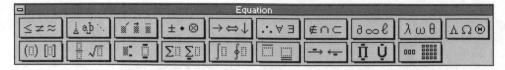

**Fig. 3.2**   The palette for the Microsoft 2.0 Equation Editor.

You can then put together collections of symbols from the palette to make up your expression or equation. Try to create the following equation

$$b = \frac{\Delta C}{\Delta Y}$$

Equation 3.1

Hint: You will need to make use of the far right hand box in the palette to create the $\Delta$ symbol and the second box in the second row of the palette to produce the effect of one expression divided by another. If you don't get quite the equation that you want the first time, don't worry. You can always double click on it to edit it.

Practice using the Equation Editor to create other expressions and equations that you have come across during your course. If you need some inspiration refer to your economics, mathematics or statistics course text.

### Tip

It may be worth creating a special document that contains the mathematical expressions and equations that you use most frequently. Then when you need them you can simply cut and paste them, rather than having to recreate them all over again. I have two such documents on my laptop – one called Mathpad which contains mathematical expressions and equations and one called Statpad which has those collections of symbols often needed in statistics and econometrics applications.

### Foreign languages and accents on text

Even when you are preparing a document in English there may be occasions when you use a word, or a person's name, that requires an accent. For example, perhaps you want to talk about an Internet Café, or write about François Quesnay and his Tableau Économique. To be able to include such accented symbols you first need to make sure that the character itself may be found in the appropriate language – here French. (Shortcut keys are also available, which may be found listed against the symbol.) To do this in Word select **T**ools, **L**anguage, and then choose the one that you want from the list. Then select **I**nsert and then **S**ymbols and you will be able to choose the symbol that you need and insert it into your document. Note: If you are likely to be doing this frequently – say you are writing a dissertation on the French economy – it might pay you to prepare a file containing the main characters that you will use so that you can just cut and paste from it, just as I suggested for mathematical symbols in the previous text box.

## Embedded objects and dynamic links between documents

If you copy and paste an object (such as an equation or a chart) from one document into another, the information will be *embedded* in the new document, but it will not be *dynamically linked* to it. This means that you will be able to edit it in the new document, just by clicking on it and then using the toolbars and menus from the original program that was used to create it. But note that the contents of the original document will be unaffected. For example, you might have created a MathPad document with all your most frequently used mathematical equations and expressions in it. You then copy and paste a formula that you need in your current document in the usual way. You could then edit the formula in your new document if it needs to be slightly different from the original (for example, you might want to use $\beta$ rather than b in Equation 3.1). The contents of the MathPad document would remain as it was.

However, there are cases where you might wish to provide a *dynamic link* between documents. This will mean that whenever the original document is updated, the information in the linked document will also automatically be modified to incorporate the changes made. To ensure that dynamic links are set up between documents you should use the *Paste Special* (rather than the ordinary Paste) option in the Edit menu. An example of a situation where this could be relevant might be as follows. Suppose that you are preparing a presentation using PowerPoint that includes some charts that you have created as part of an Excel spreadsheet file. Now suppose that you are conscious that the figures used to generate the spreadsheet chart might need to be changed at the last minute before you give the presentation (say because they have been revised or a key figure such as an interest rate used in the spreadsheet has been changed). If you have a dynamic link between the spreadsheet and presentation software files you will only need to change the information in the spreadsheet file. The chart in that file *and* the one in your presentation will then both be amended automatically. (*Note:* This, of course, assumes that you have both files on the same computer.)

### Find out

If you want to find out more about linking information across documents, go to the index in the Help menu of your word processor and type in the word "link".

## 3.2 Working with longer word processed documents

The introduction to word processing given in Chapter 2 assumed that the document you would be working on would be comparatively short – just one or two pages. However, you are quite likely to want to produce longer documents of several thousand words (perhaps also containing symbols and graphs). You will need to know about a number of other features of your word processing software and how to develop your skills in using these features. The features covered include: page numbering, centering text, creating footnotes and references, creating tables, and using the spell checker and word count tools.

In this section it is assumed that you are working on an essay for one of your courses and you have been asked to submit it in word processed form. If you have not already been set a topic to write on you might like to work on the question provided in Practical 3.2. Alternatively your lecturer may choose a topic of his/her own for you to work on.

## Practical 3.2   A word processed essay

Write an essay of no more than 2000 words to address the following question:

*Why is economics often described as the subject that studies "scarcity and choice"? Provide examples to illustrate your answer.*

Suggested references are given below, but you should find relevant material in any introductory economics textbook. If the interactive economics software WinEcon is available to you on the university computer network you should take a look at Chapter 1, "What is Economics".

Begg DKH, Fisher S and Dornbusch R (1994) *Economics*. Fourth Edition. McGraw-Hill, Maidenhead.
Lipsey RG and Crystal KA (1995) *An Introduction to Positive Economics*. Eighth Edition. Oxford University Press, Oxford.
Parkin M, Powell M and Matthews K (1997) *Economics*. Addison Wesley Longman Higher Education, Wokingham.
Sloman J (1998) *Economics*. Third Edition. Prentice Hall Europe, Hemel Hempstead.

Note: You are expected to use word processing software such as Microsoft Word or Corel WordPerfect to prepare your essay. You should submit a printout of your essay and, if requested, a floppy disk containing the file used to generate the printout. Make sure that you also keep a backup copy of the file yourself in case the disk that you submit goes missing or the files on it become corrupted in some way.

Some guidance on how you might use the word processing software in preparing your essay is given below. However, before that there are some more fundamental points that I wish to make.

Before you can start to produce your essay you must, of course, know something about the subject. So your first job must be to read the relevant sections of one or more of the recommended books. Make notes as you read, and stop and think about how the material you are reading can help you to answer the question set. When you make notes try to avoid simply copying out large sections of text (see the warning on plagiarism given below). Instead, look away from the book for a moment and try to express the point in your own words. If you understand the point being made you should be able to do that. If you can't, perhaps you should continue reading and then go back over the material a second time to make your notes.

Don't try to write the essay with your textbook open next to you (especially if you haven't already read it). You should be careful not to copy chunks of text (large or small) from the textbook into your essay as that is regarded as *plagiarism* (in plain English it is cheating!). That is why I warned you to be careful about how you take notes. You might inadvertently transfer a section of text from the book to your essay via your notes. Although you may not have intended to plagiarize, the effect will be the same as if you had just copied straight out of the textbook.

Try to create your own examples. Sloman (1998) illustrates the concept of opportunity cost using several examples relating to the decisions that a student of economics might have to make. Don't just recycle these examples. Think up your own.

## Warning. Avoid plagiarism

Plagiarism occurs when someone presents another person's work as their own. It might be copied from a book, or from another student's essay, or from something on the World Wide Web. Information technology makes it easier for people to plagiarize, simply by cutting and pasting from one electronic document to another. However, it can also make it easier to detect since sections of text can be analyzed for consistency in style, sentence lengths etc.

There is one situation where it is permissible to copy text from someone else's work. That is when you are intentionally citing someone's views or opinions and you feel that it is absolutely necessary to quote directly from them. However, this should be done sparingly. Unless the opinion is unique to the author, or he or she was the first person to express a point in a particular way, it is best to paraphrase the point that they are making (i.e. express the point in your own words). If you do quote from another author you must make sure that you provide a complete reference showing where it comes from (including page numbers). In your word processed document the quote should be in quotation marks or indented and in a different type face (font) so that it is clearly distinguishable from your words.

When you are ready you should begin to plan your essay. You might do this in your head, on a piece of paper, or even begin to *outline* your answer on the computer using the word processing software. Some people prefer to do all their preliminary work away from the computer, only moving to it when they are ready to type in their full answer. (They may, of course, still make revisions to the document after reading it through.) Others find that they can move to the computer at quite an early stage, putting down their thoughts knowing that they will probably need to revise them or move them around within the document. Of course, this is all very easy with modern computer software that allows you to copy, cut and paste within a document and between documents. You might find it helpful to have two documents: one for jotting down points and examples as they occur to you, the other which will become the final document. You can copy material from the jottings document into the draft document once you are happy with it. (Note: There are also now available brain-storming packages that allow mental mapping of ideas, e.g. MindManager, which is based on Tony Buzan's mind maps.)

*The structure and layout of your essay*

There is no single perfect way to construct an essay – essays would be very boring to read if they all looked pretty much the same – but there are a few points to keep in mind. First, and most obviously, you should answer the question that has been set. It is not enough just to latch on to one or more key words in the essay title and regurgitate an answer that you have used elsewhere (autoplagiarism!). Make sure that your answer deals with the question that has been posed. That means a *beginning* where you first identify the key concepts and points to be addressed, a *middle* where you develop these points providing explanation and illustrations, and an *end* where you provide a summary and conclusions.

If you make use of diagrams or sketches make sure that they are correctly labeled and that you interpret them in the textual part of your answer. Similarly, if you use some mathematical expressions or equations you should interpret them and integrate them into your answer. Don't just use diagrams or mathematics to decorate your answer without links to the main text. Number your equations and figures so that they can be referenced within the text.

Divide your answer up into paragraphs and try to keep your sentences reasonably short. You needn't necessarily worry about that in your first draft. You can go back and rewrite the essay to make it read better once you have a completed first draft.

Include a *bibliography* or a list of *references* at the end of your essay. It should cover all books, journal articles and papers that you have used in the preparation of the essay. Do not list items that you have not used, just to try and impress the reader. There are a number of different styles that can be used to list references. The one used by *The Economic Journal* begins with the name of the author(s), surname followed by initials, and then the date of publication. Next comes the title of the book (in italics) – if necessary you should identify the edition number. Finally you give the place of publication and the name of the publisher. For example:

Sloman, J. (1998) *Economics*. Third Edition. Hemel Hempstead, UK: Prentice Hall Europe.

If you wish to refer to a *journal article* give the title of the article after the date of publication, perhaps with the title in single quotation marks. The name of the journal comes next (in italics) and then the volume number, issue number and page numbers. Here is an example to illustrate the layout (it is worth taking a look at this paper if the journal is available in your library):

McCloskey, D. (1985) 'Economical Writing', *Economic Inquiry* Volume XXIII No. 2 (April) pp.187–222.

Increasingly people are including documents from the World Wide Web in their lists of references. After the author's name, date, title etc. you should give the full URL so that readers of your essay or paper can find the reference for themselves should they wish to. If the document provides a date when it was last modified that should be given too. For example:

Kendall, J. D. (1996) 'Enrichment Subject for Economists'. Nanyang Business School, Singapore. http://www.ntu.ac.sg/nbs/ae/ese/ Last modified August 1996.

(*Note:* This HTML document contains course material for a course on analytical, computing and writing skills for professional economists and, like the McCloskey article, is well worth a look at some point during your studies.)

If you are now ready to put together your essay in word processed form there are some things to look out for. You may be required to provide a separate cover sheet giving the course title and the lecturer's name, the title of the essay and your own name. You should check the protocol at your own institution. It may be, for example, that because of anonymous marking you will be required to give your student reference number rather than your name. It is also a good idea to include the date when the essay is due for submission. By the way, make sure that you allow yourself a day or two prior to the deadline to get your final printout. Very often at peak times the computer network is fully stretched so that it may take longer than usual to get your work printed.

Your university may provide precise guidelines on how to present your word processed essays. For example, they may require them to be double spaced with wide margins and page numbers. Perhaps quotations will required to be given in single line spacing, indented, so that they stand out from the rest of the text.

Find out how to achieve each of these effects. In Word 6, for example, each paragraph can be laid out with single, double or one and a half line spacing. Select Format and then **P**aragraph from the menu and then choose the line spacing you need; alternatively you can select a section of text and just use appropriate control keys to achieve the same effects. Use the Help system in your software to find out how to do this.

You may want some titles or headings to be centered, in bold and in a larger font. In most word processed packages you will just have to select the text you want to format and then click on the appropriate option in the formatting toolbar. Stick to standard fonts such as Times New Roman, perhaps with Arial for headings. Avoid using unusual fonts such as Algerian that are difficult to read.

Inserting page numbers is straightforward in Word. From the menu you select **I**nsert followed by Page N**u**mbers. Then you can decide where on the page you want the number to be shown (e.g. at the top or bottom of the page, centered or on the right hand side of the paper). You can also decide whether to start the page numbering on the first page or not. Practice doing this with your document when it is ready.

For some essays you may want to provide footnotes (although an alternative which is sometimes preferable is to have them all at the end as end notes). In Word you can again do this by beginning with **I**nsert in the main menu.

Occasionally you may want to create a table in your essay or report. Find out how to do this in your software and experiment with the various options available. For example, you might wish to produce a table like Table 3.1.

**Table 3.1** Population and GPD per head in selected countries.

| Country | Population (millions) | GDP per head (in US dollars) |
| --- | --- | --- |
| Arcadia | 20 | 50 000 |
| Blighty | 50 | 20 000 |
| Candia | 15 | 10 000 |

Source: fictitious.

Note: You should always give a title for the table and information about the source of any data that is shown.

---

### Tip: Style templates

For very long essays and dissertations you may want to set up a *style template* for your document. You can preset fonts for headings and subheadings to provide consistency throughout the document. You can include information such as the title and your name at the top and bottom of each page in headers and footers. Most software will have a selection of preset style templates that you can choose from, or you can define your own. If this interests you find out about it by searching for help on *style* from the Help system.

---

*Using the spell checker and word count tools*

If, as in this case, you have been given a maximum word length for your essay you can use the word count tool to see whether or not a draft version of the essay is of suitable length. Just choose **T**ools and **W**ord Count and the computer will display the total number of words (and characters) in your document.

You can also check your document for spelling mistakes and typing errors using the spell checker (in Word 6 select **T**ools and **S**pelling). The computer will work its way through your document identifying words that it doesn't recognize. You may be offered alternatives or the chance to add more specialized vocabulary to the program's dictionary. There are quite a number of terms used in economics that won't be included in the standard spell checker, but you can customize the spell checker on your own machine to include them. Some recent versions of word processing software allow the spell check to function as you are working on the document, but if this annoys you or slows you down you can usually suppress it. Recent versions of word processing software often include grammar checks that can advise you about grammatical errors or over-long sentences. Another helpful tool that is built into most word processing software is the **T**hesaurus. This allows you to find a synonym (an alternative word with a similar meaning) to prevent too much repetition. Simply highlight the word in your document and choose the Thesaurus tool to be offered an alternative.

When you have completed your document check the number of words and use the spell checker to correct any errors that you have made. Carefully read through the essay to check that you are happy with it (you may be able to do this on screen using the Print Preview facility or you may find it easier at this stage to have a printout to take away and have a look at away from the computer). When the essay is as you want it, print it out and hand it in. Don't forget to keep your own copy as backup.

## 3.3   Simple economic modeling using a spreadsheet

In section 2.2 we saw how a spreadsheet such as Excel or Lotus 1-2-3 can be used to analyze and display economic data. Another common use of spreadsheets by economists is for analyzing quantitative economic models, again displaying the information on a graph or chart. In this section we see how to build a simple quantitative economic model in a spreadsheet, to help understand the relationships involved and to support decision making. The model itself is quite a simple one – some of you would probably be able to analyze it on the back of an envelope using simple algebra. But in working on it with the spreadsheet you should be able to see the potential of this type of software for analyzing more complex models.

## Practical 3.3   Cost–volume–profit analysis on a spreadsheet

Consider a small firm producing a single homogeneous product in a competitive market where it can charge a fixed price. The firm's production costs can be divided into fixed costs (costs which must be borne each period irrespective of the quantity produced) and variable costs (costs which are related to the number of items produced).

In this problem suppose that average variable costs are constant, that is they are the same for each extra item produced so that variable costs are proportionate to output.

The problem we are going to analyze is taken from MathEcon, the interactive courseware produced by the WinEcon team and designed to accompany Jean Soper's book *Mathematics for Economics and Business* (1999). Section 2.2 of MathEcon: CVP graphical analysis works through the problem and if you have access to that software you can compare the way the problem is treated there to the way that we analyze it using Excel.

The firm has fixed costs of £1000 per month. It must spend £4 on components and £6 on labor for every unit produced; so its average variable costs (AVC) are £10. The firm can charge £15 for every unit that it sells. The questions asked in MathEcon are (i) how many units must be produced each month for the firm to break even (where total revenue = total cost) and (ii) how many units must the firm produce in order to generate profits of £500 per month?

Run Excel, or whatever spreadsheet package you have available, and begin to enter information as shown in Figure 3.3. Row 1 contains a title for the spreadsheet. The cell has been formatted to show the text in bold (select F**o**rmat C**e**lls and then Font to change the appearance of the text).

Rows 3 to 6 contain the basic parameters of the problem, as described above. The cost and revenue relationships that are based on them will be linked to the information in these cells. The information has been entered this way so that we can simply and

| | C13 | ⬇ | =$D$4*A13 | | | | |
|---|---|---|---|---|---|---|---|
| | A | B | C | D | E | F | G |
| 1 | **Simple Cost-Volume-Profit Analysis** | | | | | | |
| 2 | | | | | | | |
| 3 | Fixed cost per month in £ | | | 1000 | | | |
| 4 | Variable cost in £ per unit | | | 10 | | Price in £ | 15 |
| 5 | comprising | | components | 4 | | | |
| 6 | | | labour | 6 | | | |
| 7 | | | | | | | |
| 8 | Schedules | | | | | | |
| 9 | | | | | | | |
| 10 | Quantity | Fixed Cost | Variable Cost | Total Cost | Total Revenue | Profit | |
| 11 | Q | FC | VC | TC | TR | Π | |
| 12 | 0 | 1000 | 0 | 1000 | 0 | -1000 | |
| 13 | 20 | 1000 | 200 | 1200 | 300 | -900 | |
| 14 | 50 | 1000 | 500 | 1500 | 750 | -750 | |
| 15 | 100 | 1000 | 1000 | 2000 | 1500 | -500 | |
| 16 | 200 | 1000 | 2000 | 3000 | 3000 | 0 | |
| 17 | 400 | 1000 | 4000 | 5000 | 6000 | 1000 | |
| 18 | | | | | | | |
| 19 | | | | | | | |

◄│ ◄ │ ► │ ►│\ Chart1 \ **Sheet1** / Sheet2 / Sheet3 / Sheet4 / Sheet5 ║ ◄│

**Fig. 3.3**  The cost–volume–profit problem on a spreadsheet.

quickly see what would be the consequences of a change in any one of these values. Cell D4 contains a formula =D5+D6 rather than a specific value so that it builds on the information about the cost of labor and of components entered in the cells below it.

Next we construct the table of values containing the cost, revenue and profit schedules. Rows 10 and 11 provide text and symbolic headings for each column. Notice that you can display Greek letters in a spreadsheet. The $\Pi$ in cell F11 was entered as a P and then its appearance was changed by choosing the Symbol font via the Format Cells menu selection.

In column A, beginning with 0 in row 12, a number of possible production rates are entered. You could just enter them in equally spaced steps but I have copied the values used in the MathEcon table. Cells B12 to B17 contain the information on fixed cost. The formula =$D$3 has been entered into cell B12 and copied down the rest of the column. The dollar signs in the formula ensure that as the formula is copied down column B the absolute cell reference D3 is always used. Without the dollar signs the computer would assume that you wish your formula to always retain the same relative positions with any cells in it to that which applies in the base cell.

Cell C12 contains the formula =$D$4*A12. Copying this formula down the rest of the column works out the variable cost at each potential quantity produced. The dollar signs ensure that the AVC value held in cell D4 is always used, while the quantity values held in column A adjust automatically to their row positions. The various values that this formula gives rise to are shown in the relevant cell, while you can see the formula itself in the formula bar at the top of the spreadsheet.

The figures shown in column D (total cost = TC) are obtained by adding together the fixed and variable costs. Cell D12 contains the formula =B12+C12 which can then be copied down the rest of the column. Total revenue (TR) is price × quantity, so cell E12 has the formula =$G$4*A12, which can then be copied down the rest of the column. Finally in column F we put the formula for profit $(\Pi)$ = TR – TC. Cell F12 has the formula =E12–D12, which can then be copied down. The results should be as in Figure 3.3.

Just by glancing at the table it is clear that the firm's break-even point (where $\Pi$= TR–TC = 0 or TR = TC) is where Q = 200. At quantities below that the revenue is insufficient to cover the costs, while after that total revenue exceeds total costs (by growing amounts) so that profit is being generated. Although the table does not explicitly answer the second of our questions, it is fairly easy to work out that to obtain profits of £500 per month the firm will need to produce 300 units.

We can show this information graphically by constructing a suitable chart based on the information in cells A11 to A17 and D11 to F17. First select these cells. To select this non-contiguous area first select cells A11 to A17. Then, while pressing the Ctrl (Control) key select the remaining cells D11 to F17. Just these cells should now be highlighted and you can construct a chart based on the information held in them. Select **I**nsert **C**hart , choosing As New Sheet, and follow the steps indicated by the Chart Wizard. Confirm the cell range selected and then choose the XY chart type

(Scatter). Choose the second format which joins together the points for each series but still provides markers so that you can identify which line is which. Make sure that the computer works with the column setting for the Data Series and that it uses the first column for the X data and the first row for the legend text. (Note: Spreadsheet packages like Excel allow you to place a chart either on a new worksheet, or somewhere within the current worksheet. There can be advantages and disadvantages of each approach. Placing a chart within the current worksheet can allow you to see the effect on the graph of a parameter change "before your very eyes". However, complicated graphs may become too "bunched up" when you try to squeeze them into an existing worksheet and it may be better to put them on a separate one.)

After adding a Chart Title and a small amount of editing (you have to format the font for the profit legend as Symbol so that it shows as Π and not P, and you may choose to alter the color and style for the lines and markers, particularly if they are to be printed in black and white) you should have something similar to the chart shown in Figure 3.4.

Now we can ask some "what-if" questions. Suppose first that, perhaps due to a huge increase in demand, the market price of the product was suddenly to change to £20. What would happen to the firm's break-even quantity? Obviously it would be lower, but how much? The spreadsheet allows us immediately to find out. We simply change the entry in cell G4 to 20 and the total revenue schedule will be immediately recalculated. Total cost will now be equal to total revenue at a quantity of 100 per month. The changes will also be reflected on the graph.

Similar changes to other constants in the problem can be simulated by altering the values in the relevant cells. Of course, you may not find that the break-even quantity

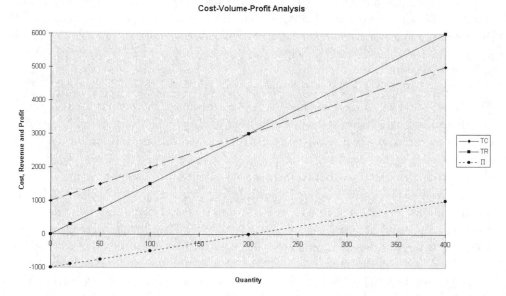

**Fig. 3.4**    The chart showing a graphical display of the cost–volume–profit schedules.

that results from one of these changes is shown in the table because we have chosen to include only a selection of Q values. If the profit figures in column F don't include a value of zero you may need to insert additional rows or extend the table out to cover higher quantities. Obviously all the formulae will need to be applied to any new rows created.

Another example of this kind of spreadsheet modeling is given in the list of exercises and mini-projects at the end of this chapter. We return to consider further uses of spreadsheets in economics in Chapter 4.

Note: You can use the Equation Editor with Excel as well as with Word. This can be very helpful for labeling mathematical expressions and equations. As with Word, just select Insert Object and then choose Equation Editor. If you are working with a different spreadsheet package such as Lotus 1-2-3 you should find out how equations can be incorporated using the software that is available to you.

## 3.4   Developing your e-mail skills

In Chapter 2 you learned how to send and receive e-mail messages and discovered some other basic features of your e-mail system (such as how to forward messages, add "signatures", delete unwanted messages and store messages that you want to keep in folders). In this section we look at some other features of e-mail systems that make them a valuable tool for economists.

First, it helps to maintain an *address book* that contains the e-mail addresses of people with whom you are in regular contact. Your e-mail software should allow you to create such an address book, adding new entries either at the keyboard or by clicking onto to the e-mail address in the From: field of a message sent to you.

### Finding e-mail addresses

If you don't know someone's e-mail address there are various ways to find it out. The first and most obvious way is through a contact with that person in some other form; by telephone or by letter or directly from them when you meet them. If you know that a person you wish to contact works at a particular university or company you might be able to find out their e-mail address via the institution's web site. Many such web sites provide searchable on-line e-mail and telephone directories. If the person you wish to contact has their own web page you might find that they have an automatic e-mail contact facility built into their web page. To use it, your web browser will need to have been properly configured to recognize your own e-mail address, but even if this has not been done you will be able to obtain the e-mail address of the person that you want to contact (just by hovering your mouse over the e-mail hot-link in the web page and noting down what it says). Another possibility if you are desperate and can't find out any other way is to e-mail someone else at the institution (e.g. the institution's webmaster or the person responsible for a department's web page) and ask them if they can let you know the e-mail address of the person you are trying to contact. Alternatively you might ask them to forward your message for you. However, you should keep this as a last resort.

There are also various other services on the web that can help you track down a person's e-mail address. Yahoo! has a people search service that you can access from the main Yahoo! web site: `http://www.yahoo.co.uk` in the UK or `http://www.yahoo.com` in the US. Alternatively, you can go straight to `http://ukie.people.yahoo.com` or `http://people.yahoo.com/`. Similar facilities can be found at `http://www.WhoWhere.com` (part of Lycos) and `http://www.Bigfoot.com/`. It is worth selecting the Advanced Search option because it will give you more fields to help you narrow down the search (for example, you might be able to specify the country or type of institution that might be included in the e-mail address). However, these tools might not be able to track down the e-mail address of the person you are looking for. Their databases are by no means comprehensive, relying mainly on submissions from people who want other people to find them, although e-mail addresses are sometimes also taken from Usenet postings or visitors to sites like Yahoo! itself. You could also try running an ordinary web page search for the person's name. If they have a web page it will probably have information about their e-mail address there.

## Sending and dealing with e-mail file attachments

Although e-mail provides an effective and simple method for individuals (and groups with a common interest – see below) to keep in touch with each other, the e-mail messages themselves will only be able to contain plain unformatted (ASCII) text. However, most modern e-mail systems will now allow you to attach other files to an e-mail message. This means that all kinds of file types, such as Word documents, Excel workbooks, image files, even audio and video files can be sent from one person to another as e-mail attachments. This won't help if the recipient doesn't have a copy of the software package that was used to create the file, or at least one that will enable them to view it. If you do plan to send say a spreadsheet file to someone as an e-mail attachment, it may be worth checking with them first that they have the software to work with it. You should check too that they have the same version of the software that you have. If not it may be possible for you to save your file in the format of an earlier version so that the recipient can read it, although some features may be lost in the process.

The e-mail software at the sender's end will encode the file, turning it into basic ASCII text. When the e-mail message arrives, the recipient will be able to decode the file and turn it back into exactly the same format it had when it was created. There are various encoding–decoding protocols, although the most commonly used one now is MIME (Multipurpose Internet Mail Extensions). Modern e-mail software will look after the encoding–decoding process automatically, although when you send the file you may be asked to indicate the file type. You will, of course, also need to be able to tell the computer where to find the file that you wish to send, i.e. provide the full path to the folder or directory on the A, C or network drive where the file is saved.

## Some points to keep in mind when working with e-mail file attachments

*File size*

Files produced by word processing, spreadsheet and other applications packages can be quite large. It is not a good idea to send a message with a large number of file attachments or several messages in quick succession to the same person as this could easily fill up their mail box and prevent other messages from getting through to them. However, you may be able to mitigate this problem by making use of file compression or "zip" utilities (see the text box on p. 86 for more details). Again, though, you will need to check that the recipient of the file also has the relevant software for unzipping the file.

*Viruses*

There have been a number of scares recently about viruses that have been transmitted across the Internet contained in e-mail file attachments. Word documents are especially implicated here as several of the most widespread viruses are built into macros (automated procedures) that are contained in such files. Viruses can be plain annoying, displaying some message or image on your computer screen, but they can also be devastating, wiping out all the files on a computer hard disk and even the whole of a network to which the computer is attached.

To protect yourself against viruses you should have on your system an up-to-date version of one of the recognized virus checkers (see the text box on dealing with computer viruses), but there are some additional precautions that are worth taking when sending or receiving e-mails containing file attachments.

When sending a file, check if you can that it is virus free. If it is a Word file you could save the file in RTF (rich text format). This will retain the formatting that you added to your text but remove any macros that may have been infected with a virus.

When receiving a file as an e-mail attachment do not open it immediately from within the e-mail software. Instead save it, if possible to a floppy disk, and then check the disk for viruses before you open the file. This is a nuisance. It is very convenient to be able to open files directly from within the e-mail software, but the risk of virus problems easily outweighs this convenience. If you are concerned that you may have a virus in a file that has been sent to you and you are not sure what to do, contact your computing help desk or IT administrator.

*If you want to forward a message with a file attachment*

If you have received an e-mail message with a file attachment and you want to send the file on to a third person, you will need first to save the file attachment on your own system and then send a new message to the third person, attaching the file yourself. File attachments cannot be sent on as part of a forwarded message.

*Don't send file attachments when you don't need to*

If the file that you want to send consists entirely of text, with no mathematical symbols, embedded equations or graphics, and if it is comparatively short, it is not worth sending it as a file attachment. It is better simply to save a version of the file in plain text form, or to copy and paste the text directly into your e-mail message box. You will avoid any potential problems of file incompatibility, viruses etc., and be sure that the recipient of your message can read what you have to say. On several occasions I have been sent file attachments that I could not initially read (because they had been prepared using software that I didn't have or a later version of the package that I did have). After going to considerable lengths to convert the file into a form that I could read I then discovered that it consisted entirely of text which could have been sent as a normal e-mail message.

## Zip files and compression utilities

When files are to be stored in an archive, or moved across the Internet as e-mail attachments, it is desirable that they should be as small as possible. Using software such as PKZIP or WinZip it is possible to compress or "zip" files so that they occupy the minimum amount of space. Then when you want to decompress or unzip the files you can use the PKUNZIP command or WinZip to return the file to its full size. With the Windows WinZip software it is even possible to create self-extracting zipped files so that the recipient of the file need not have the compression software on their system. A self-extracting zip file is an executable file (.EXE file) that includes both a zip file and the software to extract or unzip the contents of the zip file. Just double click on it in Windows Explorer to run it and the contents will be extracted.

Note: You can also compress collections of files together in a single zipped file. WinZip can also handle UUencoded, XXencode, BinHex and MIME files (used primarily to transfer files by e-mail).

For more information find out whether the WinZip utility is available on your system. If it is, look at the Help that it offers. If not, go to `http://www.winzip.com`.

## Viruses and virus checkers

Computer viruses are deliberately programmed pieces of code that are attached to otherwise normal files and they are designed to infect computer systems and to spread across them. Some are relatively benign, causing a message to be displayed on the screen but creating no real problem for the computer system itself. However, others can have devastating effects, wiping out files and requiring many hours of support staff time to re-establish computer systems.

Some of the most common viruses are Word macro viruses such as the WM/Cap virus. This works by infecting the standard Word template file, NORMAL.DOT, so that when new Word files are created they will contain the virus-causing macro. Then if you share this file with someone else you will spread the virus to their system. The so-called Melissa virus (or W97M.Mailissa) spreads itself in a different way. When a user opens an infected document the virus will attempt to e-mail a copy of the document to up to fifty other people using the Microsoft Outlook e-mail system.

If you are working in a university lab it will probably have virus protection software installed that can scan the computer memory and drives for known viruses. If it encounters a virus it will warn you about it and it may be able automatically to remove the virus from the file (to "dis-infect" the file). If you are working at home it is a good idea to install a virus protection program. There are a number of such programs now available, such as Dr Solomon's FindVirus and Norton AntiVirus. As new viruses are coming along all the time you will need to keep the software up to date. Often you can download the latest version directly from the company's web site. For more information on viruses and how to protect yourself against them go to one of the following web sites:

```
http://www.drsolomon.com/
http://www.symantec.co.uk
http://www.nai.com
```

## The Millennium bug

The so-called Millennium bug, or Y2K bug, is not a computer virus at all. It is simply the name given to what happens to computer systems when they are unable to recognize the year 2000 in a date and read it instead as 1900, or some other year. The problem arises because some older software which is still in use tended to use only two digits to refer to a year (1963 was represented by 63, for example). So when the system encounters 00 it is unable to recognize this as referring to the year 2000. To be fair to the programmers responsible for this, at the time that they were working computer memory was very much at a premium. By using two digits rather than four to refer to each year they were able to save memory. They also expected that their programs would be replaced before the arrival of the new millennium.

Three types of software can be affected. BIOS software (Basic Input Output System – the tiny program that boots up your computer when it is first switched on), the Windows operating system (Apple computers are pretty much immune to this problem) and applications programs (particularly spreadsheet-based programs that call on date fields). If you are using modern computers and software the Millennium bug is unlikely to be a problem for you. You can check the Action2000 web site for further information if you are concerned:
`http://www.bug2000.co.uk`

## Practical 3.4   Sending and receiving a file attachment

For this practical you will need to team up with a fellow student on your course, or a friend at another institution that you know has e-mail. Each of you will need to have on your computer hard disk, the network drive or a floppy disk, a file that has been produced by your word processing or spreadsheet software. It could, for example, be a file that was created as a result of one of the previous practicals.

You should check that the person who is to receive the file has a copy of the relevant application that was used to produce it. If they have a different piece of word processing or spreadsheet software they might still be able to deal with the file. For example, Excel can read Lotus 1-2-3 files and Word can read WordPerfect files, provided that they were not created with the very latest version of the software which may not be recognizable in the current version of the alternative software package. One way to ensure that you don't run into any problems is to save your file in the format of an earlier version (say Excel version 2 or Word 6), or in the case of word processed documents as an RTF file as suggested above. Or, if you know what package they have at their end and your software allows you to save in that format, you could do that to minimize problems for them. Of course, if you are students working on the same network such problems won't arise, but you should be prepared for them as you might meet them on other occasions.

Load your e-mail software and begin a new message. Enter the recipient's e-mail address and give the subject as `Practical 3.4`. In the message box enter a brief message, greeting your friend and telling him or her that a file is attached (give a brief description of what the file is about). Complete everything you want to say in the message box. Then click on the icon or menu option in your e-mail software (mailer) that enables you to send file attachments. In the relevant dialog box indicate where on your system the file is located (give the full path name – for example, it could be C:\book\chapter3\prac3.xls). You may be able to select the file by browsing through the disks and folders available to you. When you have located the file you want, click the button to upload it. If the computer offers a variety of file types and you recognize one that is appropriate, for example Excel-sheet, you should select it. If not choose the option to let the mailer decide. If the computer offers a list of encoding options (UUencoding, BinHex, MIME etc.) and you are confident which one is to be used you can select it. If not just choose the option "Mailer decides". When all the options are set click on the Send button and your message will be sent, together with the file attachment.

Depending on the mailer software that you are using the process may be slightly different. If you are unsure what to do, as always, have a look at the on-line Help that the software provides.

Next, as the recipient of a message with a file attachment from your friend, check that you can download the file that he/she has sent you. Remember, it is safer to save the file and check it for viruses, rather than opening it immediately while still in the mailer system. If you are working on-line via a modem it also makes sense to minimize the time that you are connected to the phone line.

If you run into any problems in sending or receiving e-mail attachments, recheck what you have done and look again at the mailer Help system. If you still can't sort it out contact your lecturer or local computer help desk.

## E-mail discussion lists, newsletters and awareness services

As well as being used to send private messages to individuals or groups of people, e-mail tools can be used to maintain links between groups of individuals with a common interest through mail lists (or discussion lists), newsletters or awareness services. Subscribers to electronic newsletters and awareness services simply receive regular postings providing material on a particular subject. But mail list subscribers can participate actively, sending (posting) messages to the list which will then be forwarded (distributed) to all other subscribers to the list. A distinction can thus be made between the one-way or closed services newsletter and awareness services, where subscribers receive e-mail from those who run the list but cannot participate directly themselves, and two-way or open mail lists which thrive on user involvement.

## Mail lists

Some of the first mail lists that were set up were maintained manually by individual enthusiasts. List owners created a special e-mail address for subscribers to send their messages to and then used the Distribution list function in their e-mail software to create a list name that could be entered into the mailer's To: field, so that they didn't have to type in all the individual subscribers' e-mail addresses each time. Effectively subscribers sent their contributions to the list owner who then forwarded them to everyone on the list.

Nowadays most mail lists are automated so that they do not require manual intervention – a piece of *list management software* will do the job instead, relaying all messages that are sent to the list to everyone that subscribes to it. However, there is likely still to be an individual list owner who you can contact if you have problems, or if you wish to complain that contributions to the list are offensive or inappropriate in some other way. Some lists are moderated – that is contributions are not forwarded to the list until they have been vetted by the list editor.

In the UK a huge number of academic mail lists are operated by Mailbase at the University of Newcastle (at the time of writing there are over 2000 lists with over 160 000 subscribers worldwide). You can get full details of all the Mailbase lists and help about how the system operates by visiting the Mailbase web site at `http://www.mailbase.ac.uk`.

One list that you might like to subscribe to is the *cti-econ* list, which is owned by staff at the Institute for Learning and Research Technology at the University of Bristol. This is a mail list for people who are interested in the use of computers and IT in learning and teaching economics.

To join the list send the following two line message to mailbase@mailbase.ac.uk:

```
join cti-econ <Your First Name> <Your Family Name>

stop
```

You put your actual name in the message, not your e-mail address. The system will recognize this automatically from your e-mail message header. The second line of the message (`stop`) is particularly important if you have configured your mailer to include a signature at the end of your e-mail messages. This word stops the system before it comes to the signature, which it would not be able to interpret. Do not include any other words – not even "please" or "thank you" – as this message will be read and interpreted by a computer program, not a person.

If you wanted to join any of the other Mailbase mail lists you would send a similar message to mailbase substituting the appropriate list name. If at some point you want to leave a list you send a similar message to mailbase with the simple format:

```
leave <listname>

stop
```

There is no need to include your name this time.

---

**Important**

When you want to leave a list remember to send this message to the main Mailbase e-mail address, not to the list itself.

When you first join a mailbase list you will receive a message from mailbase asking you to confirm your details. This allows the system to check your e-mail address. You will then be sent a message welcoming you to the list which will include a brief explanation of how the list operates, including instructions on how to leave the list (so this is one message you should not delete). You will then be able to post messages to the list. To do this, compose and check your message and then send it to the list address; for example, messages for cti-econ list should be sent to:

cti-econ@mailbase.ac.uk

Remember to include some text on the subject line indicating what your message is about. Your message will then be distributed to all members of the cti-econ list.

---

**Tip**

When you first join a mail list it is sensible simply to read other messages sent to the list to gauge the level and tone of the list before you send any messages yourself. (Being on a list without sending a message is sometimes referred to as "lurking".) For lists managed by Mailbase you can browse or search through the list archives by going to the Mailbase web site. This can help you avoid irritating other list members by sending a message on a topic that has already been thoroughly aired.

---

Mailbase is not the only system that provides e-mail discussion lists of interest to economists. Many US based lists use other list management systems such as listserv or majordomo. Mail lists running under these systems operate in much the same way as those in the Mailbase system, although you will need to type `subscribe` (rather than `join`) when joining the list and `unsubscribe` (rather than `leave`) when leaving a list.

The cti-econ web site provides a good place to start a search for relevant e-mail discussion groups. It has a list of around forty mail lists of interest to economists at `http://www.ilrt.bris.ac.uk/ctiecon/resources/mlists.htm`. It also provides links to two directories of mail lists with which you can use keyword searches: L-soft's CataList directory `http://lsoft.com/catalist.html` and Liszt `http://www.liszt.com`.

Another excellent point of departure if you are looking for a mail list devoted to your special topic in economics is Bill Goffe's *Resources for Economists* web page `http://econwpa.wustl.edu/EconFAQ/EconFAQ.html`, which is mirrored in the UK at `http://netec.mcc.ac.uk/EconFAQ/EconFAQ.html`. If you follow the links (e.g. to `http://netec.mcc.ac.uk/EconFAQ/MailUsenet/MailLists/index.html`) you can find information about a large number of economics mail lists, organized by their *Journal of Economic Literature* (JEL) headings.

## Mail list digests

Some mail lists offer a digest service. This means that if you subscribe to this version of the list you won't receive every new message when it is sent to the list. Instead, at the end of every day or perhaps every week, you will receive a single message which batches together all the messages sent to the list over the relevant period in digest form. This can be a good idea for mail lists that have a lot of "traffic", i.e. a lot of messages are sent to the list each day.

### Warning

Mail lists can often generate huge numbers of messages, many of which are opinionated or contain inaccurate information. Professional and scholarly mail lists are generally very good, but you should remember that individual messages are not usually subject to checking or editorial control. However, the mail list itself offers its own process of self-correction in that errors will usually be seized upon and pointed out by other subscribers.

### Lists of subscribers

Most mail lists maintain a list of subscribers and their e-mail addresses that you can access. This can be helpful if you wish to maintain contact with some subscribers "off-list".

## E-mail newsletters and current awareness lists

Several of the entries in the cti-econ list are not true mail lists in that they don't allow subscribers to post messages to them. Instead, either all subscribers are sent a periodic newsletter (e.g. the bi-weekly Scout Report for Business and Economics – `http://scout18cs.wisc.edu`), or on the basis of keyword information provided by subscribers they provide targeted news (e.g. Economics Working Papers, which notifies subscribers about new working papers in economics that have been added to the Economics Working Papers Archive at the University of Washington, St Louis – `http://econwpa.wustl/edu/`). These newsletters and awareness services provide a very convenient way of keeping up to date in your subject. Incidentally, all members of the cti-econ mail list will automatically be sent copies of the monthly CTI-ECON Newsletter.

## Newsgroups

Newsgroups have many of the characteristics of e-mail discussion lists in that they offer a means by which a group of enthusiasts about a particular topic or subject area can exchange information, ideas, opinions and other material, but they work in a different way. However, they operate more like bulletin boards and messages are posted on the system for subscribers to view, rather than being sent to their e-mail box. There are many thousands of newsgroups covering a wide range of subjects, grouped together in *hierarchies*. Some are rather esoteric – bizarre even – with just a few subscribers. *Usenet* refers to the worldwide collection of computers that host newsgroups.

You will need a software application called a *newsreader* to be able to view newsgroups. The latest versions of the two most popular browsers, Netscape and Internet Explorer, both have newsreaders built into them (respectively Collabra and Outlook Express). However, they will need to be configured to identify you and your e-mail address before you can use them. For further information on newsgroups see Stein (1999), Chapter 12.

## Summary

This chapter has shown you how to build on the basics and develop your skills, as an economist, with standard office software. Explanations and illustrations have been provided to demonstrate how to incorporate graphics images and equations into word processed documents and how to use spreadsheets to help you analyze quantitative economic models.

## Exercises and mini-projects

1. Try to create each of the following equations using your word processing software. (Hint: you will probably be able to create the first five just by combining normal text with subscripts and superscripts and the relevant Greek and mathematical characters produced with the Symbols font. To produce the remaining equations you are more likely to need the Symbols palette or the Equation Editor.)

   (i)     $TC = 120 + 45 Q - Q^2 + 0.4 Q^3$

   (ii)    $C = a + b Y_d$

   (iii)   $M = p_x x + p_y y$

   (iv)    $\Pi = TR - TC$

   (v)     $Q = L^\alpha K^\beta$

   (vi)    $\sqrt{x} = x^{0.5}$

(vii)    $\partial y / \partial x \leq 0$

(viii)   $\sum_{i=1}^{n} x_i$

(ix)    $x = \dfrac{-b \pm \sqrt{b^2 - 4ac}}{2a}$

(x)     $V_t = V_0 (1 + R)^t$

(Note: if you don't get quite the expression you want the first time, don't worry. You can always double click on it to edit it.)

2. Sometimes you will be asked to produce written material in the form of a report rather than an essay. For such a report it may be better to structure the material using a numbered list of points (or even a list of bullet points).

Produce a brief word processed report (no more than two pages) on one of the following topics:

(i)      the difference between microeconomics and macroeconomics
(ii)     the difference between GDP and GNP, real and nominal
(iii)    the difference between a model and a theory
(iv)    the comparative performance of two countries, regions or industries over the last decade.

3. A simple macroeconomic model is built on a relationship between consumption (C) and national income (Y) of the form C = a + b Y where a and b are constants. Here a represents autonomous consumption and is assumed to be greater than 0. The constant b is the marginal propensity to consume, i.e. the proportion of any additional unit of income that will be consumed so 0 < b < 1. The level of aggregate demand in the economy (AD) is C plus I (investment), which is assumed here to be entirely autonomous – its value is taken as given and it is unaffected by changes in C or Y.

Equilibrium in the model occurs where Y = AD and is usually illustrated on a "Keynesian cross" diagram where AD is plotted against Y and equilibrium is where this line crosses the 45 degree line (which traces out the condition Y = AD). Consult almost any introductory economics textbook if this is not familiar to you.

Based on the parameter values given below, construct a spreadsheet model to generate schedules of values for Y, C, I and AD over a range of values from Y = 0 to 100 (going up in steps of 10). Produce a chart that illustrates the relationships graphically.

Initial parameter values: a = 10;  b = 0.8; I = 5.

Identify the equilibrium value of Y. Then conduct "what-if" exercises to simulate the effects of each of the following changes: (i) I increases by one unit to 6; (ii) b goes down to 0.75.

**4.** Go to the Mailbase website at `mailbase@mailbase.ac.uk` or the section of Bill Goffe's "Resources for Economists" page that lists economics mail lists.

Search through the mail lists and identify one that interests you. Join the list by sending the appropriate message. If you can, search through the list's archives and make a mental (or actual) note of some of the issues that have been discussed. Note: Do not send any messages to the mail list. After a few days send a message to leave the mail list.

# CHAPTER 4

# Spreadsheets for economists

## Objective

The objective of this chapter is to extend the reader's skills in working with spreadsheets for economics related tasks. Skills covered are:

- the use of statistical functions for analyzing and summarizing economic data, including cross-tabulations for categorical data and regression analysis on a spreadsheet
- financial analysis on a spreadsheet
- optimization using a spreadsheet
- working with matrix models using spreadsheets
- working with dynamic economic models using spreadsheets

Economists use spreadsheets for a wide range of tasks. As we have already seen in the previous two chapters, a spreadsheet package provides a convenient environment not only for analyzing and charting data, but also for formulating and analyzing quantitative economic models. In this chapter we shall look at some further examples of each of these types of application, demonstrating the flexibility and power of the spreadsheet for quantitative economic analysis.

## A brief history of spreadsheets

The original idea for an electronic (computer-based) spreadsheet came from an American, Dan Bricklin. While at the Harvard Business School where he was studying for an MBA, Bricklin was required to undertake a number of case studies based on real company data. Students were asked to consider the implications of possible changes to some of the data values ("what-if" exercises) and this meant that they had to perform many long, complicated and tedious calculations. In this type of exercise it would be very easy to make a mistake somewhere in the calculations. Even a single error could throw out all the rest of the values and yet be hard to detect.

Bricklin had quite a bit of experience of working with word processors and he began to visualize "a word processor that would work with numbers", that is, a computer package with a simple user interface that could hold all the data and formulae for a quantitative problem of the type he had been working on, and immediately recalculate all the results if any of the basic inputs was changed. His original prototype program, written in BASIC on an Apple computer, provided a 10×10 grid of 100 cells with columns labeled A, B, C etc. and rows labelled 1, 2, 3 etc. Although there was no scrolling, let alone any of the graphics and other features that we now take for granted, the basic structure of the electronic spreadsheet could be seen in this simple program.

Bricklin brought in his friend Bob Frankston to produce the code for a working version of the program which they called VisiCalc. Rather than market the software themselves they signed up with a company called Personal Software which launched VisiCalc as the first commercial spreadsheet package, running on Apple II computers, in 1978. The program was an immediate success, enjoying a symbiotic relationship with the Apple computer, and Personal Software changed its name to VisiCorp.

The success of VisiCalc spawned a range of rival products as other companies launched their own spreadsheet packages for different machines and operating systems. In 1981 the first version of SuperCalc was released by the Sorcim Corporation, while around the same time Microsoft brought out Multiplan.

A major advance took place in 1982 with the launch of Lotus 1-2-3, which was the first spreadsheet to integrate graphical displays. Along with limited database management facilities, it provided the third feature in the "1-2-3" package of worksheet, database and graphics. The package was also easier to use than some of the previous spreadsheet programs and incorporated extensive 'Help' facilities.

Successive releases of different spreadsheet packages have included more and more built-in functions and procedures while the Windows environment has allowed program designers to make the software easier to use with toolbars, icons and Function Wizards. Excel has come to be the dominant spreadsheet package, mainly because it is part of the Microsoft family of programs rather than due to any inherent superiority in its features. Lotus 1-2-3 is still available while Quattro is also a widely used spreadsheet.

Users quickly recognized the potential of spreadsheet software, not only for financial and business calculations, but for a wide range of applications. Books and articles have appeared describing the use of spreadsheets in subjects as varied as science and engineering, geography, statistics and, of course, economics.

While the term "spreadsheet" is used to refer to any computer package of this type, the files that are produced are called worksheets or workbooks (a collection of worksheets). You can usually tell which spreadsheet was used to create a worksheet or workbook by the file extension that it has been given. For example, the extension .XLS would go with Excel worksheets while Lotus 1-2-3 will produce an extension of the form .WK* (where the last character will depend on the version of the software being used).

Although some features may be lost, it is usually possible to load a file produced with one spreadsheet package into another. It should also be relatively easy to see how instructions which are given to construct, say, an Excel worksheet would need to be modified for use with a different spreadsheet package.

## 4.1   Analyzing and summarizing economic data

## Practical 4.1   GDP per capita in OECD countries

Table 4.1 gives comparative data on GDP per capita in 29 OECD countries in 1997. The figures are in thousands of US dollars, based on current exchange rates.

There is clearly a large variation in GDP per capita across these countries. The lowest figure is for Turkey while the highest is for Luxembourg. It is hard to take in all the information just by looking at the table. Fortunately spreadsheet packages contain a number of functions and tools that can help us analyze the data in various ways. So run your spreadsheet software and enter the information with the country names in column A and the GDP figures in column B. Remember to include a title for the table. You could put it in row 1 of the spreadsheet, perhaps placing the first row of the table with the information for Canada in row 3. Once the information has been entered, save the worksheet (call it perhaps oecdgdp.xls) so that if anything goes wrong as you attempt to analyze the data you can always call it up again in its basic form.

Now we will use the spreadsheet to sort the data, ranking the countries in descending order of GDP per capita. In Excel to do this first select all the cells containing both the country names and the figures and then choose **D**ata followed by **S**ort. In the dialog box make sure that you select column B to sort by and click on the radio button to choose **D**escending. Make sure also that the radio button next to No Header Ro**w** is also on. Other spreadsheet packages will have similar commands.

When you click **OK** the table should be rearranged to show the countries in descending order of GDP per capita, with Luxembourg at the top and Turkey at the bottom. It is now much easier to see that there are five countries with a GDP per capita above 30 000 US dollars per year (with the US itself just under that figure)

**Table 4.1**   GDP per capita in OECD countries in 1997[a].

| | |
|---|---:|
| Canada | 20.1 |
| Mexico | 4.3 |
| US | 29.3 |
| Japan | 33.2 |
| Korea | 9.6 |
| Australia | 21.2 |
| New Zealand | 17.3 |
| Austria | 25.5 |
| Belgium | 23.8 |
| Czech Republic | 5.1 |
| Denmark | 32.2 |
| Finland | 23.3 |
| France | 23.8 |
| Germany | 25.5 |
| Greece | 11.4 |
| Hungary | 4.5 |
| Iceland | 27.3 |
| Ireland | 21.1 |
| Italy | 19.9 |
| Luxembourg | 37.3 |
| Netherlands | 23.3 |
| Norway | 34.8 |
| Poland | 3.5 |
| Portugal | 10.2 |
| Spain | 13.5 |
| Sweden | 25.7 |
| Switzerland | 35.9 |
| Turkey | 3.0 |
| United Kingdom | 21.7 |

Source: OECD National Accounts, Main Aggregates, Volume 1 obtainable
from http://www.oecd.org/std/gdpperca.htm
[a] In thousands of US dollars, based on current exchange rates

while at the other extreme there are four countries where GDP per capita is under 5000 US dollars per year (with the Czech Republic only just above that figure).

Table 4.1 presents the data with the countries in the same order as it was made available on the OECD web site. It is not exactly in alphabetical order but appears to group the countries first by geographical regions and then alphabetically within the various regions. If you did wish to order the countries alphabetically you could do that using the spreadsheet's data sorting facility. Try it as an exercise.

Next let's see how you can use built-in spreadsheet formulae to compute the average or mean of the values in the table. Underneath the table enter the text Mean value = into a cell in column A and then in the cell next to it in column B enter the formula =AVERAGE(B4:B32) – if your GDP figures are in a different block put in the first and last cell addresses in the block instead of B4 and B32. When you press **Enter** you should see the value 20.3 displayed.

If you are too lazy to type in the formula to compute the mean, or if you have forgotten the formula, modern spreadsheets have a Function Wizard to do all the hard work for you. In Excel highlight the block of cells that you want to use and then click on the Function Wizard icon $f_x$. (You may have to use **I**nsert Function to activate this feature.) In the dialog box select the function name AVERAGE (in the function category Statistical) and in the second step indicate the block of cells to use. Try using the function MEDIAN and interpret the value that is produced – if you don't know what the median of a set of numbers is, the spreadsheet's **H**elp feature should be able to tell you. Notice that, amongst others, there are functions to return the largest (MAX), the smallest (MIN), the standard deviation, the variance and a measure of skewness for the values in a block of cells. There may be occasions where you would find such functions useful. Another thing you can do for a set of data such as this is to get a full table of summary statistics. To do this in Excel select **T**ools, **D**ata **A**nalysis and then Descriptive Statistics. Make sure that you put a mark against Summary Statistics before clicking **OK**.

Quite often economists faced with a set of observations on a particular variable – here the variable is GDP per capita – want to collect together the observations in a *frequency table*, counting the number of observations falling into various classes. Then this information can be displayed visually as a *histogram*. Spreadsheets such as Excel

## Warning

If you check the OECD National Accounts or look at the web site, you will find that the figure quoted for GDP per capita for the OECD overall (in US\$ '000) is not 20.3 but 22.4. This is partly accounted for by the fact that, as a footnote to the OECD table indicates, the figure given on the web site for some reason excludes Korea, the Czech Republic, Hungary and Poland. However, there is another factor that we should have thought of, even if all countries had been included. This is that the figures in the table are ratios, showing each country's GDP divided by the population of the country. The populations in the various countries vary considerably and a more suitable average for the whole OECD would take this into account, that is it would take the ratio of the sum of GDP in the whole of the OECD and divide by the total population of the OECD. As some basic algebra or a simple numerical example will confirm, this is not the same as the average of the GDP per capita figures across countries. Without all the original data to hand we cannot check what difference this would make, but we should be aware of a possible distortion in our calculations. Just because a computer can work out a value for you doesn't mean that the result will be meaningful!

Note: The OECD also shows the GDP per capita figures based on current purchasing power parities, rather than current exchange rates. If you don't know what this means, consult your economics textbook.

can do this for you; however, first you must set up *limits* for the classes (or the *bins* as they are called in spreadsheet terms).

When you classify data it is not necessary for the class intervals all to have the same width. However, in this case we will set up eight classes, each five units wide. Our classes will go from 0 up to 5; from 5 to 10; from 10 to 15; from 15 to 20; from 20 to 25; from 25 to 30; from 30 to 35 and from 35 to 40. This may be slightly too many classes, given the amount of data. However, it will be interesting to count up the number of OECD countries with GDP per head in each of these classes.

Somewhere in the spreadsheet (e.g. cells G4:G11) you need to enter values corresponding to the upper limits of the class intervals or bins. So enter into these cells the numbers 5, 10, 15, 20, 25, 30, 35 and 40. Now you can use the histogram tool. If you are using Excel select **T**ools, **D**ata Analysis and then **H**istogram (the procedure is likely to be very similar in other spreadsheet packages). In the dialog box enter the first and last cell address for the GDP values in the Input range (e.g. B4:B32). In the bin range enter the first and last cell address for the bin values (e.g. G4:G11). You have several options for the Output range. You can put the table and chart in a new sheet, or by giving a cell address in an empty part of the existing sheet the results can be copied in there. Say you wanted to put them in the current worksheet, beginning in cell A40. Type that address into the dialog box and make sure that the Chart Output option is selected. Then click **OK**. You should get a frequency table counting the values in each class, and to the right of it a histogram illustrating this visually.

If you want to edit the graph, say replacing the default title of Histogram with "GDP per capita in OECD countries", you simply click on the object and put in the text that you want. Figure 4.1 shows an edited version of the histogram I created.

Note that the spreadsheet histogram is not quite the same as would be shown in a statistics textbook in that the bars shown are not right up next to each other. However, this chart does provide a helpful graphical view of the frequency table. Note also that if an observation corresponds to a bin value (upper limit) it is assigned to that class. In other words if you wanted a value of 5 to go into the second class rather the first

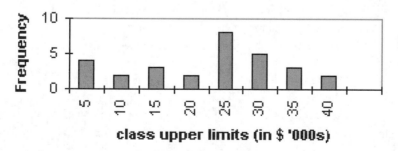

**Fig. 4.1**   Histogram showing the frequencies of GDP per capita in OECD countries.

one, etc., bin values would have to be specified as 4.9, 9.9, 14.9, 19.9, 24.9, 29.9, 34.9 and 39.9. In this case it would make no difference as none of the GDP per capita values falls exactly on a class limit.

## 4.2   Cross-tabulation

## Practical 4.2   The position of women in economics departments

Suppose you have been looking at a university department's web page which lists staff alphabetically by name, and gives an indication of their position in the department (showing who is a Professor, a Senior Lecturer and ordinary Lecturer). You notice that of the twenty staff listed six are women, but only one of the four Professors is a woman. You decide to investigate the relationship between position and gender more systematically. (Note: the information here is entirely fictitious. However, it is not out of line with the findings of a study of UK economics departments conducted on behalf of the Royal Economic Society. See Booth and Burton (1999).)

You enter the person's name, gender and position into a spreadsheet as shown in Figure 4.2.

|    | A | B | C |
|----|---|---|---|
| 1  | Name | Gender | Position |
| 2  | Allen | M | S |
| 3  | Friedman | M | L |
| 4  | Frost | F | L |
| 5  | Harris | F | L |
| 6  | Hendrie | M | P |
| 7  | Hunt | M | S |
| 8  | Jackson | F | S |
| 9  | Jones | M | L |
| 10 | Kaplanski | M | S |
| 11 | Khan | M | P |
| 12 | Koopman | M | L |
| 13 | Lee | M | L |
| 14 | Liu | F | S |
| 15 | Murphy | M | S |
| 16 | Osborne | F | P |
| 17 | Patel | M | S |
| 18 | Panagiotis | M | L |
| 19 | Rossi | M | L |
| 20 | Schwartz | M | P |
| 21 | Smith | F | L |

**Fig. 4.2**  Staff names showing gender and position.

What you need to do is to draw up a table, known as a *contingency table*, which has two columns to distinguish the gender of the individuals and three rows to distinguish the staff according to their position or status. The table would show the number of cases falling into each two-way category. Now with a small data set such as we have here it is easy enough just to count up the cases manually. However, most spreadsheet packages can do the job automatically and this can be very helpful when you have a large number of cases.

The procedure in Excel is as follows. Go to an area of the worksheet where you would like the table to appear, say cell E1. From the menu bar select **D**ata and then **P**ivot Table. The PivotTable Wizard should show the screen corresponding to the first of four steps that you need to complete. Make sure that the Microsoft Excel List or Database radio button is on and click on the Next button. You will be asked for the worksheet range that contains the data you want to use. Enter B1:C21 and then click on the Next button. You should see on screen the box for the third step as shown in Figure 4.3.

Click and drag the Gender button into the **C**OLUMN area and then click and drag the Position button into the **R**OW area. Then click and drag the Position button into the **D**ATA area. Clicking on the Next button takes you to the box for the final step. Here you should make sure that the starting cell is where you want the table to begin. You should also deselect the Save Data with Table Layout option. When you

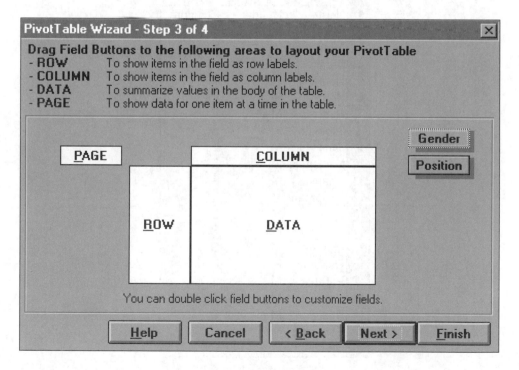

**Fig. 4.3**   PivotTable Wizard Step 3.

| Count of Position | Gender | | |
|---|---|---|---|
| Position | F | M | Grand Total |
| L | 3 | 6 | 9 |
| P | 1 | 3 | 4 |
| S | 2 | 5 | 7 |
| Grand Total | 6 | 14 | 20 |

**Fig. 4.4**   Contingency table produced by Excel.

click on the **F**inish button you should see a table resembling the one in Figure 4.4. The table confirms our earlier impression that females are underrepresented as a proportion of total staff and this increases at the higher grades.

Unfortunately the rows have been ordered alphabetically. If you wanted to have them in order of status you would need make sure that the contents of column C contained labels that would reflect this ordering. For example, they could read "1:Professor", "2:Senior Lecturer" and "3:Lecturer". You could put the labels in column B as Male and Female, if you wish, to change the Gender headings in the table from M and F.

There are various options available to you with tables of this sort. For example, you can get the computer to show the entries as percentages of the total. Select the table you have created and then click on the right mouse button. Select Options and scroll down in the Show Data as: window until you get to % of Total. When you click **OK** the entries will be shown as percentages of the total. For information on further variations on what you can do, click on the **H**elp button in the first of the four PivotTable Wizard windows.

---

**Tip**

With much larger databases containing many more cases and fields (variables) it makes sense to keep the data in a separate file from the worksheet where the cross-tabulations are undertaken. For more advanced analysis of data of this type it may be better to use a proper statistics package such as SPSS (see Chapter 5).

---

## 4.3   Regression on a spreadsheet

The example given in section 4.2 looked at a situation where we wanted to analyze two categorical variables to see if there was any relationship between them. Many economic variables are quantitative in nature and the main tool used by economists to investigate relationships between quantitative variables is regression analysis. Most spreadsheet packages contain commands for running regressions, and although for more advanced work it will be advisable to use a dedicated statistics or econometrics package (see Chapter 5), for some simple applications a spreadsheet will be perfectly adequate. Regular spreadsheet users will be comfortable with the spreadsheet environment and will be able to make use of all the other spreadsheet functions (especially those for creating graphs) to augment the basic results.

## Practical 4.3   Carbon monoxide emissions in the European Union

Consider the data in Table 4.2, which provides information on gross domestic product at market prices, in millions of ECUs, and carbon monoxide emissions in millions of tonnes (CO) for the 15 European Union countries in 1997 (source: Eurostat, New Cronos Database http://europa.eu/int/en/comm/eurostat/).

**Table 4.2**   CO emissions and GDP for EU countries in 1997.

| Country | GDP | CO |
| --- | --- | --- |
| Austria | 182.01 | 56.7 |
| Belgium | 213.7 | 111.3 |
| Denmark | 140.05 | 59.9 |
| Finland | 104.68 | 56.4 |
| France | 1223.15 | 347.5 |
| Germany | 1853.34 | 848.9 |
| Greece | 105.71 | 78.2 |
| Ireland | 66.62 | 31.9 |
| Italy | 1011.86 | 405.1 |
| Luxembourg | 13.91 | 8.7 |
| Netherlands | 318.3 | 170.9 |
| Portugal | 88.63 | 47.9 |
| Spain | 472.04 | 238.1 |
| Sweden | 202.01 | 53.6 |
| United Kingdom | 1134.03 | 532.3 |

You are asked to examine the hypothesis that there is a relationship between CO and GDP. If such a relationship exists a model of it could be used to predict the consequences for CO emissions of increases in GDP.

Using your spreadsheet software begin a new worksheet and enter the data in cells A1 to C16. First, examine the data graphically. You need to plot what is called a *scatter diagram* or an *XY graph*, that is you should plot the values of the CO variable against the values of the GDP variable. Here, GDP is the X variable (to be plotted on the horizontal axis); CO is the Y variable (to be plotted on the vertical axis).

In Excel you can use the Chart Wizard to help you with this. Select cells B1 to C16 and click on the chart icon. Use the mouse to move to an empty part of the worksheet (say cell A19) and click on the mouse. (Alternatively you can **I**nsert the chart on a new separate worksheet within the workbook.) The box for Step 1 (of 5) of the Chart Wizard will appear. The range for B1:C16 should already be showing. If not, enter it now. Click Next and the box for Step 2 will open offering you a variety of chart types. Click on XY (**S**catter) and then Next to move on to Step 3. You now have a variety of formats for the XY graph to choose from. Select format number 1 and click Next to move to step 4. A box with a sample chart will now appear. Make sure that the radio button next to Data Series in **C**olumns is showing, and that the first column is to be used for the X data. The computer will probably also have the first row marked to be used for Legend Text. Click Next to move to the box for the final step. Here you can add a Chart Title; put something like CO emissions and GDP in EU countries in 1997. Then add titles for the axes: GDP for the X axis and CO for the Y axis.

You don't need a legend here so you can move the radio button to **N**o. Click the button marked **F**inish and you should get a graph something like Figure 4.5 appearing in your worksheet.

If you feel that the graph is too small you can increase its size by pointing the mouse at the bottom right hand corner so that a two-headed arrow appears. Hold the mouse down and stretch the graph towards the bottom right of the screen and the graph size will be increased proportionately. If you increase it too much you can click on the bottom right corner and move the mouse back upwards and to the left. If you just want to expand (or decrease) one of the two dimensions of the graph, go to the mid point of the right side or bottom of the graph until you see the double-headed arrow and stretch or reduce the graph as required.

As you should know by now, you can edit individual parts of the graph, for example to change the text in the title, or the font used, or to change the color or style

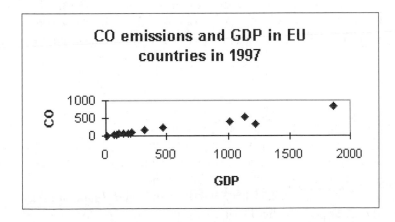

**Fig. 4.5** XY (scatter plot) of CO emissions and GDP.

of the marker used to plot the points. If you feel that any such changes are needed make them now and then save the worksheet.

Looking at the scatter diagram it certainly appears that there is a relationship between CO emissions and GDP. In general the larger the GDP figures the higher the CO emissions. Although the figures are not exactly linearly related, there is no obvious evidence of any nonlinearity. As a working hypothesis it might therefore be reasonable to assume that the following model is an adequate description of the data.

$$Y_i = \alpha + \beta X_i + u_i \qquad \text{for } i = 1,...,15 \qquad \text{Equation 4.1}$$

where $Y_i$ denotes CO emissions in country i, $X_i$ denotes GDP in country i, $\alpha$ and $\beta$ are constant parameters (to be estimated) and $u_i$ is a disturbance term that accounts for all the influences on CO emissions other than GDP. Although the disturbances are not directly observable it seems reasonable to assume that while for some countries they may be positive and for others they may be negative, on average they will be zero. We can also assume, at this stage, that their values are unrelated to the size of GDP.

Expressing the same model in slightly more accessible notation, and recognizing that the $\alpha$ and $\beta$ parameters would respectively measure the intercept and slope of the relationship when displayed graphically, one can write

$$CO = \text{intercept} + \text{slope GDP} + \text{disturbance} \qquad \text{Equation 4.2}$$

Now we want to estimate the values of $\alpha$ and $\beta$ (intercept and slope) from the data. This is where regression analysis comes in. Regression analysis seeks to account for variations (around the mean) in a *dependent* variable in terms of the variations in the *independent* variable. Here CO is the dependent variable and GDP is the independent variable. The model assumes that causation runs from the right hand side to the left hand side of the equation.

The principle that is used in fitting basic regression models is that of *least squares*. That is, a line will be fitted to the scatter of points such that the sum of the squares of the vertical distances between the original points and the fitted line is minimized.

In terms of the algebra, estimates of $\alpha$ and $\beta$ will be chosen, call them a and b, to minimize

$$\sum_{i=1}^{15}(Y_i - \hat{Y}_i)^2 \quad \text{or} \quad \sum_{i=1}^{15}(Y_i - a - bX_i)^2 \qquad \text{Equation 4.3}$$

where the fitted line has the equation $\hat{Y}_i = a + bX_i$

Spreadsheet packages such as Excel have built-in regression commands that can be used to obtain the estimated intercept and slope values (as well as some other statistics that can be used to help assess the suitability of the model).

From the **T**ools menu select **D**ata Analysis and then Regression. (*Note:* If Data Analysis doesn't appear in the **T**ools menu you may need to install it by selecting **T**ools and then Add-**I**ns.) You will need to input the Y range (the cells containing the observations of the dependent variable – here C2:C16) and the X range (the cells containing the observations of the independent variable – here B2:B16). The regression output can either go somewhere else in the current worksheet (in which case you will need to enter the address of the top left hand cell for the range to be used) or you can put it in a separate worksheet within the workbook. You can even ask the computer to put the results in a completely different workbook. Here we choose the middle option. As you can see in Figure 4.6, it is also possible to get some additional information on the residuals. We will take a closer look at this in a minute – for now just click on the indicators next to the Residual Plots and Line Fit Plots. Click **OK** and the computer will start executing the command. For a few moments various results and graphs will flash up on the screen until eventually the process is complete and a new worksheet will appear containing all the results.

The summary output should be something like that shown in Figure 4.6. (Some of the columns have been widened to show all the information that is in them.)

There is a lot of information here. To begin with let's just focus on what we were trying to find, namely estimated values for the intercept and slope or X variable

SUMMARY OUTPUT

| *Regression Statistics* | |
| --- | --- |
| Multiple R | 0.9730247 |
| R Square | 0.946777 |
| Adjusted R Square | 0.942683 |
| Standard Error | 56.884494 |
| Observations | 15 |

ANOVA

| | *df* | *SS* | *MS* | *F* | *Significance F* |
| --- | --- | --- | --- | --- | --- |
| Regression | 1 | 748 306.8624 | 748 306.9 | 231.2554 | 1.17E-09 |
| Residual | 13 | 42 065.99365 | 3235.846 | | |
| Total | 14 | 790 372.856 | | | |

| | *Coefficients* | *Standard Error* | *t Stat* | *P-value* | *Lower 95%* | *Upper 95 %* |
| --- | --- | --- | --- | --- | --- | --- |
| Intercept | 6.002644 | 19.5910697 | 0.306397 | 0.764154 | -36.3213 | 48.32657 |
| X Variable 1 | 0.4147747 | 0.027275098 | 15.20708 | 1.17E-09 | 0.35585 | 0.473699 |

**Fig. 4.6** Summary regression output for Excel. (continued overleaf)

RESIDUAL OUTPUT

| Observation | Predicted Y | Residuals |
|:---:|:---:|:---:|
| 1 | 81.495791 | -24.7957907 |
| 2 | 94.640002 | 16.65999849 |
| 3 | 64.091843 | -4.19184343 |
| 4 | 49.421262 | 6.9787384 |
| 5 | 513.33434 | -165.834342 |
| 6 | 774.72122 | 74.17877754 |
| 7 | 49.84848 | 28.35152044 |
| 8 | 33.634936 | -1.73493578 |
| 9 | 425.69659 | -20.5965916 |
| 10 | 11.77216 | -3.07216032 |
| 11 | 138.02544 | 32.87456284 |
| 12 | 42.7641 27 | 5.135872647 |
| 13 | 201.7929 | 36.30709748 |
| 14 | 89.791285 | -36.191285 |
| 15 | 476.36962 | 55.93038097 |

**Fig. 4.6**  Summary regression output for Excel. (continued)

coefficient. These values are contained in the third of the four main blocks within the output, and are given as

Intercept      6.002644

and

X Variable 1 0.4147747

The results tell us that the fitted model is given (approximately) by the equation $\hat{Y}_i = 6.03 + 0.415X_i$ . Interpreting these values we find that there is a certain amount of CO (just over 6 million tons) that seems to occur on average irrespective of GDP. This is our estimate for $\alpha$ and would be the intercept on the vertical axis of the graph.

The X variable coefficient, or slope coefficient – our estimate for $\beta$ – is about 0.415. This suggests that in EU countries on average, for every extra million ECU that is added to GDP a further 0.415 million tons of CO will be generated.

Before we look at some of the other figures in the table let's turn our attention to one of the graphs that has been plotted automatically for us. Figure 4.7 shows the graph plot which contains the fitted or predicted Y values as well as the observed Y values.

It would be better if these values had been joined together and plotted without the markers. To modify the graph in that way double click on the predicted values. The Format Data Series box should open and you can change the radio button for Line

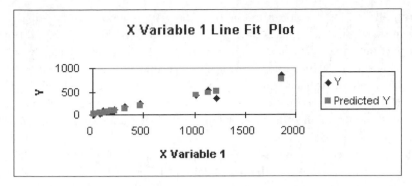

**Fig. 4.7**  Scatter diagram including fitted (predicted) Y values.

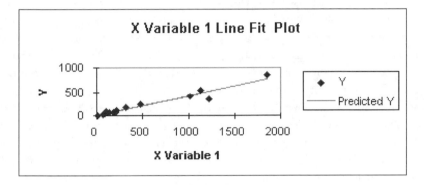

**Fig. 4.8**  Scatter diagram including fitted line.

from None to Automatic and for Marker to None from Automatic. When you click *OK* the graph should appear as in Figure 4.8 (you can edit other features such as the Title, Axis titles etc. if you wish).

The fitted line has been chosen so that it minimizes the sum of the squares of the positive and negative deviations of the actual points from the line. At first sight the model appears to fit the data quite well with none of the points too far away from the fitted line.

A statistic that is used in regression analysis to indicate how well a set of data are fitted by a model is $R^2$, R-squared (or R-square as Excel calls it). Also known as the *Coefficient of determination*, this is the ratio of two sums of squares. The numerator is the sum of squares of the fitted values around the mean value of Y. The denominator is the sum of squares of the actual values around the mean value of Y.

$$R^2 = \frac{\sum_{i=1}^{n}(\hat{Y}_i - \overline{Y})^2}{\sum_{i=1}^{n}(Y_i - \overline{Y})^2}$$

Equation 4.4

This statistic must be non-negative (it is the ratio of two sums of squares) and it will be unit free (the same units of measurement are used on the top and bottom of the ratio). The biggest value it could have would be 1, and that would only occur if all the actual and fitted values of Y corresponded so that all the actual points fell on the fitted line (a highly unlikely situation). More generally, R-squared will take a value somewhere between nought and one. Its value will indicate the goodness of fit of the model to the data, giving the proportion of the total sum of squares that can be explained by the model.

Here we can see that the value of R-squared is 0.946777 which indicates that nearly 95% of the variation in the dependent variable (CO) around its mean can be explained by or attributed to variations in GDP. This seems to be very strong evidence that the model is a good one. However, one would be very ill-advised to judge a regression model solely on the basis of its R-squared value (more on this later). (*Note:* The ANOVA or analysis of variance table decomposes the total sum of squares into the regression (or explained) sum of squares and the residual sum of squares. As can be confirmed, R-squared = 748 306.8624/790 372.856.)

We can test the hypothesis that $\beta = 0$ (which would imply no relationship between CO and GDP) using either the t-statistic or the F-statistic. Here we will use the t-statistic. It can be shown (see the web site or any statistics or econometrics textbook) that the ratio of the difference between the estimated coefficient and the true parameter value to the estimated standard error of the coefficient estimate will have a Student's t distribution. So if the null hypothesis is true, i.e. $\beta = 0$, the calculated t-statistic (which would now just be the coefficient estimate divided by standard error) would be expected to be very small. On the other hand, if this ratio is, in absolute value, much bigger than zero we would be inclined to reject the null hypothesis and accept the alternative, i.e. $\beta \neq 0$.

Before the current generation of software became available it was necessary to look up the critical t-value in a set of t tables. Taking the relevant number of degrees of freedom (i.e. the number of observations minus the number of parameters to be estimated – so here the degrees of freedom = 15 – 2 = 13) and the chosen significance level (i.e. the probability or risk of incorrectly rejecting the null hypothesis – usually set at 5% or 0.05 but split between the two tails would leave 0.025 in each tail) one would look up the value in the table. If the absolute value of the calculated t-ratio is greater than the value from the tables, then one would be able to reject the null hypothesis and accept the alternative, i.e. one would conclude that there was a significant relationship between the variables. Now the tabulated t-value for 13 degrees of freedom with 0.025 in each tail is 2.16. Our results show a t-statistic of 15.2071 so we are comfortably able to reject the null hypothesis and accept that the results are significant.

Modern software, including Excel, is able to show the P-value or probability value for a statistic such as this which means that we don't need to refer to tables any more. The P-value is the probability of getting a t-value greater than the one obtained, given the null hypothesis. So if this is less than 0.025 then we can confidently reject the null hypothesis and accept the alternative at the 5% significance level. Here the P-value is shown as 1.17 E-09 – which means $1.2 \times 10^{-9}$ (or 0.000000001). This is certainly a lot smaller than 0.025 and so we can conclude that the estimate of the slope coefficient is significantly different from zero.

(*Note:* If we have a strong theoretical reason for discounting on a priori grounds the possibility that β could be negative, we could conduct a one-tailed rather than a two-tailed test. The critical value for this test would leave all 5% in the right hand tail and thus lower the value that the calculated t-statistic would have to exceed – with our degrees of freedom it would be 1.771.)

The standard error of the X coefficient indicates the precision of our estimate of β. We can construct a 95% confidence interval for β by taking the point estimate, plus or minus the product of the estimated standard error and the value of t that leaves 2.5% of the t distribution in each tail. Here that would be $0.4147747 \pm 0.27275098 \times 2.16 = [0.35585, 0.473699]$ These lower and upper 95% values are also shown in the summary output table (Figure 4.6).

A similar analysis can be carried out with the Intercept estimate. The t-statistic and P-value for this parameter suggests that it is not significantly different from zero. An alternative model might apply the restriction that $\alpha = 0$, i.e. force the regression line through the origin. If you look again at the Regression dialog box you will see that it is possible to implement this in Excel – you simply put a mark in the space next to the Constant is **Z**ero in the Input part of the window. However, if you do work with a strictly proportional model of this form you will not be able to interpret R-squared in the way that we could here.

An important part of any regression analysis is a consideration of the residuals. This can help diagnose any problems that there might be with the model and perhaps point to possible ways in which the model can be improved. The residuals are the differences between the actual and the fitted Y values, often denoted by the letter e. They can be regarded as estimates of the unobservable disturbances (the u values). The final part of the summary output gives a full list of fitted (Predicted) Y values and Residuals by observation.

The residual plot shows the residual values plotted against the X values (here GDP) – see Figure 4.9.

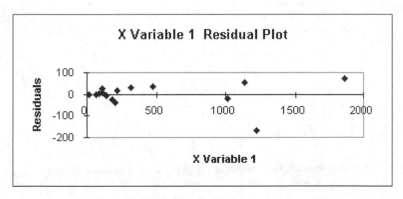

**Fig. 4.9** Residual plot.

When we originally specified the model we made the assumption that the disturbances were unrelated to the size of GDP. Although we can't observe the u values we can examine the residuals and see if there is any evidence of a relationship between their values and those of GDP (X). While the residual plot does not provide any evidence of a relationship between the e and X values on average, it does suggest that the variance of the error term might be higher for larger values of X (what econometricians call *heteroskedasticity*). The points are spread more widely around the horizontal axis for higher values of GDP than for lower ones. This may mean that the simple linear functional form is inadequate – perhaps it might be worth trying a power function formulation instead (which would imply a linear relationship between the logarithms of the variables). Or it might mean that one would need to use an estimating procedure other than that of the simple least squares regression – one that took into account the heteroskedasticity. We defer further discussion of both these matters until Chapter 5. Dedicated statistics and econometrics packages (unlike spreadsheets) will have a much richer range of options for diagnostic testing and procedures for dealing with heteroskedasticity (and other) problems.

## Regression results from other spreadsheets

The regression results generated by some other spreadsheet packages are less extensive and have a slightly different look to them. For example, the results obtained using Lotus 1-2-3 for the simple regression of CO on GDP are shown below. You still get the least squares estimates for the intercept (constant) and the X coefficient) as well as R-squared. Although you get the standard error of the X coefficient you don't get the t-value or t-probability value. Of course, it is easy to add an extra row to calculate the t-value by entering a formula to divide the X coefficient by its standard error.

```
                    Regression Output

Constant                        6.00264

Std Err of Y Est.               56.8845

R Squared                       0.94678

No. of Observations                  15

Degrees of Freedom                   13


X Coefficient(s)0.41477

Std Err of Coef.0.02728
```

# Practical 4.4   A simple model of the UK consumption function

The data for the model we have just been considering is cross-section data, that is it consists of observations on variables taken across individuals, households, firms, industries or, as in this case, countries at a single point in time or for a single time period. Economists often also study time series data, that is where the values for each variable consist of observations made for successive time periods or for points in time. Consider the data in Table 4.4, where Y is real personal disposable income in the UK and C is real consumers' expenditure in the UK (both variables in £ millions, 1990 prices).

**Table 4.3**   Annual data on real personal disposable income and real consumers' expenditure in the UK.

|      | Y       | C       |
|------|---------|---------|
| 1985 | 309 734 | 276 742 |
| 1986 | 323 394 | 295 622 |
| 1987 | 335 720 | 311 234 |
| 1988 | 356 714 | 334 591 |
| 1989 | 370 932 | 345 406 |
| 1990 | 378 638 | 347 527 |
| 1991 | 378 154 | 340 037 |
| 1992 | 385 757 | 339 652 |
| 1993 | 393 256 | 348 164 |
| 1994 | 399 572 | 357 845 |
| 1995 | 412 376 | 364 046 |
| 1996 | 427 690 | 376 648 |

Source: UK National Accounts (Blue Book) 1997 and MIDAS September 1998.

Here the frequency of the data is annual, but time series data can also be quarterly, monthly, weekly or for some financial series at even higher frequency such as every hour or minute. As we shall see in more detail in Chapter 5, with time series data the order and position of observations makes a difference in a way that it does not with cross-section data. The observations on the two variables for the countries in Table 4.2 can be ordered in any way you choose: alphabetically, geographically, by the size of CO or by the size of GDP. Each observation is considered to be independent of every other observation. With time series data the order is important. Each time period occurred in a particular relation to all other time periods. 1995 came after 1994 but immediately before 1996 and any trend that is apparent in a series is something that we must taken into account when analyzing the series, or its relationship with another series. With quarterly or monthly data we may also have to take account of seasonal patterns in the data. However, we will not concern ourselves with such matters here, except to be aware that when fitting regressions to two series that both exhibit trends, there is a danger of spurious regression results being obtained and that accompanying statistics such as R-squared may be misleading.

Most introductory textbooks on economics initially propose a simple theory to explain how consumption is determined in an economy. They assume the existence of a linear consumption function of the form

$$C = \alpha + \beta Y \qquad\qquad \text{Equation 4.5}$$

where $\alpha$ denotes autonomous consumption, that is the amount of consumers' expenditure that will occur whatever the level of income ($\alpha \geq 0$). $\beta$ can be interpreted as the marginal propensity to consume, that is the proportion of any additional income that will be consumed at the margin, $\Delta C/\Delta Y$. By working with a linear relationship we are assuming that the marginal propensity to consume ($\Delta C/\Delta Y$) is a constant. We also assume that $\beta$ is positive but less than one ($0 < \beta < 1$), which means that we expect consumers to spend some (perhaps most) but not all of any extra income that they receive.

We can use a spreadsheet package to obtain estimates of $\alpha$ and $\beta$ and to evaluate the adequacy of the simple linear consumption function model. Of course, since we would not wish to claim that consumers' income is the only factor that can affect their consumption, and we must also allow for the possibility of measurement errors in the variables, we would include a disturbance term in the model which then becomes

$$C_t = \alpha + \beta Y_t + u_t \qquad\qquad \text{Equation 4.6}$$

(because we have time series data we have used a t subscript to denote a typical time period – t = 1985…1996).

Before running the regression let us again examine the data graphically. This time not only can we look at a scatter diagram of C against Y, but we can also view a time series plot of each series.

Enter the information in Table 4.3 into cells A1:C14 of a new worksheet. Then select all of that range and click on the Chart Wizard. Then choose **I**nsert **C**hart **A**s New Sheet. Follow the steps, this time selecting Line and then format 1 (with Markers and the points joined together but with no grid lines). Add a Title and Axes titles and you should get something rather like Figure 4.10 (although I have edited the formatting of some of the objects to make the graph more suited to a black and white display).

It is clear from the graph that the C and Y series follow each other rather closely over the time period with both series showing a slight upward (although not constant) trend.

Figure 4.11 shows a scatter diagram (XY plot) of C against Y. Again I have modified the diagram provided by the Chart Wizard slightly, not only to display the graph better in black and white, but also to begin the horizontal and vertical axes at 25 000

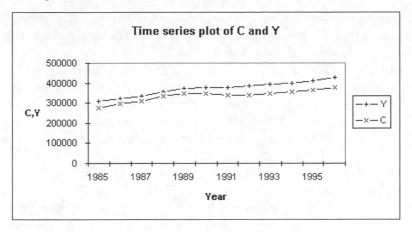

**Fig. 4.10** Time series plot of C and Y.

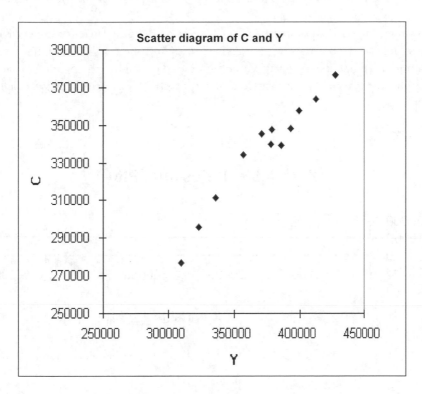

**Fig. 4.11** Scatter diagram of C and Y.

rather than zero. To do this point in turn at each axis, click the mouse and select Format Axis. Click on the Scale tab and make sure that the Minimum is selected with a figure of 25 000 entered into the box.

The graph confirms the close positive relationship between the series, although there is a slight suggestion of nonlinearity. For the moment we will move on and fit a linear regression line through the points.

As before, select **T**ools **D**ata Analysis and Regression, with cells B2:B13 as the X input range and C2:C13 as the Y input range. I suggest that you again put the results into a new worksheet. The full summary output is not reported here, but these results should show an estimated value of 44 529.7 for the autonomous consumption and 0.78336 for the marginal propensity to consume. These values satisfy our a priori requirements ($\alpha \geq 0$; $0 < \beta < 1$)

So, rounding the values slightly, the fitted regression equation would be

$\hat{C} = 44530 + 0.783Y$.

The R-squared is 0.94726 (indicating that nearly 95% of the variation in C around its mean can be explained by the model). The t-statistics for the intercept and X coefficient are respectively 2.03578 and 13.4022 (the P-values are 0.06913 and 1E-07), which suggests in each case that one can reject the null hypothesis that the true regression parameter is zero.

However, the residual plot (Figure 4.12) shows a definite cause for concern about the specification we have used. There is a clear pattern here suggesting that a simple linear model estimated in this way with time series data might be providing misleading ideas about the marginal propensity to consume in the UK. Spreadsheet packages are

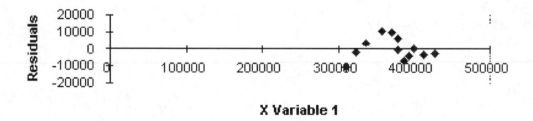

**Fig 4.12** Plot of the residuals against Y for the simple UK consumption function model.

limited in terms of the diagnostic tests and graphics that are available and anyone who wishes seriously to build a model of UK consumers' expenditure would be advised to approach the matter using a dedicated econometrics package which is designed for the task, employing more sophisticated econometric specifications and techniques (and rather more observations). We will return to this in Chapter 5.

# Practical 4.5   A simple Cobb–Douglas production function

Before moving on we will give one further example of the use of a spreadsheet for estimating a regression model, showing how one can transform data prior to the application of a least squares regression, and how spreadsheets can estimate multiple regression models as well as simple ones (that is, ones which are not limited to a single X variable).

The data in Table 4.4 are indexes of output, and of the capital and labor inputs in US manufacturing industry for the years 1899 to 1922. They are the original values

**Table 4.4** The Cobb–Douglas production function data.

| Date | Output | Capital | Labor |
|------|--------|---------|-------|
| 1899 | 100 | 100 | 100 |
| 1900 | 101 | 107 | 105 |
| 1901 | 112 | 114 | 110 |
| 1902 | 122 | 122 | 118 |
| 1903 | 124 | 131 | 123 |
| 1904 | 122 | 138 | 116 |
| 1905 | 143 | 149 | 125 |
| 1906 | 152 | 163 | 133 |
| 1907 | 151 | 176 | 138 |
| 1908 | 126 | 185 | 121 |
| 1909 | 155 | 198 | 140 |
| 1910 | 159 | 208 | 144 |
| 1911 | 153 | 216 | 143 |
| 1912 | 177 | 226 | 152 |
| 1913 | 184 | 236 | 154 |
| 1914 | 169 | 244 | 149 |
| 1915 | 189 | 266 | 154 |
| 1916 | 225 | 298 | 182 |
| 1917 | 227 | 335 | 196 |
| 1918 | 223 | 366 | 200 |
| 1919 | 218 | 387 | 193 |
| 1920 | 231 | 407 | 193 |
| 1921 | 179 | 417 | 147 |
| 1922 | 240 | 431 | 161 |

used in the classic study of production functions undertaken by Charles Cobb and Paul Douglas and published in the *American Economic Review* in 1928.

As a result of examining this data Cobb and Douglas put forward their now famous functional form for a production function.

$$Q = AK^\alpha L^\beta$$                                                   Equation 4.7

Here Q denotes the output of the firm, industry or economy and K and L denote respectively the capital and labor inputs, with A as simply a scaling constant. The parameters $\alpha$ and $\beta$ can be interpreted as the elasticity of output with respect to capital and the elasticity of output with respect to labor respectively. Their sum provides an indication of the nature of returns to scale for the production process and if this should turn out to be unity (one) it would imply constant returns to scale; that is, if each of the inputs, labor and capital, were to be increased by a common proportion, then the output would also increase by this proportion. If $\alpha + \beta < 1$ this would suggest decreasing returns to scale (output would go up but by a smaller proportion than the inputs), whereas if $\alpha + \beta > 1$ there would be increasing returns to scale (output would increase more than proportionately).

## Constant elasticity regression models

With an equation of the form $Q = f(K,L)$ the elasticity of Q with respect to K is defined as $\dfrac{\partial Q}{\partial K}\dfrac{K}{Q}$. (This is the limit, as DK tends to zero, of $[\Delta Q/Q]/[\Delta K/K]$).

If one first differentiates the equation $Q = AK^\alpha L^\beta$, with respect to K, one obtains $\alpha AK^{\alpha-1}L^\beta$. Multiplying by the ratio K/Q this simplifies to $\alpha$. In a similar way the labor elasticity of output for this functional form can be found simply to be $\beta$. For this reason log-linear specifications such as the one used here are sometimes called constant elasticity regression models. Readers who are confident in their use of partial differentiation may like to check these results for themselves.

Now although Equation 4.7 is not linear in form, it is possible to convert it to linearity by taking logarithms.

Since $\log XY = \log X + \log Y$ and $\log X^n = n \log X$ (for any base) if we apply a logarithmic transformation to Equation 4.7 we get (if you need a refresher course on logarithms you could look at the appropriate section in MathEcon):

$$\log Q = \log A + \alpha \log K + \beta \log L$$                         Equation 4.8

The logarithm of the constant A is just another constant (say c). Logarithmic transformations of the variables Q, K and L just produce new variables – say q, k and l – so the model can be written as

$$q = c + \alpha k + \beta l \qquad\qquad \text{Equation 4.9}$$

which is clearly linear in form.

So if we have data on Q, K and L we can first obtain three new series, q, k and l, based on the logs of these variables and then regress q on k and l to get estimates of α and β (and indirectly of α + β).

Begin a new worksheet and enter the data in Table 4.4 to cells A1:D25.

Our first task is to create three new series, to be held in columns E, F and G, containing the logarithmic transforms of the original series. In cells E1:G1 put text labels as headings for the new series: logQ, logK and logL. In cell E2 enter =log(B2) and then copy this down the rest of the column to cell E25. Similarly in cells F2 and G2 put =log(C2) and =log(D2) and then copy down. The resulting figures should all be 2.something because the logarithmic transformation has used the base e, i.e. these are the natural logarithms. (You can also use a spreadsheet to get common logarithms to the base 10 if you prefer, by putting =LOG10(B2) etc. Although the estimate of the intercept constant – logA or c – will be different, the base that you choose to work with will have no effect on the estimates of α and β.)

Now you can run the regression. When you get to the Regression window put cells E2:E25 as the Y input range and F2:G25 for the X input range. You should find that the estimates of α and β, the coefficients of X Variable 1 and X Variable 2 respectively are 0.23113 and 0.81222. This implies a figure of 1.04335 for the measure of returns to scale (you can put a formula into the worksheet to calculate this sum if you like – all the numbers in the summary output table are treated as values and can be used as inputs into formulae).

Although this figure is a little in excess of one, the difference is not very much. If you have enough expertise in econometrics you may know how to test to see if this difference is significant. At first sight the results would appear to provide some support for the view that, at least for that period in the US, manufacturing industry was subject to constant returns to scale. However, as we can see in Figure 4.13, the residuals when plotted against time, show a distinctive pattern with alternating blocks of positive and negative values. This phenomenon is referred to as *autocorrelation*, and it is again indicative of some form of misspecification. Modern approaches to the empirical examination of production functions consider functional forms that are rather more flexible than the simple Cobb–Douglas form. When working with time series data one would also have to formulate the models in such a way as to overcome problems of spurious regressions due to trends in the series.

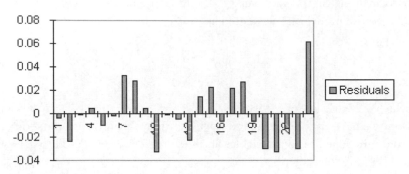

**Fig. 4.13**   Residual plot from the log-linear Cobb–Douglas regression.

### A model which incorporates the restriction of constant returns to scale

Back in the 1920s Cobb and Douglas did not, of course, have access to spreadsheet packages or indeed any form of computer software to help them fit their model to the data. Because the least squares regression estimates had to be obtained "by hand", that is with pencil, paper and the direct application to the data of addition, subtraction, multiplication and division operations, they worked with a slightly different model that incorporated the restriction of constant returns to scale. This allowed them to use a simple bivariate regression model, that is one with just a single explanatory variable. Once the model was fitted it was then judged, in a rather casual way by modern standards, by how well it appeared to fit the data – again at that time modern ideas of regression diagnostics had not been developed.

Beginning with Equation 4.5, if we impose the restriction $\alpha + \beta = 1$ we can substitute $1 - \alpha$ for $\beta$ into the equation giving $logQ = logA + \alpha logK + (1 - \alpha)logL$. Expanding the final term and subtracting $logL$ from both sides of the equation one gets $logQ - logL = logA + \alpha logK - \alpha logL$ or $log(Q/L) = logA + \alpha log(K/L)$.

If one now applies suitable log transformations to calculate the values of the dependent and independent variables for this regression model, one can estimate $\alpha$ directly from the simple model $Y = c + \alpha X + u$ (where $Y = log(Q/L)$, $X = log(K/L)$ and $u$ is a disturbance term).

## 4.4   Financial analysis on a spreadsheet

Spreadsheets provide a very convenient tool for those wishing to conduct financial analysis of various kinds. Most spreadsheet packages incorporate many standard financial computational procedures as built-in functions. In a moment we will look at a couple within Excel. First, however, consider the simple worksheet shown in Figure 4.14.

This worksheet has been constructed to calculate the future value of a deposit that is placed in an account paying out a fixed compound rate of interest at the end of each year. If you regularly needed to do this type of calculation but the deposit, the interest rate and the number of years are going to be different each time it might be worth setting up a worksheet such as this that you could use.

Cell D3 is where you enter the initial deposit. Notice that although the formula bar shows that a value of 100 has been entered here the cell itself is showing £100.00. This is because this cell has been formatted to display the contents as currency with a format code £#.##, i.e. pounds sterling to the nearest penny. Cell D7, which shows the result of the calculation, is formatted in a similar way. (Use **F**ormat **C**ell and then choose the Number Tab and Currency.) Cell D4 is where you enter the annual interest rate, here assumed to be 10% or 0.1. Cell D5 is where you enter the number of years, currently set at 12.

Next, notice that in the formula bar when the cell D3 is highlighted you can see the word DEPOSIT over on the left hand side. This is because in designing the worksheet, I have given the cell D3 the name DEPOSIT to make the contents of the worksheet easier to interpret. Although you can't see it I have also named cell D4 INTRATE, while D5 is named YEARS. To give a worksheet cell a name, simply go to the cell, select **I**nsert **N**ame and then use **D**efine or **C**reate. For full details search for help on Name from the Help Index.

Now to calculate the future value of a DEPOSIT left for a certain number of YEARS in an account paying a compound interest rate of INTRATE each year we must use the formula =DEPOSIT*(1+INTRATE)^YEARS (^ means raise to the power of) and so this is what has been entered into cell D7. Of course, you could also put =D3*(1+D4)^D5 but you would have to remember what each item in the formula represents.

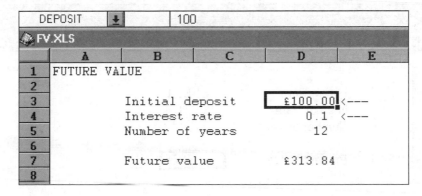

**Fig. 4.14** Calculating the future value of a deposit.

## Help

Do you understand the derivation of this formula? If not, begin with a simple example where you deposit £100 at 10% per year for two years. After one year the account will contain your deposit of £100 plus the interest earned, which is 10% of £100, i.e. £10 = £110 in all. At the end of the second year the interest due will be 10% of £110, which is £11. Adding this to the £110 gives £121. Notice that this is £100 × (1 + 0.1) × (1 + 0.1) or £100 × (1 + 0.1)$^2$. Every further year that you leave the money in the account its value will increase by the factor (1 + 0.1) so after N years it will be worth £100 × (1 + 0.1)$^N$.

If you replace the particular value £100 with D (for deposit) and 0.1 with R (for interest rate) you get the formula we are using.

Now let us look at the problem the other way round and ask how much we would need to deposit in an interest earning account, given a fixed interest rate R each year, if we wish to accumulate a future sum of F in N years time (where the future amount F, the interest rate R and the number of years N will be our data inputs).

Algebraically if $F = P \times (1 + R)^N$ then $P = F / (1 + R)^N$; or in words:

Present Value = Future Sum/(1 + Interest Rate)^Number of Years

Figure 4.15 displays a worksheet that will do this. You can even use strings of words for cell names provided that you connect them together using the underscore symbol_. (You can't have spaces in names.)

| D7 | ↓ | | =Future_Sum/(1+Interest_Rate)^Number_of_Years | | | |
|---|---|---|---|---|---|---|

**PV.XLS**

| | A | B | C | D | E | F | G |
|---|---|---|---|---|---|---|---|
| 1 | PRESENT VALUE | | | | | | |
| 2 | | | | | | | |
| 3 | | Future Sum | | £100.00 | | | |
| 4 | | Interest Rate | | 0.1 | | | |
| 5 | | Number of Years | | 12 | | | |
| 6 | | | | | | | |
| 7 | | Present Value | | £31.86 | | | |
| 8 | | | | | | | |

**Fig. 4.15** Worksheet to calculate the present value of a future sum.

# Practical 4.6 Investment appraisal and the net present value of an Investment Project

The concept of present value is central to the economist's view of investment decision making because it enables an agent to evaluate on a common basis a series of payments or receipts that are expected at different points in time. A sum of, say, £500 available in one year's time would not have the same value to an investor as £500 now (quite apart from any problems of inflation). If the rate of interest is non-zero the investor could deposit a sum less than £500 in an interest earning account which would grow to £500 by the end of the year. You can use the worksheet we have just created to see how this varies with the rate of interest.

Now suppose an investor is faced with two mutually exclusive investment projects, A and B. Project A requires a payment of £1000 now but is expected to generate net flows of benefits of £500 at the end of year 1, £700 at the end of year 2 and £500 at the end of year 3. Project B requires a payment of £600 now but is expected to generate net flows of benefits of £400 at the end of year 1 and £800 at the end of year 2 (nothing in year 3). Which project should the investor choose? The present value criterion for investment appraisal would recommend that the project with the greater net present value (NPV) is chosen, where the NPV of a project is defined as

$$\sum_{t=1}^{3} \frac{\text{Benefit}_t}{(1+\text{Interest rate})^t} - \text{Initial payment} \qquad \text{Equation 4.10}$$

Even when we know the initial payment and the expected net benefits we can't make a decision until we know what interest rate to use in the formula. Interest rates can change so we might choose to evaluate the NPVs for each project at a variety of interest rates to see how sensitive the decision is to the assumption made.

Figure 4.16 shows part of a worksheet that has been constructed to help with this problem.

Cells B9 to B12 and D9 to D12 contain the values for the initial cost of the projects and the expected net benefits. Cell D3 holds the assumed interest rate value and this is then used to calculate a discount factor = 1/(1 + interest rate). Discounted net benefits can then be obtained by multiplying each year's figures by the discount factor an appropriate number of times. So, for example, the figure in cell B17 is found by entering the formula =B10*D4 while B18 is =B11*D4*D4. The NPV for each project can then be found as the sum of the relevant entries. So, as can be seen, the NPV for project A = SUM(B16:B19).

With an interest rate of 10% the NPV for project B is the greater so that project would be chosen. However, for some lower interest rates the NPV for project A would be the greater. To see exactly what the relationship is between the NPV and the interest rate for each project one could produce a table of values or even a graph (Figures 4.17 and 4.18).

As can be seen clearly from Figure 4.18, if the interest rate is high enough the NPV falls to zero before becoming negative. Here this happens first for project A. The

| B21 | | | | =SUM(B16:B19) | |
|---|---|---|---|---|---|
| | **A** | **B** | **C** | **D** | |
| **1** | NPV : | | worksheet on investment appraisal | | |
| **2** | | | | | |
| **3** | | | Assumed interest rate is | 0.1 | |
| **4** | | | Implied discount factor | 0.909091 | |
| **5** | | | | | |
| **6** | | | Undiscounted net benefits | | |
| **7** | | | Project A | | Project B |
| **8** | | Year | | | |
| **9** | | 0 | −1000 | | −600 |
| **10** | | 1 | 500 | | 400 |
| **11** | | 2 | 700 | | 800 |
| **12** | | 3 | 500 | | 0 |
| **13** | | | | | |
| **14** | | | Discounted net benefits | | |
| **15** | | | | | |
| **16** | | 0 | −1000 | | −600 |
| **17** | | 1 | 454.5455 | | 363.6364 |
| **18** | | 2 | 578.5124 | | 661.157 |
| **19** | | 3 | 375.6574 | | 0 |
| **20** | | | | | |
| **21** | NPV | 408.7153 | | | 424.7934 |

**Fig. 4.16**   Part of the NPV worksheet.

interest rate where the NPV = 0 is called the internal rate of return or IRR for short. Spreadsheets such as Excel include a built-in function that will calculate this value for you. The format for this function is =IRR(range,guess) where the range is the block of cells containing the cost and benefit figures – so for project A that would be B9:B12. Notice that you must also provide a guess or estimate of the internal rate of return since the program will compute this value iteratively.

| C29 | | | =($B$9)+($B$10/(1+A29))+($B$11/(1+A29)^2)+($B$12/(1+A29)^3) | | | |
|---|---|---|---|---|---|---|
| | **A** | **B** | **C** | **D** | **E** | **F** |
| **24** | NPV as function of the interest rate | | | | | |
| **25** | | | | | | |
| **26** | Assumed | | Project A | Project B | | |
| **27** | interest rate | | | | | |
| **28** | 0 | | 700 | 600 | | |
| **29** | 0.01 | | 666.5518135 | 580.2764 | | |
| **30** | 0.02 | | 634.1753926 | 561.0919 | | |
| **31** | 0.03 | | 602.8248593 | 542.4262 | | |
| **32** | 0.04 | | 572.4567592 | 524.2604 | | |
| **33** | 0.05 | | 543.0299104 | 506.576 | | |
| **34** | 0.06 | | 514.5052627 | 489.3556 | | |
| **35** | 0.07 | | 486.8457679 | 472.5828 | | |
| **36** | 0.08 | | 460.0162577 | 456.2414 | | |
| **37** | 0.09 | | 433.9833316 | 440.3165 | | |
| **38** | 0.1 | | 408.7152517 | 424.7934 | | |
| **39** | 0.11 | | 384.1818444 | 409.6583 | | |
| **40** | 0.12 | | 360.3544096 | 394.898 | | |
| **41** | 0.13 | | 337.2056356 | 380.4996 | | |
| **42** | 0.14 | | 314.7095193 | 366.4512 | | |
| **43** | 0.15 | | 292.841292 | 352.741 | | |

**Fig. 4.17**   Table of NPV values for different interest rates.

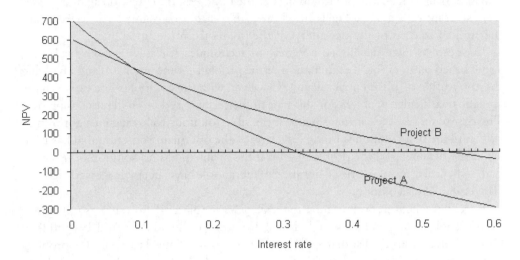

**Fig. 4.18**   Net present value graphs.

This example illustrates the dangers of ranking projects on the basis of their IRRs. Although the IRR is greater for project B, when interest rates are below about 8% project A actually has the higher NPV.

Excel also has a built-in function to compute the NPV of a project. However, this function only evaluates the present value of the terms which are in the future and does not incorporate the initial cost, which will still have to be deducted (or added in as a negative amount). So instead of the calculations leading up to our formula in cell B21, we could instead enter the formula =NPV(B3,B3:B12)+B9.

---

**Tip**

There are a number of other built-in functions for financial calculations that you might like to investigate. However, as can be seen from the case of the NPV function, it is important that you understand exactly what the function is doing and you are advised always to experiment with simple numerical examples where you can see what is happening before relying on built-in functions as part of more elaborate worksheets.

---

## 4.5   Optimization in a spreadsheet

As a subject economics is almost everywhere concerned with optimization. Economic agents are assumed to be maximizing or minimizing some function of their choice variables, possibly subject to one or more constraints. Firms maximize their profits, consumers maximize their utility (subject to their budget). In regression analysis, as we have seen in section 4.3, a line is fitted through a scatter of points so as to minimize the sum of squares of the deviations of the points from the fitted line.

Economists have developed a variety of techniques for solving such problems, some based on a graphical examination of the problem, some analytical and involving the application of differential calculus. However, with the computer one can examine specific quantitative problems of this type numerically, based on an iterative approach. The computer searches amongst various possible solutions following an algorithm or rule until the best solution is found (in terms of the optimizing criterion that has been set at the beginning of the problem) – or, if the problem has no solution or has been badly specified, until a preset number of iterations have been processed without convergence to a solution.

Excel has a built-in optimization tool called *Solver*. (Note: If Solver does not appear on the Tools menu you may have to install it. Select **T**ools and then Add-**I**ns and then choose Solver from the list that appears.) To use it you will need to set up the problem so that the computer knows which is the *target* cell and whether the value in the cell is to be maximized, minimized or made as close as possible to some specified value. You will also have to specify which cells can have their values changed in order to arrive at the optimum solution (the *changing cell(s)*) and any additional *constraints* that might apply.

We will look at three examples to illustrate how the Solver tool works, beginning with another look at least squares regression. This will not only help to acquaint you with the use of Solver, but also enhance your understanding of regression analysis.

## Practical 4.7   Least squares regression again

Begin a new worksheet and start to enter text, values and formulae as shown in rows 1 to 8 of Figure 4.19. The contents of cells in the block A1:B7 and C3:E3 are exactly as they appear (text and values). But cell C4 should contain the formula =$B$1+$B$2*A4. Similarly cells C5:C7 should also contain suitable formulae to produce fitted values for Y, based on the intercept and slope parameters held in cells B1 and B2 (the values placed there are not, at the moment, the least squares estimates but guesses whose values can be altered).

In cell D4 enter the formula =B4-C4. The residual or value of e is the difference between the actual and fitted values of Y. You can copy this formula into cells B5:B7 to get the rest of the e values.

In cell E4 enter the formula =D4*D4 and then copy it down into E5:E7. This gives the squared errors. Then in cell E8 put the formula =SUM(E4:E7). This is the sum of the squares of the errors and is what we want to minimize when we fit a least squares regression line.

I have also incorporated a small graph which shows both the actual Y values and the fitted Yhat values, plotted as a scatter diagram so that you can see the effects of varying

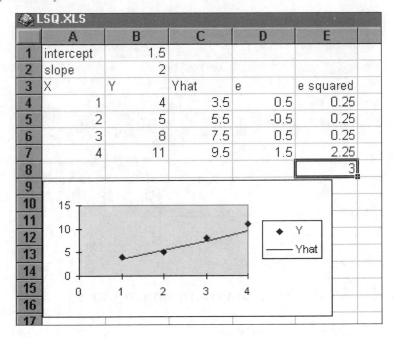

**Fig. 4.19** The least squares regression worksheet for use with Solver.

the values of the intercept and slope of the fitted line, but this is not absolutely necessary. Use the Chart Wizard to construct a graph based on cells A4:C7 and then select the XY format. I have also edited the graph so that the Yhat values are shown connected by a line but without markers. (Yhat denotes the fitted or predicted values of Y.)

Now before we try out the Solver look first at the effects of manually adjusting the values in cells B1 and B2. Watch what happens to the sum of squares of errors (in cell E8) if you change the contents of B1 to 2 or the contents of cell B2 to 2.5. One of these changes reduces the value in E8 while the other change increases it.

The least squares regression line chooses values for B1 and B2 so as to minimize the contents of E8. We can use the Solver to get the best or "optimum" solution. Select **T**ools and then Solver and make the settings as shown in Figure 4.20.

Now click the **S**olve button and after a few moments you should find that the Intercept and Slope values have been changed to 1 and 2.4 respectively so that the sum of squares is reduced to 1.2. Another dialog box will be on screen and this will allow you either to save the optimum solution or to reset the values to what they were. You can get various reports on the optimization as well.

If you want to you can use the regression command just to check that the estimates are the same. In fact, the least squares regression routine uses an analytical rather than an iterative approach, based on an exact solution to the minimization problem using calculus. The Solver tool doesn't, of course, give you all the additional regression statistics. However, you can use the Solver tool for problems that don't have analytical solutions.

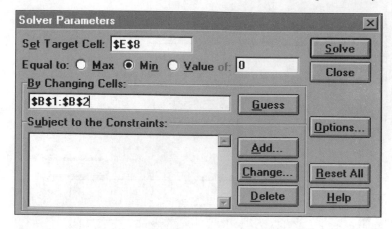

**Fig. 4.20**   Setting the Solver parameters.

# Practical 4.8   A linear programming problem

Consider the following hypothetical problem.

A firm produces two products, Bits and Bobs, using three inputs, card, paint and glue.
To produce each Bit requires 4 units of card and 1 unit of paint (but no glue).
To produce one Bob requires 2 units of card, 1 unit of paint and 3 units of glue.
Today the firm has available 32 units of card, 10 units of paint and 21 units of glue.
Per unit profit is £1.20 for each Bit and 90p for each Bob.
How many Bits and how many Bobs should be produced in order to maximize the firm's profit and what will be this profit?

This is an example of a simple linear programming problem. Linear programming problems involve a (linear) *objective function* of the *choice variables* in the problem which has to be maximized or minimized. There will also be a number of linear *inequality constraints* and *non-negativity conditions* for the choice variables which have to be satisfied.

Here there are two choice variables – the number of Bits and the number of Bobs to be produced. The objective function is the total profit function – a linear function of the choice variables, where the coefficients are given by the per unit profit rates on Bits and Bobs. There are three inputs and the amounts of these that are used up each day will depend upon the number of units of Bits and Bobs that are produced – in each case a linear combination of these amounts where the coefficients are given by the input requirements. The amount of each input that is used cannot exceed the amount that is available – although it might be optimal not to use up every unit of all the inputs. The non-negativity conditions require that the outputs of Bits and of Bobs cannot be less than zero.

**BITSBOBS.XLS**

| | A | B | C | D | E | F | G |
|---|---|---|---|---|---|---|---|
| **1** | Linear programming problem | | | | | | |
| **2** | | | | | | | |
| **3** | Quantities produced | | | Profits per unit | | Profit = | |
| **4** | Bits = | 0 | | 1.2 | | 0 | |
| **5** | Bobs = | 0 | | 0.9 | | | |
| **6** | | | | | | | |
| **7** | Inputs | Used in the production of | | | | Available | |
| **8** | | Bits | Bobs | Altogether | | | |
| **9** | Card | 0 | 0 | 0 | | 32 | |
| **10** | Paint | 0 | 0 | 0 | | 10 | |
| **11** | Glue | 0 | 0 | 0 | | 21 | |

**Fig. 4.21**  Initial worksheet for the linear programming problem.

The solution to this problem can be obtained using Excel's Solver tool. First, though, we must construct a worksheet containing the information for the problem.

Begin a new worksheet and enter information as shown in Figure 4.21. The cells contain the text and values are as shown, with the exception of those which contain formulae as specified below.

| Cell | Formula |
|---|---|
| F4 | = B4*D4+B5*D5 |
| B9 | =4*B4 |
| C9 | =2*B5 |
| D9 | =B9+C9 |
| B10 | =1*B4 |
| C10 | =1*B5 |
| D10 | =B10+C10 |
| B11 | =0*B4 |
| C11 | =3*B5 |
| D11 | =B11+C11 |

Cell F4 calculates the profits based on the number of Bits and Bobs that are produced. Initially it is assumed that no units are being produced, as reflected in cells B4 and B5. Cells B9 to D9 show how much card is used up in the production process at current rates (again initially zero because B4 and B5 have the value 0 to begin with). Similarly the cells in columns B to D of rows 10 and 11 reflect the use of paint and glue given the current production mix.

Now call up the Solver and make the settings for the Target Cell and the Changing cells as shown in Figure 4.22. Make sure that the radio button specifies a **Max**.

To enter each of the constraints you will need to click on the **Add** button. Another dialog screen will be displayed with a space to put the value or cell reference for the

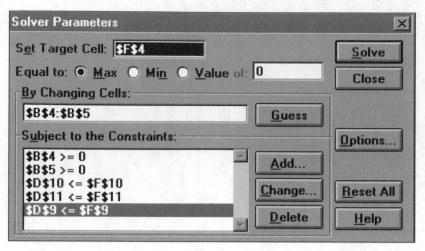

**Fig. 4.22**   Solver parameter settings for the linear programming problem.

left hand side of the inequality, a space to put the value or cell reference for the right hand side of each inequality and in the middle a scrolling list for you to specify the form of each inequality.

The first two constraints shown are the non-negativity conditions, which ensure that the computer will exclude all solutions involving negative quantities of Bits and Bobs. Each of the other constraints reflects the requirement that the amount of card, paint and glue that is used cannot exceed the amount available (we are assuming here that unused resources from previous days cannot be saved for use later on).

When all the settings are as shown in Figure 4.22 you can click on the **S**olve button. The solution you should get has 6 units of Bits and 4 units of Bobs being produced, with a total profit of 10.8. At this solution all of the card and paint available will be used, but only 12 units of glue.

Using a spreadsheet to solve a linear programming problem it is very easy to see how the solution will vary if the initial conditions change in any way. All you have to do is to edit the information in the cells and rerun the Solver. Try making each of the following changes. Observe the result and interpret what is happening.
(i) D2 = 4; (ii) F9 = 36; (iii) B11 = 0.5*B4.

## Practical 4.9   Portfolio selection

Suppose an investor holds two stocks with slightly different expected rates of return and risk. Stock A has an expected return of 0.2 (20%) but has a standard deviation around that value (a measure of risk) of 0.75 (75%). Stock B has a slightly lower expected return of 0.16 (16%) but there is also a lower standard deviation at 0.5 (50%). Suppose the investor initially holds equal amounts of the two stocks (i.e. equal

| C6 | ↓ | | =SQRT((D3*D3*C3*C3)+(D4*D4*C4*C4)+(2*D3*D4*C3*C4*E3)) | | | | |

**PORTFO.XLS**

| | A | B | C | D | E | F | G | H |
|---|---|---|---|---|---|---|---|---|
| 1 | PORTFOLIO | | | | | | | |
| 2 | | Return | Risk | Weights | Correlation | | | |
| 3 | Stock A | 0.2 | 0.75 | 0.5 | -0.6 | | | |
| 4 | Stock B | 0.16 | 0.5 | 0.5 | | | | |
| 5 | | | | | | | | |
| 6 | Portfolio | 0.18 | 0.30104 | 1 | | | | |
| 7 | | | | | | | | |

**Fig. 4.23**  Worksheet for the portfolio selection problem.

weightings of 0.5 each). This initial information has been entered into cells B3 to D4 in a worksheet as shown in Figure 4.23.

The expected return for the overall portfolio is just the weighted average of the individual returns. So cell B6 holds the formula =B3*D3+B4*D4. However, the expected risk of the overall portfolio is given by quite a complicated (nonlinear) formula which depends not only on the risks of the individual stocks and how much of each is held in the portfolio, but also on the correlation between the expected returns on the different stocks – here assumed to be –0.6 (–60%) as shown in cell E3. Cell C6 contains that formula which is written more formally below:

$$\sigma_p = \sqrt{w_1{}^2\sigma_1{}^2 + w_2{}^2\sigma_2{}^2 + 2w_1 w_2 \sigma_1 \sigma_2 \rho_{12}} \qquad \text{Equation 4.11}$$

where $\sigma_1$ denotes the standard deviation for stock 1; $\sigma_2$ denotes the standard deviation for stock 2; $\sigma_p$ denotes the standard deviation for the portfolio; $w_1$ and $w_2$ are the weights; and $\rho_{12}$ denotes the correlation between the two returns. (See, for example, Blake (1990).)

Try changing the weights of shares in the portfolio to see how the risk and return vary (make sure that the weights always add up to 1 – you can keep track of this by putting the formula =D3+D4 in cell D6). You can also try changing the correlation to see how this can affect the portfolio risk. Before going on, however, make sure that the original values as shown in Figure 4.23 are restored.

We can see that the current shareholding gives an overall rate of return for the portfolio of 18% but with a risk of over 30%. Suppose the investor wants to get the best possible return, but doesn't want the risk to rise above 27.5%. How much of each stock should the investor hold? We can use Solver to find out. Set the Target Cell as B6 and the cells that can be changed to D3 and D4. Then enter constraints to ensure that the individual weights are between 0 and 1, that their sum is 1 and finally that the portfolio risk (in cell C6) is ≤0.275.

When you run the Solver you should get weights of 0.434855 and 0.565145 respectively, with a portfolio rate of return of 0.177394. The risk constraint is binding at 0.275.

# 4.6 Working with matrices in a spreadsheet

Many linear economic models are written in the form of matrix equations. They can then be manipulated and solved using matrix algebra operations. Spreadsheet packages such as Excel contain matrix handling functions and it is comparatively easy to set up and solve linear economic models within a worksheet.

To begin with consider the system of equations in three unknowns, $x_1$, $x_2$ and $x_3$

$$2x_1 + x_2 = 6$$
$$- x_1 + 4x_2 + x_3 = 1$$
$$x_1 + 2x_2 - x_3 + 2$$

Such a simple system of equations can easily be solved using ordinary algebra. However, the point of working with this example here is to demonstrate the matrix method so that you can see how to apply it to much bigger systems.

The equations can be expressed in matrix form as $\mathbf{Ax} = \mathbf{b}$ where $\mathbf{x}$ is a $3 \times 1$ column vector whose elements are the unknowns $x_1$, $x_2$ and $x_3$, $\mathbf{b}$ is a $3 \times 1$ column vector whose elements are the right hand side constants 6, 1 and 2, and $\mathbf{A}$ is a $3 \times 3$ matrix whose elements are the coefficients of the x values in the equations (arranged in rows to reflect the positions that they have in the system of equations).

Now a matrix equation of the form $\mathbf{Ax} = \mathbf{b}$ (where, as here, $\mathbf{A}$ is square) can be solved for $\mathbf{x}$ by pre-multiplying both sides by the inverse of $\mathbf{A}$, $\mathbf{A^{-1}}$. Since the product of $\mathbf{A}$ and $\mathbf{A^{-1}}$ is $\mathbf{I}$, the identity matrix, and the identity matrix times $\mathbf{x}$ is just $\mathbf{x}$ we find the solution as $\mathbf{x} = \mathbf{A^{-1}b}$.

If you are unfamiliar with this, or have forgotten the details, review the relevant material by looking at your favourite Mathematics for Economists textbook, or go to the web site for my course *Further Mathematics for Economists* (Econ257) at http://www.pbs.port.ac.uk/econ/~judge/econ257/.

We can use the spreadsheet package to find the inverse for us, and then (post)multiply it by the vector $\mathbf{b}$ so as to obtain the solution in the form of the vector of x values. Begin a new worksheet and enter the text and values in rows 1 to 8 as shown in Figure 4.24. (I have made the title in the first line appear in bold using **F**ormat C**e**lls and then changing the settings on the Font tab. It is not necessary to do this, but you may wish to experiment with the formatting possibilities of your spreadsheet so that you can improve the look of the screen and print versions.)

Now go to cell A9 and select the block A9:C11. Call up the Function Wizard (**I**nsert **F**unction) and select the Math & Trig function category and then Function **N**ame MINVERSE. Put A4:C6 into the place for the array required and click **Finish**. The elements of the inverse matrix should then appear.

To (pre)multiply the vector of constants by this inverse go to cell F9 and select F9:F11. Again call up the Function Wizard but this time choose MMULT from the list of Function Names. Enter cells A9:C11 as the first array and cells F4:F6 as the second array. The solution values 2.75, 0.5 and 1.75 should appear. Check that these values do

| | A | B | C | D | E | F |
|---|---|---|---|---|---|---|
| | **LINEQU.XLS** | | | | | |
| **1** | Linear Equation solution using matrix algebra | | | | | |
| **2** | | | | | | |
| **3** | A (matrix of coefficients) | | | | b (vector of constants | |
| **4** | 2 | 1 | 0 | | 6 | |
| **5** | -1 | 4 | 1 | | 1 | |
| **6** | 1 | 2 | -1 | | 2 | |
| **7** | | | | | | |
| **8** | Inverse of A | | | | | |
| **9** | 0.5 | -0.08333 | -0.08333 | | $x_1 =$ | 2.75 |
| **10** | 0 | 0.166667 | 0.166667 | | $x_2 =$ | 0.5 |
| **11** | 0.5 | 0.25 | -0.75 | | $x_3 =$ | 1.75 |

**Fig. 4.24**  Matrix equations on a spreadsheet.

give the solution by substituting them back into the left hand sides of the equations. Just to round off the worksheet I also entered some text in cells E9:E11. Notice that you can have subscripts in the text in a spreadsheet cell – use **F**ormat C**e**lls again.

## Practical 4.10   A simple macroeconomic model

Now consider the following simple three equation macroeconomic model given in Thomas (1989), p. 268.

C = 80 + 0.8Y − 0.5R
I = 2000 − 2R
Y = C + I + G

where C is consumers' expenditure, I is private investment expenditure, G is government expenditure, Y is national income and R is the interest rate.

This model has three *endogenous* variables (determined within the model) – C, I and Y. R and G are *exogenous* (given from outside the model) and the model is presently written in *structural form*. Thomas shows that the model can be written as a matrix equation of the form $\mathbf{Ay} + \mathbf{Bx} = \mathbf{0}$ or $\mathbf{Ay} = -\mathbf{Bx}$, where $\mathbf{y}$ is a vector of the endogenous variables, $\mathbf{x}$ is a vector of the exogenous variables and $\mathbf{A}$ and $\mathbf{B}$ are coefficient matrices.

Here we have

$$A = \begin{bmatrix} -0.8 & 0 & 1 \\ 0 & 1 & 0 \\ 1 & -1 & -1 \end{bmatrix} \quad B = \begin{bmatrix} 0.5 & 0 & -80 \\ 2 & 0 & -2000 \\ 0 & -1 & 0 \end{bmatrix}$$

$$y = \begin{bmatrix} Y \\ I \\ C \end{bmatrix} \quad x = \begin{bmatrix} R \\ G \\ 1 \end{bmatrix}$$

so that

$$\begin{bmatrix} -0.8 & 0 & 1 \\ 0 & 1 & 0 \\ 1 & -1 & -1 \end{bmatrix} \begin{bmatrix} Y \\ I \\ C \end{bmatrix} = \begin{bmatrix} 0.5 & 0 & -80 \\ 2 & 0 & -2000 \\ 0 & -1 & 0 \end{bmatrix} \begin{bmatrix} R \\ G \\ 1 \end{bmatrix}$$

Now to solve for the endogenous variables in terms of the exogenous ones, i.e. to get the *reduced form*, all we have to do is to multiply both sides of this equation by the inverse of **A** to get $\mathbf{y} = -\mathbf{A}^{-1}\mathbf{Bx}$. We can use the spreadsheet to do the matrix inversion and matrix multiplication for us to get the matrix of multipliers
$$\mathbf{M} = -\mathbf{A}^{-1}\mathbf{B}.$$

Begin a new worksheet and enter the text and values in rows 1 to 8 (note cell E8 contains the text –**M** as we first get that rather than **M** itself when we multiply $\mathbf{A}^{-1}$ by **B**).

| | A | B | C | D | E | F | G |
|---|---|---|---|---|---|---|---|
| **THOMAS.XLS** | | | | | | | |
| **1** | Simple macro model from Thomas (1989) | | | | | | |
| **2** | | | | | | | |
| **3** | A | | | | B | | |
| **4** | -0.8 | 0 | 1 | | 0.5 | 0 | -80 |
| **5** | 0 | 1 | 0 | | 2 | 0 | -2000 |
| **6** | 1 | -1 | -1 | | 0 | -1 | 0 |
| **7** | | | | | | | |
| **8** | A⁻¹ | | | | -M | | |
| **9** | 5 | 5 | 5 | | 12.5 | -5 | -10400 |
| **10** | 0 | 1 | 0 | | 2 | 0 | -2000 |
| **11** | 5 | 4 | 4 | | 10.5 | -4 | -8400 |

**Fig. 4.25**  Getting the reduced form coefficient matrix for the simple macro model.

Use the Function Wizard to get the inverse of the block A4:C6 and place it in cells A9:C11. Then use it to multiply the values in block A9:A11 by E4:G6, putting the result in cells E9:E11. If you want the elements of the **M** matrix itself you must change all the signs. Having done that you would obtain the reduced form solution as:

$$\begin{bmatrix} Y \\ I \\ C \end{bmatrix} = \begin{bmatrix} -12.5 & 5 & 10\,400 \\ -2 & 0 & 2000 \\ -10.5 & 4 & 8400 \end{bmatrix} \begin{bmatrix} R \\ G \\ 1 \end{bmatrix}$$

How should you interpret this? The values in the **M** matrix give the impacts on each of the endogenous variables of a unit change in the various exogenous variables. Coefficients in row i column j pick up the effect on endogenous variable i of a change in endogenous variable j. So for example the −2 value tells us that the impact on I of a one unit increase in R is a fall of 2 units. The final column of the matrix is the constant intercepts of each of the reduced form equations.

There are, many other potential applications of matrices in economics where a spreadsheet can be used. For example in an earlier book (Judge, 1990) I showed how one can use a spreadsheet when working with input–output models. Excel also includes TRANSPOSE and MDETERM functions that you can use. If you need to add or subtract matrices simply define the formula for the first cell in the matrix and copy across and down.

If you plan to make extensive use of matrix models in your work you will probably be better off using a mathematical processing package like *Mathcad* or *Mathematica* rather than a spreadsheet (see Chapter 7). These can handle analytical as well as numerical solutions, i.e. the cells of the coefficient matrices can be unspecified parameters rather than numerical values. However, for many quantitative economic applications the matrix functions in a spreadsheet provide a very convenient set of tools with which to work.

## 4.7 Dynamic economic models in a spreadsheet

## Practical 4.11 A simple multiplier–accelerator model

Consider a simple multiplier–accelerator model which takes the form

$$C(t) = bY(t)$$
$$I(t) = v[Y(t) - Y(t-1)]$$
$$AD(t) = C(t) + I(t) + A(t)$$
$$Y(t) = AD(t-1)$$

where $C(t)$ is consumption in period t, $I(t)$ is planned investment expenditure in period t, $Y(t)$ is national income in period t, $A(t)$ is other autonomous elements of demand

and AD is aggregate demand in period t. b and v are parameters: b is the marginal propensity to consume, v is the accelerator coefficient or the capital–output ratio. Requiring a constant capital–output ratio such that $K(t) = v\, Y(t)$ would mean that $I(t) = v\,[Y(t) - Y(t-1)]$ since $I(t) = K(t) - K(t-1)$.

Such models provide one possible mechanism whereby cycles can occur in the macroeconomy (although today's generation of economists is working with rather more complex models of the business cycle that can also account for the asymmetries that are observed with upswings typically being longer than downturns).

Nevertheless students of economics will usually still encounter the multiplier–accelerator model and we use it here to illustrate how dynamic economic models can be analyzed within a spreadsheet. The model is dynamic (rather than static) in form because the values of variables in the model depend also on past period values. Compare this with the simple macromodel considered in the last section where, implicitly, any change in an exogenous variable had an immediate impact on the endogenous variables. In dynamic models adjustment to new conditions takes time. The system may start to move towards a new equilibrium, but will probably never reach it because a further change in conditions occurs before equilibrium can be attained.

In the multiplier–accelerator model income will tend to fluctuate around its equilibrium value through the combination of the multiplier (operating via the marginal propensity to consume, b) and the accelerator (operating through the accelerator coefficient, v). Equilibrium is the level of income that, if reached, the economy will remain at. Thus it has $Y(t) = Y(t + 1) = ... = Y^* = A/(1 - b)$.

Begin a new worksheet and enter text and values into rows 1 to 15 as shown in Figure 4.26, except for those cells specified below where a formula is to be entered. (You may also wish to widen column A and reduce the size of column B in accordance with the way I have shown it.)

| Cell | Formula |
| --- | --- |
| B9 | +C4 |
| B10 | +C5 |
| B15 | +C6/(1 - C4) |

Now we will extend the worksheet to construct a table of values that shows how the variable evolves over time. Enter column headings in row 17 as follows:

| Cell | Entry |
| --- | --- |
| A17 | t |
| C17 | Y |
| E17 | C |
| F17 | I |
| G17 | A |
| H17 | AD |

| | A | B | C | D | E | F |
|---|---|---|---|---|---|---|
| 1 | Simple multiplier-accelerator model | | | | | |
| 2 | | | | | | |
| 3 | | | Parameters | | | |
| 4 | Consumption b = | | 0.75 | | | |
| 5 | Investment   v = | | 0.85 | | | |
| 6 | A = | | 610 | | | |
| 7 | | | | | | |
| 8 | | | Model equations | | | |
| 9 | C(t) = | 0.75 | Y(t) | | Consumption function | |
| 10 | I(t) = | 0.85 | [Y(t) - Y(t-1)] | | Investment function | |
| 11 | AD(t) = | | C(t)+I(t)+A(t) | | Aggregate demand | |
| 12 | Y(t) = | | AD(t-1) | | Output | |
| 13 | | | | | | |
| 14 | Equilibrium income | | | | | |
| 15 | Y* = | | 2440 | | | |

**Fig. 4.26**  Part of the multiplier–accelerator worksheet.

Now in cells A18 to A60 place values from –2 up to 40. Next enter the following values and formulae:

| Cell | Entry |
|---|---|
| C18 | =600/(1–C4) |
| E18 | =$C$4*C18 |
| F18 | 0 |
| G18 | 600 |
| H18 | =E18+F18+G18 |
| C19 | =H18 |
| E19 | =$C$4*C19 |
| F19 | =$C$5*(C19–C18) |
| G19 | 600 |
| H19 | =+E19+F19+G19 |
| G20 | =$C$6 |

Now copy cell entries as follows:

| Cells to copy from | Cells to copy to |
|---|---|
| C19 | C20:C60 |
| E19 | E20:E60 |
| F19 | F20:F60 |
| H19 | H20:H60 |
| G20 | G21:G60 |

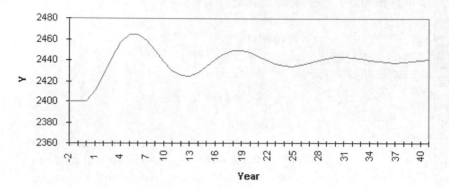

**Fig. 4.27**  Time path of national income.

If you have done everything correctly you should now have a table showing the values of each of the variables from period t = −2 until period t = 40. Following the increase in autonomous demand in period 0 income increases moving towards the new equilibrium value of 2440. But there are (damped) oscillations as it fluctuates around the new equilibrium reflecting the ups and downs of investment which in turn goes through periods of positive and negative values. In this model consumption responds immediately to income, investment responds to changes in income and income responds with a one period lag to aggregate demand.

It's easier to see what is going on if we look at the graph. Use the Chart Wizard to plot Y against t to get a graph something like that shown in Figure 4.27.

In these models interest focuses on how different values of b and v affect the properties of the model. The model reduces to a second-order difference equation in Y and one can analyze it mathematically to discover which range of values produces damped oscillations (as here) and which produces explosive oscillations. However, within a spreadsheet we can conduct "what-if" experiments by varying the values of b and v (within sensible ranges) and viewing the results. Try each of the following combinations and consider the results.

| Experiment | b | v |
| --- | --- | --- |
| 1 | 0.75 | 1 |
| 2 | 0.75 | 1.2 |
| 3 | 0.9 | 0.85 |
| 4 | 0.5 | 0.85 |

This example should give you an idea of how to set up dynamic models within a spreadsheet. Much more complex models can be dealt with. For example, in Judge (1990) I extended a model rather like the one described here to create a "flexible multiplier–accelerator" model where the simple consumption function used here is replaced by a permanent income/adaptive expectations consumption function of the form $C(t) = b\,Y^{p}(t)$. The investment function too was made more flexible so that investors reacted less sharply to changes in national income. A copy of the worksheet constructed in this case is available on the web site for this book.

## Summary

This chapter has described a number of spreadsheet applications of interest to economists, showing how spreadsheets can be used for data analysis, problem solving and model analysis. By working through these examples you will have been able to extend your spreadsheet skills. You will probably also have thought of various other possible uses for spreadsheets in economics.

The examples covered here (and in Chapters 2 and 3) do not make use of all the features that are available in Excel or comparable spreadsheets. For example, we have not attempted to look at the use of spreadsheet *macros* (a facility whereby a sequence of steps can be encapsulated in a procedure that can be stored and then called up as required). We will return briefly to them in Chapter 7 but you can find out more about these and other spreadsheet features by using the package's Help feature.

For further examples of the use of spreadsheets in economics keep an eye on the on-line journal *CHEER (Computers in Higher Education Economics Review)*. An interesting example of a dynamic economic model that has been described there is Whitmarsh (1991).

## Exercises and mini-projects

1. Staff in a company have been sent a questionnaire asking them whether or not they have received any IT training. The questionnaire also asks respondents to indicate their gender, status in the company (junior or senior) and their employment mode (full-time or part-time). The results for one branch are shown in the table below.

| Employee | IT training | Gender | Status | Employment mode |
|:---:|:---:|:---:|:---:|:---:|
| 1 | Yes | Male | Senior | Full-time |
| 2 | Yes | Male | Junior | Full-time |
| 3 | Yes | Female | Junior | Full-time |
| 4 | No | Female | Junior | Part-time |
| 5 | No | Female | Junior | Part-time |
| 6 | No | Male | Junior | Part-time |

| 7  | No  | Female | Junior | Full-time |
|----|-----|--------|--------|-----------|
| 8  | Yes | Male   | Junior | Full-time |
| 9  | Yes | Female | Junior | Full-time |
| 10 | Yes | Male   | Junior | Full-time |
| 11 | No  | Male   | Junior | Part-time |
| 12 | No  | Male   | Junior | Full-time |
| 13 | No  | Female | Junior | Part-time |
| 14 | Yes | Male   | Senior | Full-time |
| 15 | Yes | Male   | Junior | Full-time |
| 16 | No  | Female | Senior | Full-time |

Begin a worksheet and enter these data in cells A1 to E17. Use the spreadsheet's PivotTable Wizard (or equivalent tool) to produce contingency tables showing IT training responses cross-tabulated against each of the other variables. Briefly summarize your findings.

2. The table below provides information for 1997 on the following variables for each state in the United States (including the District of Columbia):
Unemployment – the percentage of the labor force that is unemployed
Poverty – the percentage of households classified as having income below the poverty line
Crimes – the total number of recorded crimes
Households – the number of households in thousands
Source: Bureau of Labor Statistics and Bureau of Census. (Data available from "The Dismal Scientist" web site at http://www.dismal.com)

| State | Unemployment | Poverty | Crimes | Households |
|-------|--------------|---------|--------|------------|
| Alabama     | 4.7 | 15.7 | 211 188   | 1624.2   |
| Alaska      | 6.6 | 8.8  | 32 110    | 214.3    |
| Arizona     | 4.7 | 17.2 | 327 734   | 1687.4   |
| Arkansas    | 4.4 | 19.7 | 119 052   | 950.7    |
| California  | 5.2 | 16.6 | 1 569 490 | 11 100.5 |
| Colorado    | 2.9 | 8.2  | 181 041   | 1502.4   |
| Connecticut | 3.4 | 8.6  | 130 286   | 1230.6   |
| Delaware    | 3.6 | 9.6  | 37 612    | 275.6    |
| Florida     | 4.1 | 14.3 | 1 065 609 | 5648.2   |
| Georgia     | 3.7 | 14.5 | 433 563   | 2722.6   |
| Hawaii      | 5.5 | 13.9 | 71 492    | 388.5    |
| Idaho       | 4.9 | 14.7 | 47 495    | 429.6    |
| Illinois    | 4.4 | 11.2 | 611 589   | 4352.5   |
| Indiana     | 3   | 8.8  | 261 902   | 2208.8   |
| Iowa        | 2.6 | 9.6  | 108 827   | 1102.8   |
| Kansas      | 3.4 | 9.7  | 118 422   | 981.8    |
| Kentucky    | 4.4 | 15.9 | 122 205   | 1477.8   |

| Louisiana | 4.4 | 16.3 | 280 671 | 1571.8 |
|---|---|---|---|---|
| Maine | 4.3 | 10.1 | 38 896 | 482.9 |
| Maryland | 3.8 | 8.4 | 287 969 | 1871 |
| Massachusetts | 3.1 | 12.2 | 224 848 | 2322 |
| Michigan | 3.9 | 10.3 | 480 579 | 3575.7 |
| Minnesota | 2.5 | 9.6 | 206 833 | 1763.4 |
| Mississippi | 4.8 | 16.7 | 126 452 | 978.9 |
| Missouri | 3.5 | 11.8 | 260 081 | 2952.2 |
| Montana | 5.1 | 15.6 | 38 753 | 340.8 |
| Nebraska | 2.6 | 9.8 | 70 982 | 631.5 |
| Nevada | 4.3 | 11 | 101 702 | 619.2 |
| New Hampshire | 2.5 | 9.1 | 30 963 | 438.6 |
| New Jersey | 4.7 | 9.3 | 326 711 | 2888.5 |
| New Mexico | 6.1 | 21.2 | 119 483 | 619.2 |
| New York | 5.1 | 16.5 | 709 328 | 6737 |
| North Carolina | 3.1 | 11.4 | 407 743 | 2796.1 |
| North Dakota | 2.7 | 13.6 | 17 380 | 246.6 |
| Ohio | 4.1 | 11 | 505 005 | 4259.6 |
| Oklahoma | 3.5 | 13.7 | 182 258 | 1265 |
| Oregon | 5.1 | 11.6 | 203 328 | 1249.3 |
| Pennsylvania | 3.8 | 11.2 | 412 463 | 4593.9 |
| Rhode Island | 3.7 | 12.7 | 36 069 | 377.8 |
| South Carolina | 4.2 | 13.1 | 230 637 | 1376.3 |
| South Dakota | 2.5 | 16.5 | 23 948 | 273.1 |
| Tennessee | 3.8 | 14.3 | 295 873 | 2040.9 |
| Texas | 4.9 | 16.7 | 1 065 357 | 6893.5 |
| Utah | 3.2 | 8.9 | 123 447 | 639.4 |
| Vermont | 2.8 | 9.3 | 16 658 | 226.5 |
| Virginia | 3 | 12.7 | 261 022 | 2511.1 |
| Washington | 4.5 | 9.2 | 332 466 | 2139 |
| West Virginia | 6.7 | 16.4 | 44 839 | 714.2 |
| Wisconsin | 3.4 | 8.2 | 190 133 | 1942.5 |
| Wyoming | 4.9 | 13.5 | 20 068 | 183.7 |
| Washington DC | 6.5 | 21.8 | 52 049 | 231.3 |

Begin a new worksheet and enter the data into cells A1:E52. Create a new variable in column F called CPH showing Crimes/Households.

(a) Use your spreadsheet to find for each series the Minimum, Maximum, Mean, Median and Standard deviation. What is the best measure of crimes per household for the entire USA?

(b) Use your spreadsheet to rank the data by state according to the size of the variable CPH. Which states have (i) the highest value, (ii) the lowest value, (iii) the value closest to the average?

(c) Use your spreadsheet to construct a frequency table and histogram for CPH. Write a brief report summarizing your findings.

3. Use the regression commands with the above data to investigate whether there is any evidence to support the hypothesis that crimes per household can be explained by unemployment. Are the results any better if you use the poverty rate as the

explanatory (independent) variable? Write a brief report on your findings. Hint: construct scatter diagrams of CPH against each independent variable.

**4.** The data in the table below give real personal disposable income (Y) and real personal consumption expenditure (C) for the US for the years 1985-1997 (both variables in $ billions, 1992 prices). Use your spreadsheet to estimate a simple consumption function as we did for the UK in Practical 4.4. What immediate problem is raised by your results?

| | Y | C |
|------|--------|--------|
| 1986 | 4076.8 | 3708.7 |
| 1987 | 4154.7 | 3822.3 |
| 1988 | 4325.3 | 3972.7 |
| 1989 | 4411.7 | 4064.6 |
| 1990 | 4489.6 | 4132.2 |
| 1991 | 4483.5 | 4105.8 |
| 1992 | 4605.1 | 4219.8 |
| 1993 | 4666.7 | 4343.6 |
| 1994 | 4772.9 | 4486 |
| 1995 | 4906 | 4605.6 |
| 1996 | 5043 | 4752.4 |
| 1997 | 5183.1 | 4913.5 |

Source: The Economic Report of the President, 1999, Table B31, p. 363. Available at http://www.access.gpo.gov/eop/.

**5.** The table below gives data on the demand for beef in Greece for the years 1966 to 1987, together with the price of beef paid by consumers, the price of lamb and consumers' income. Use your spreadsheet to estimate a simple linear demand function of the form:

Demand = $a_0$ + $a_1$Price + $a_2$ PLamb + $a_3$Income.

Provide a brief report on your findings.

| Year | Demand | Price | PLamb | Income |
|------|--------|-------|-------|--------|
| 1966 | 101.6 | 232 | 196 | 1043.3 |
| 1967 | 115 | 226.5 | 197 | 1098.9 |
| 1968 | 129.1 | 222.9 | 196.6 | 1169.4 |
| 1969 | 141.6 | 213.5 | 194.1 | 1284.8 |
| 1970 | 157.3 | 239.6 | 214.4 | 1406.7 |
| 1971 | 133.6 | 263.8 | 209.9 | 1541.4 |
| 1972 | 133.3 | 273.9 | 226.6 | 1684.4 |
| 1973 | 122.1 | 309.6 | 253.5 | 1892 |
| 1974 | 141 | 286.1 | 269.3 | 1708.1 |
| 1975 | 164.1 | 265.6 | 255.8 | 1485.8 |
| 1976 | 201.6 | 256 | 298 | 1900.5 |
| 1977 | 211.1 | 249.6 | 291.5 | 1986 |

| 1978 | 247.2 | 238.2 | 311 | 2118.6 |
| 1979 | 225.7 | 272.9 | 332.6 | 2159.2 |
| 1980 | 219 | 266.8 | 342.6 | 2080.1 |
| 1981 | 155 | 292 | 370.5 | 2105.8 |
| 1982 | 194.2 | 325.1 | 381.5 | 2137.8 |
| 1983 | 216.8 | 318.5 | 362.5 | 2065.1 |
| 1984 | 202.5 | 300.2 | 364.7 | 2131.4 |
| 1985 | 202 | 287.5 | 345.2 | 2214.8 |
| 1986 | 207.8 | 253.9 | 295.1 | 2099.4 |
| 1987 | 246.9 | 234 | 282.8 | 2050.2 |

Source: Lianos and Katranidis (1993). Demand in thousands of tons. Prices in drachmas per kilo (deflated by an overall index of prices, 1982 = 100). Income in thousand drachmas (deflated by an overall index of prices, 1982 = 100).

**6.** Construct a worksheet to compare the net present values of two investment projects with initial costs and expected flows of benefits as shown.

|  | Project 1 | Project 2 |
| --- | --- | --- |
| Initial cost | £600 | £600 |
| Benefits after 1 year | £200 | £575 |
| Benefits after 2 years | £600 | £200 |

Which project is preferred if the interest rate is 12%? Would the ranking of the projects be the same at all interest rates? Explain. (*Hint:* produce a graph of the NPV against the interest rate for interest rates between 0 and 20%.)

**7.** Create a worksheet similar to that described in Practical 4.7 to allow you to alter parameter values for a least squares regression model. This time, though, the model will have the simple nonlinear form $Y = aX^b$. The values for the variables and the initial parameter settings are shown below. Note: The formula in cell C5 should be +$b$2*(A5^$b$3). This formula can then be copied into cells C6:C9.

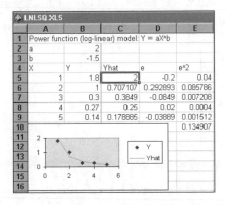

**Fig. 4.28**  Power function (log-linear model) regression using Excel Solver.

Use Excel Solver (or the equivalent device within your spreadsheet) to select values for a and b so as to minimize the contents of cell E10. If you can, include a chart such as the one shown in Figure 4.28 so that the actual and fitted values of Y (Yhat) can be seen plotted against X. What values do you get for a, b and $\Sigma e^2$? After re-reading this chapter you realize that the functional form used here is log-linear. Create new columns containing LN(X) and LN(Y) and use the built-in regression function to estimate the equation LN(Y) = LN(a) + b LN(X) + error. Then recover your estimate of a by applying an exponential to your estimate of LN(a).

Why are the two sets of estimates of a and b obtained in this question not the same?

8. The Top Star Computer Company would like to determine how many desktop and laptop personal computers to manufacture during the current production period. Both models use a Pentium microprocessor. The assembly times are one and a half hours for each desktop and three hours for each laptop computer. The firm has available 3400 microprocessors and 6000 hours of assembly time for the current production period. The profit contributions are £500 for each desktop and £750 for each laptop. The firm believes that it can sell as many units as it produces.

Formulate the problem as a linear program and use Excel Solver (or the equivalent for your spreadsheet) to solve the problem.

9. You have read in your econometrics textbook that the least squares regression estimates can be found from the data using the matrix equation $\hat{b} = (X^T X)^{-1} X^T y$, where y is a column vector of the values of the dependent variable, X is a matrix containing the values of the dependent variables arranged in columns and beginning with a column of ones and $\hat{b}$ is a column vector of the least squares estimates.

Use your spreadsheet's matrix commands to compute the least squares estimates for the X matrix and y vector shown below. Check your results using the built-in regression command.

$$X = \begin{bmatrix} 1 & 4 \\ 1 & 6 \\ 1 & 12 \\ 1 & 16 \\ 1 & 20 \\ 1 & 30 \end{bmatrix} \quad y = \begin{bmatrix} 2 \\ 5 \\ 4 \\ 8 \\ 6 \\ 10 \end{bmatrix}$$

10. Create a worksheet to analyze the time path of P(t), t = 1,...,40 for the simple cobweb model of the market for a prouct where:

$QD(t) = 15 - 5\ P(t)$
$QS(t) = -1 + 3\ P(t-1)$
$QD(t) = QS(t)$

Examine the properties of the model if the coefficient of $P(t-1)$ in the supply equation were to be (a) 4.5, (b) 5 (c) 6.

# CHAPTER 5

# Statistics and econometrics software

## Objectives

The objectives of this chapter are to

- make the reader aware of the wide range of statistical and econometrics software that is used by academic and professional economists in their work
- identify some of the key features and capabilities that can be found in the best known statistics and econometrics packages
- ensure that the reader is prepared to work with packages in both interactive and batch mode
- illustrate how statistics and econometrics packages can be used in a range of econometric modeling applications

## 5.1 Introduction. Dedicated statistics and econometrics packages

Although, as we have seen, it is possible to use spreadsheet packages for basic data analysis, graph plotting and even simple econometric modeling based on least squares regression, most economists use packages that are dedicated to statistical and econometric work for everything other than these very basic tasks. The range of software available is enormous. Some of the best known packages are listed in Table 5.1. (Further details of these and many other statistics and econometrics packages can be found on my web site. Other well-known packages that might be used at your university are LIMDEP, SORITEC, Statgraphics, Systat and TROLL.)

As a student of economics you are likely to be expected to work with at least one of these packages. Your lecturer will, no doubt, provide you with instructions on how to access and work with the packages that are used on your course. However, it will be helpful for you to have an awareness of the features and capabilities of some other software in this area as you may have to switch to a different package if you move on to postgraduate studies, or if you work as an economist in a public or private sector organization after graduation. It could even be that your current lecturer leaves your university on a permanent or temporary basis before the end of your course and his/her replacement favors a different package!

Statistics and econometrics software comes in all forms and sizes, often with versions to run on a number of different platforms (hardware and operating systems). There are some very large general purpose packages which can be used to undertake many different

**Table 5.1** Some of the most widely used statistics and econometrics packages for economists.

| Name | Brief description |
|------|-------------------|
| 1. Econometric Views (EViews) | State of the art econometric techniques with good graphics; object oriented Windows interface. http://www.eviews.com/ |
| 2. Microfit | Versatile interactive menu-driven program for econometric modeling with emphasis on dynamic models based on time-series data. Windows and DOS versions available. http://eee4.co.uk/ep/prodsupp/humanities/microfit/ |
| 3. Minitab | General purpose statistical software. First developed over 25 years ago as a teaching tool. http://www.minitab.com/ |
| 4. PcGive | Versatile interactive menu-driven program for econometric modeling with emphasis on dynamic models based on time-series data. Uses the GiveWin user interface, running under Windows. http://timberlake.co.uk/ |
| 5. RATS | Regression Analysis of Time Series. Comprehensive time-series and econometrics software package. Command language gives flexibility. http://www.estima.com/ |
| 6. SAS | Statistical Analysis System. Powerful integrated statistical analysis system. http://www.sas.com/ |
| 7. SHAZAM | Multipurpose econometrics software package from Canada, but widely used around the world; command language activates pre-programmed routines. http://shazam.econ.ubc.ca/ |
| 8. SPSS | Statistical Package for the Social Science. Comprehensive general purpose statistics package. http://www.spss.com/ |
| 9. STATA | Flexible programmable statistics package. http://www.stata.com/ |
| 10. TSP | Time Series Processor. Well established command driven econometrics software available on a wide range of platforms. http://www.tspintl.com/ |

**Find out**

Which statistics and econometrics software packages are you expected to work with? Which version of each program is installed on the university system? Is there any documentation (printed or on-line) available to you to help you develop your expertise?

If you have a moment, why not send me an e-mail giving me the answers to these questions as I would be interested to know which packages are being used and where.

types of econometric and statistical estimation and testing procedures (e.g. SAS and SPSS). There are also some much more specialized programs that are designed principally for use with a particular type of model or methodological approach (Microfit and PcGive, for example, have been developed primarily to provide a user-friendly framework within which to formulate and test dynamic econometric models based on time series data).

Some packages have been specifically designed to run on PCs under Windows, taking advantage of the graphical interface so that instructions can be issued by clicking on an icon or menu bar. Data and results can be cut and pasted between windows (and even across software applications) and there will usually be excellent high resolution graphics to augment the basic results – EViews merits special mention here, although both Microfit and PcGive also have good user-friendly features.

Many other packages are *command driven*, that is the user must type in a command which contains appropriate *keywords* and has the correct *syntax* in order to get the computer to do anything. Sometimes these command line programs have only a *text-based user interface*, and with only crude character based graph plots they betray their history as pre-Windows programs. However, there can be advantages in working with software that responds to instructions that are issued in a sequence of carefully structured commands. What one has, in effect, is a *programming language* to work with (and one that may be easier to learn and use than the more fundamental programming languages such as Fortran or C). Usually it is possible to work with such programs either in *interactive mode* (each instruction is immediately executed and then the computer waits for the next instruction) or in *batch mode* (a full set of commands is put together in the form of a program held in a file – when the file is called up the computer follows the instructions one by one with no further human intervention). This method of working obviously requires one to anticipate the sequence of instructions that one wants to give. But it can be particularly convenient if you want to run a number of regressions based on slightly different data sets (say using the same series but using a variety of different time periods or using different but similar series, say relating to different sectors or countries). Rather than having to work through the process manually one instruction at a time, you can collect together the instructions in sequence and then get the computer to run through them in one go. The file containing the instructions may include lines that are very similar and the programming can be speeded up by copying and editing lines of the program in a text editor (or any word processor provided that you remember to save the file in text only format). Because you will usually save the program it can be used again at a later date, say if new data have become available. Or having run the program if you realize that a change needs to be made (say you want to use a slightly different set of independent variables in a regression) it is a simple matter to edit and rerun the program.

When working with command line programs it is easy to make a mistake, either through a typing error, or because of a failure on the part of the user to understand the required structure of a command. This kind of mistake will result in an *error message*. Error messages generated by recently released versions of software packages have become easier to understand than those for earlier versions, but they can still sometimes be cryptic and require you to look them up in the manual to find out exactly what the problem could be.

> **Tip**
>
> If you are learning how to use a command line package it can be worthwhile to try out some of the example programs that are printed in the manual or made available as files to accompany the package. To build up your confidence you can then amend them in various ways and look to see whether the new version of the program works in the way that you expect.

Most of the econometrics software packages that are based on the use of commands have extensive vocabularies of keywords enabling a wide variety of procedures to be invoked. As beginners you will probably not have cause to use very many of them, but as you become more experienced you will find that you will want to incorporate more and more of them into your programs. It is just like learning and using any language. You can even program completely new procedures that are not available as such within the package, by putting together sequences of commands to produce a particular effect. This kind of command driven package can actually be more powerful and flexible than a point and click icon or menu driven program that offers only a set of "canned" routines.

For advanced work econometricians and applied economists sometimes find it worthwhile to move even further away from the standard packages with their built-in routines and use a matrix programming language such as GAUSS, Ox or S-Plus. These languages are focused more specifically on statistical and numerical functions than generic programming languages such as Fortran or C. They are also easier to learn and have their own mutual support network of users who are willing to provide advice and share code via e-mail discussion lists and newsletters.

In this book it has usually been assumed that you will be working on a Windows-based PC of some kind. However, the econometrics software that you are asked to use could be installed on a mainframe computer or a large server attached to the network and run under the UNIX operating system (or its freeware counterpart Linux). If this is the case you may still be able to work from your desktop PC, which will function as a workstation,

> **Tip**
>
> When writing program files containing commands and keywords make sure that you include adequate documentation so that if you (or somebody else) looks at the program some weeks or months later you are able quickly to interpret what is being done. Most statistics and econometrics packages that are based on the use of commands of this type will have a facility for adding *remarks* or *comments*, that is blocks of text that will be ignored by the computer but can be read by you.

but you will need to familiarize yourself with some basic UNIX commands. There are also some econometrics packages still around that were written for the MS-DOS environment. You can usually run these in a DOS window on your PC – or a special front end such as TSP's "Through the Looking Glass" may have been provided. (MS-DOS – the text-based Disk Operating System for PCs that was the dominant operating system in the days before Windows. To find out how to run programs in a DOS window call up the Windows Help system and use the Index to search for information on MS-DOS.)

## 5.2 Preparing to use statistics and econometrics software: some preliminary considerations

The correct way to conduct statistical analysis or undertake econometric modeling is first to formulate the hypothesis to be tested or the model to be investigated and then to collect data that can be used for this purpose. It may be, of course, that once you have examined the available data other possibilities will be suggested to you. However, while it is certainly desirable to examine the basic properties of the data (both graphically and through the calculation of summary descriptive and test statistics) before the main work is begun, from a statistical point of view it is a good idea to use only part of any data that you have for this purpose and to retain sufficient observations to provide an independent test of hypotheses or models whose construction has been influenced by the data. In any event what I am suggesting is that some careful thinking should be done before you sit down at the computer. You need to consider what you are attempting to do.

### Data and data files

The data that you use will either be *primary* data – collected by you say through a survey – or it will be *secondary* data – data collected by someone else but made available to you. Secondary data could come from an official government or international agency, or it might have been obtained from some other private source. In any case you should pay very careful attention to data definitions and other features of the data (for example, what units of measurements have been used and, if adjustments have been made to express a series in constant prices or in a common currency, how this has been done).

Data can be *cross-section* in form (each observation of every variable relates to a different individual, sector or country, for example, for a particular period or at a specific point in time) or it can be *time-series* data (each observation of every variable relates to a particular time period, perhaps annual, quarterly or some other frequency). As mentioned in Chapter 4, cross-section data can be entered in any order but time series observations must be placed in sequence. A particularly interesting type of mixed cross-section and time series data set is *panel data*, where there are several observations collected over time for a number of individuals. It is unlikely that you will come across panel data unless you are taking an advanced course in econometrics. Special techniques are needed to analyze such data.

Increasingly data is available to you already in electronic form, from a CD-ROM or computer disk or in a file downloaded over the Internet. A variety of formats might be used and we will consider some of the possibilities in a moment. Most statistics and econometrics packages will be able to read in data that has been provided in this way, but there are some points to look out for.

If you have collected the data yourself, or if the data has been provided to you only in printed form, you will need to enter the values at the keyboard to create your data file. Although most statistics and econometrics packages have data entry capabilities, it could be worthwhile to set up a datafile outside of these packages, because it is often easier to edit mistakes within a spreadsheet or simple text editor than it is in proprietary statistics and econometrics software data entry modules. You might also wish to keep your data file in a "neutral" form so that you can use it with several different statistics or econometrics software packages. However, if you do take this approach you will need to check carefully what formats and *what versions* of any spreadsheet software your statistics and econometrics software will accept. New versions of software packages are coming out all the time and your spreadsheet might be a version that has arrived since the statistics or econometrics software that you are using was written. For this reason it is a good idea to save any data files that are created within a spreadsheet for use with other software in an early version format – say Lotus 1-2-3 version 1 or 2 (.WKS or .WK1) or Excel version 2.1 using the Save **A**s rather than the **S**ave command from the menu.

If you do use a spreadsheet to create your data file there are some other conventions that you should be aware of if you want to go on to use it with statistics or econometrics packages. The file should have a standard structure with each column holding the values of a particular variable – row 1 would have the text providing the name for the variable while the rest of the column contains the respective values (by time period for time series data, by case for cross-section data). Column A should begin with a blank cell and then contain text strings to identify each observation. For time series data it would give the year followed by a colon or a hyphen and then the period within the year. For example, '1999:3 or '1999-3 could be used to identify the third quarter of 1999. Only numerical values should be contained in the heart of the worksheet – not the results of formulae. It is better to use the facilities within the statistics or econometrics package for any transformations that you need to make (see below). If there are any formulae in the worksheet, the statistics or econometrics

> **Tip**
>
> If a data file is provided to you in a spreadsheet format that is not accepted by your statistics or econometrics package, provided that you have a spreadsheet package that will recognize it, you can load up that software and the file and then save the data in an earlier format that can be used by the other program. Or, if the statistics or econometrics program is Windows based, you may be able to copy and paste the data into it from your spreadsheet.

software could fail to read the file. (You could create formulae within the spreadsheet and then format the relevant cells as values, but I recommend that you avoid using this approach, doing the minimum work with the spreadsheet and entering only text and values.) You should not use the spreadsheet to do anything else such as create graphs or add any explanatory text. There must be no blank rows or columns within the block, which must be contiguous. The file should be saved as a single worksheet of a suitable version as explained above – *not as a workbook file*.

Figure 5.1 illustrates an acceptable spreadsheet format.

| ROSES.XLS | A | B | C | D | E |
|---|---|---|---|---|---|
| | | roses | price | pcarn | income |
| 1 | | | | | |
| 2 | 1971:3 | 11484 | 2.26 | 3.49 | 158.11 |
| 3 | 1971:4 | 9348 | 2.54 | 2.85 | 173.36 |
| 4 | 1972:1 | 8429 | 3.07 | 4.06 | 165.26 |
| 5 | 1972:2 | 10079 | 2.91 | 3.64 | 172.92 |
| 6 | 1972:3 | 9240 | 2.73 | 3.21 | 178.46 |
| 7 | 1972:4 | 8862 | 2.77 | 3.66 | 198.62 |
| 8 | 1973:1 | 6216 | 3.59 | 3.76 | 186.28 |
| 9 | 1973:2 | 8253 | 3.23 | 3.49 | 188.98 |
| 10 | 1973:3 | 8038 | 2.6 | 3.13 | 180.49 |
| 11 | 1973:4 | 7476 | 2.89 | 3.2 | 183.33 |
| 12 | 1974:1 | 5911 | 3.77 | 3.65 | 181.87 |
| 13 | 1974:2 | 7950 | 3.64 | 3.6 | 185 |
| 14 | 1974:3 | 6134 | 2.82 | 2.94 | 184 |
| 15 | 1974:4 | 5868 | 2.96 | 3.12 | 188.2 |
| 16 | 1975:1 | 3160 | 4.24 | 3.58 | 175.67 |
| 17 | 1975:2 | 5872 | 3.69 | 3.53 | 188 |

**Fig. 5.1** A small spreadsheet datafile prepared for use with other statistics or econometrics software. (Source: Gujarati, 1995.)

The variables are defined as follows:

roses      quantity of roses sold in dozens
price      average wholesale price of roses in $ per dozen
pcarn      average wholesale price of carnations in $ per dozen
income      average weekly family disposable income in $ per week.

The data are for the Detroit metropolitan area in the United States.

**Exercise**

Use your spreadsheet package to create a data file containing the information shown in Figure 5.1. Make sure that when you save the file it is in a format that can be read by your statistics or econometrics package.

Some statistics and econometrics packages have their own data file formats. If you are working only with one package to analyze your data it can be all right to save data in such a format, but if you were considering using another package too you would be better saving the data in spreadsheet or text form.

**Some file formats that you might encounter.**

Space delimited or free format (e.g. .TXT or .PRN) – spaces are used to separate the data entries
Comma delimited (e.g. .CSV) – commas are used to separate the data entries
GiveWin (.BN7 holds the data and .IN7 contains information about the variables in the file) Microfit (.FIT)
RATS (.RAT)
TSP (.TLB)
GAUSS (.DAT contains the data, .DHT specifies the form of the data)
Note: only the first two types of file are "human readable", i.e. outside the particular package.

## Missing values

Sometimes a data file will have missing values for some observations. In most modern software packages you can leave an entry blank and the software will recognize that the value is missing. But you may have to be careful to check that this is interpreted correctly as a missing value rather than a zero when you ask the statistics or econometrics software to undertake some analysis using the variable concerned.

## Sample information

With some statistics and econometrics software you will need to provide the program with information about the data file when you load it. For example, if it is time series data such things as the sample period concerned and the frequency of the observations (annual, quarterly, monthly etc.) will have to be identified to the program before the file is loaded. You may also need to list the names of the variables to be loaded from the data file. (Be careful to check whether there are any restrictions on the names that you can use for variables. Some packages restrict variable names to a limited number and set of characters. You will also have to avoid the use of names that are used as keywords in commands. For example, LOGL might be used to stand for the log likelihood function so you would not be able to use it as the label for the variable that is the logarithm of labor – LNL might be a suitable alternative. Actually there can be occasions where this approach can give you extra flexibility. For example, you might have a very large data file containing many different variables but for a particular session you might want only to load a subset of them (it will save you memory if you don't load the whole file). With packages that don't allow you to load only specified variables from a file you would have to create a separate file outside the package that contains only the set of variables that you want to use for the particular session.

> **Tip**
>
> Always make several backup copies of data files and do not keep them in the same place. This can apply particularly to primary source data files and to files that you may wish to work with again and again. If you use your statistics or econometrics software to create new variables, don't forget to re-save the data file so that these additional variables are immediately available to you at your next session.

## Other file types

In addition to data files you will need to be aware of other types of file when you work with statistics or econometrics packages. As we noted in section 5.1, many such packages collect together the instructions or commands in the form of a program which would usually be saved as a file. Such files will be referred to variously by different software packages as the *program file* or the *input file*, and there may be a required extension for these files so that a particular software package can recognize them. They will be pure (ASCII) text in format and can be created, read and edited using any text editor or word processor. Make sure, however, that you save such a file in pure text form if you use a word processor to create or edit a program file.

The results of the analysis that you conduct with your statistics or econometric software take two basic forms – text and graphics. The output from the regressions, any statistical tests that you conduct, etc. – the results – will consist only of text and values. You will be able to view it on the screen or you can send it to an *output or results file* that can then be saved for incorporating into a report or editing before printing. Like the input file this will be pure ASCII text and will be recognizable outside the software that was used to create it. Graphics images created by the software will also appear on screen and you will also be able to save them. Different packages offer different sets of options for graphics file types and you need to think carefully before making your selection. Some will allow you to save in formats that can be edited or enhanced using graphics software such as Paint or PaintShop Pro while others can only be printed or copied into a document as a complete image. For example PcGive/GiveWin offers Windows Metafile (.WMF), Enhanced Windows Metafile (.EMF), Encapsulated PostScript (.EPS) and GiveWin's own format (.GWG). The only one of these formats that can be loaded back into GiveWin for later viewing is the .GWG format. So if you think that you might want to do that, the .GWG format would be the preferred option. However, if what you want is a format that can be pasted into a word-processed report one of the other formats would be required. Of course, with Windows programs such as this both text and graphics can be copied and pasted into another application such as a word processor via the clipboard.

## 5.3   Becoming familiar with statistics and econometrics software

Most statistics and econometrics packages will have a variety of support materials to help you become familiar with the software. There will be a manual, possibly divided up into several sections such as "Getting Started", "User Manual" and "Reference Manual". Although software users sometimes consider consultation of the manual as an admission of defeat, it really does pay at least to browse through it when you are starting with a new package. However, you might find that when a software package has been installed on a network for a large number of users there are only a limited number of manuals available so that you will have to manage without one.

> **Find out**
>
> Does your software have an on-line introduction that steps you through its basic features, or a set of example problems from which you can deduce some of the basic principles? Even if these features do not come with the program you may find them at the software publisher's web site.

Your lecturer will probably prepare an introduction to the use of the software for you, again either in printed form or, increasingly, in an electronic form that can be accessed from the web. You will certainly need to find out the particular details that will be unique to the way that the package is accessed at your university. For some packages, in addition to the official manuals, there are books that have been written to demonstrate the use of the package. For example, Walter Enders has written a book based around the use of RATS (Enders, 1996). It is also worth looking at reviews of the package you will be working with. *The Economic Journal*, the *Journal of Applied*

*Econometrics*, the *Journal of Economic Surveys* and *CHEER* (*Computers in Higher Education Economics Review*) all carry regular software reviews.

You may be given some problems to work on, as part of your statistics or econometrics course. Perhaps this will also entail finding appropriate data to use before you start with the package. Beginning students may find it worthwhile to try to replicate a set of published results, from either a textbook or a journal. Many textbooks provide the data for their worked examples on a disk or via their web sites. Although comparatively few journals publish the data used with the article itself, increasingly journals require authors to provide the data set so that it can be made available electronically via the web. Don't be too ambitious to begin with – many published articles will make use of large data sets and advanced techniques and you will need to master rather more elementary procedures before you can move on.

In this chapter you will be provided with several examples of published articles where the data used have been made generally available. Work through the practicals to check that you can produce the results using your software. Due to space restrictions only two packages will be illustrated in this book – TSP and PcGive. However, if you are working with a different package it should be possible to deduce what you would have to do to produce the desired effect using your software. You will also be able to find examples of the use of some of the other packages on the book's web site.

## Practical 5.1   Cigarette consumption in Turkey

A number of papers have been published over the years attempting to disentangle the different influences on the demand for cigarettes in various countries. The object is usually to see to what extent consumers have responded to price changes and whether other factors, such as anti-smoking health education campaigns or advertising restrictions, have affected demand. One fairly recent paper of this type by Aysit Tansel used Turkish data and she helpfully included the data set used in her study (see Table 5.2) (Tansel, 1993). We will use this as a case study to illustrate how two different econometric software packages, TSP and PcGive, can be used to work on problems of this type. However, before we look at the use of the packages themselves let us consider what Tansel has done in more detail.

Tansel follows the usual approach in modeling exercises of this type and bases her specification on demand theory so that the quantity of cigarettes consumed is expressed as a function of the price of cigarettes and consumers' income. No other price variables are needed because cigarettes are considered to have no close substitutes or complements. Because demand theory relates to the behavior of an individual, Tansel needs to express both the cigarette consumption variable and the income variable that she uses in her regressions on a per capita basis – in the case of income the aggregate series is divided by the whole population while aggregate cigarette consumption is just divided by the population over 15 (which is used to proxy the population of potential smokers). Both the income and price variables are also expressed in real

**Table 5.2**  Data from Tansel's study of cigarette demand in Turkey.

|      | Q     | Y    | P     |
|------|-------|------|-------|
| 1960 | 1.86  | 2561 | 1.362 |
| 1961 | 1.917 | 2560 | 1.363 |
| 1962 | 1.981 | 2652 | 1.361 |
| 1963 | 1.937 | 2840 | 1.454 |
| 1964 | 1.924 | 2882 | 1.62  |
| 1965 | 1.947 | 2900 | 1.688 |
| 1966 | 2.039 | 3167 | 1.664 |
| 1967 | 1.985 | 3220 | 1.76  |
| 1968 | 2.018 | 3350 | 1.812 |
| 1969 | 2.016 | 3443 | 1.984 |
| 1970 | 2.114 | 3546 | 1.996 |
| 1971 | 2.144 | 3826 | 1.926 |
| 1972 | 2.223 | 4014 | 1.875 |
| 1973 | 2.357 | 4109 | 1.869 |
| 1974 | 2.574 | 4304 | 1.813 |
| 1975 | 2.403 | 4526 | 2.008 |
| 1976 | 2.456 | 4784 | 2.148 |
| 1977 | 2.517 | 4869 | 2.075 |
| 1978 | 2.593 | 4906 | 2.347 |
| 1979 | 2.723 | 4786 | 1.875 |
| 1980 | 2.347 | 4638 | 2.145 |
| 1981 | 2.527 | 4714 | 2.279 |
| 1982 | 2.413 | 4808 | 2.392 |
| 1983 | 2.346 | 4844 | 2.23  |
| 1984 | 2.206 | 5006 | 2.106 |
| 1985 | 2.107 | 5132 | 2.714 |
| 1986 | 2.024 | 5409 | 2.539 |
| 1987 | 2.165 | 5672 | 2.967 |
| 1988 | 2.082 | 5723 | 3.968 |

Q, cigarette consumption per adult (kg); Y, per capita real GNP in Turkish liras (1968 prices); P, real price of cigarettes (the retail price of cigarettes divided by the consumer price index (1975)).

terms so as to remove the effects of inflation. Usually when you collect data for use in your work you will begin with unprocessed data and one of the first things you will use the econometrics software to do is to create the new derived variables that you require. For example, if you have one series giving the price of cigarettes in current or nominal prices and another series that is the consumer price index you would divide the former by the latter to obtain the real price series. Since on this occasion we already have the data that we require, these transformations will not be needed. However, as we shall see in a moment, we will still have to use our software to create some other new and derived variables before we can run our regressions.

Tansel works with a log-linear regression model (so that the regression coefficients can be interpreted as elasticities). So we will need to use our software to generate new series which are the logarithms of the series in the data file. In PcGive (actually in the GiveWin front end that is used with PcGive) there is a handy *Calculator* tool that we can use to do this, but in TSP we will have to type in a command of the form GENR LNQ = LOG(Q); (you can leave out the GENR keyword – short for generate).

Next we must use our software to create some *dummy variables* that are needed in the regression to capture the possible effects of health awareness and anti-smoking campaigns that were brought in during the time period being analyzed. Dummy variables are variables that we construct to reflect possible shifts in the relationship due to qualitative differences between observations. A dummy variable will take either the value 1 or 0 in each time period, representing the presence or absence of the effect. Two such variables are needed here. The first, which will take the value zero for the years 1960–1981 inclusive and 1 thereafter, is used to see if the health warning that was printed on cigarette packages from the end of 1981 onwards had any impact on consumption. The second, which will take the value zero for the years 1960–1985 inclusive and 1 thereafter, is used to see if the anti-smoking health campaigns of 1986 and 1988 had any effect. In PcGive the Calculator tool can again be used to create these new variables. TSP requires the use of commands to produce the same effect.

In common with many other previous studies, Tansel incorporates a *lagged dependent variable* in her regression – that is, she includes the lagged value of lnQ amongst the variables on the right hand side of the regression equation. This is supposed to reflect the habit-forming nature of smoking. So Tansel's model does not assume that when income or the price changes, consumers will move immediately to their new long-run equilibrium position. Rather, because they find it hard to make the full adjustment, initially there will only be *partial adjustment* towards the new equilibrium. This allows us to distinguish in our model between the *short-run* elasticities (which are the coefficients of the current period price and income variables in the regression equation) and the *long-run* elasticities, which will be equal to the short-run elasticities divided by one minus the coefficient of the lagged dependent variable (which by assumption will be in the region 0 to 1). Note that in the long run all adjustment will be complete so that $\ln Q_t$ and $\ln Q_{t-1}$ will both take the same value, just equal to lnQ, say. Equating them in Equation 5.1 and subtracting the $\beta_5 \ln Q$ term from both sides means that the lnQ will have a coefficient of $(1 - \beta_5)$ on the left hand side of the equation. When the equation is solved for lnQ by dividing both sides by $1 - \beta_5$ all the coefficients of the remaining variables on the right hand side of the equation will measure the long-run effects.

If we include a disturbance term, the regression model we want to estimate will take the form:

$$\ln Q_t = \alpha + \beta_1 \ln P_t + \beta_2 \ln Y_t + \beta_3 D82\_88_t + \beta_4 D86\_88_t + \beta_5 \ln Q_{t-1} + u_t$$

Equation 5.1

Depending on the software that you use it may not be necessary to create a new variable for the lagged dependent variable. You might, however, be able to get the program automatically to incorporate such a variable when the regression model is formulated. In addition, some software packages will automatically compute the long-run elasticities. Care may be needed to specify correctly the sample period to be used for the regression. Since there will not be a value of $\ln Q_{t-1}$ for 1960 you will only have 28 years, data for use in the regression.

If you were to look at Tansel's paper you would see that before running her regressions she plotted the Q, P and Y series and discussed the trends that were exhibited. Such time series plots can suggest possible modifications to the specification (see section 5.4 for a discussion of the problems of working with trending data). They can also alert you to possible errors that might have crept into the data set that need to be corrected before you proceed. It can also be worthwhile to get the computer to produce some summary descriptive statistics for the variables in your data set.

One of the advantages of working with dedicated econometrics packages is that they can produce for you a wide range of diagnostic test statistics that can help you to assess the suitability of the model. If you look at Tansel's paper you will find that her results include tests for autocorrelation, heteroskedasticity, normality of the residuals etc. You will need to consult an econometrics textbook to help you understand such results properly, but modern software such as PcGive helpfully attaches asterisks to the diagnostic test statistics to indicate that the null hypothesis (of no autocorrelation – or serial independence, homoskedasticity or normality) should be rejected at the 5% (one asterisk) or 1% (two asterisks) level of significance. Since you will be looking for a model that is free of such problems you will be hoping that the diagnostic statistics are all satisfactory. If not you will need to consider possible modifications of your model.

When you look at the regression results themselves the first thing that you should do is to examine the signs and magnitudes of the regression coefficients. Here we will expect the price coefficient to be negative and probably quite small (indicating an inelastic response, especially in the short run). We anticipate a positive coefficient for income, again less than one in absolute value. The coefficients of the dummy variables are both expected to be negative, indicating a downward shift in demand as a result of the anti-smoking measures that were introduced towards the end of the period. The coefficient of the lagged dependent variable must be between zero and 1. The closer it is to zero the faster will be the adjustment to equilibrium following a change in any of the other variables. Values for estimated parameters that are not plausible might indicate problems with the model being used – unless of course they are not significantly different from zero (see below).

The overall significance of the regression equation can be established using the F-statistic. Large values suggest that the model has some overall relevance, although precisely how big the F-value needs to be in order to establish significance (at the 5% level) depends of course on the degrees of freedom. Modern software will also provide a probability or P-value that will measure the probability of a type I error, that is the probability of incorrectly rejecting the null hypothesis (of no relationship). Provided that this is below 0.05 the test shows significance at the 5% level.

You can judge the significance of individual variables (or more correctly of their coefficients) by looking at t-values (or, if they are shown, the t-probability values that go with them). As we saw in Chapter 4, under the null hypothesis that an underlying parameter is in fact zero the t-ratio (which is the coefficient estimate divided by its standard error) will tend to be quite close to zero. Large t-values (in absolute terms) suggest that the null hypothesis can be rejected – again the exact critical value will depend on the degrees of freedom, although values greater than 2 are likely to indicate significance. Alternatively you can look at the t-probability values and see if they are small enough to consider the result significant.

If a t-value, or t-probability value, suggests that a coefficient is not significantly different from zero you may consider dropping the relevant variable from the model (although you would first wish to be sure that the t-value was not affected adversely by any multicollinearity in the sample data – that is strong correlation amongst the right hand side variables). When Tansel estimates the model described by Equation 5.1 she finds that the t-value for the D86_88 dummy is rather low, so she excludes this variable from the model and runs a second regression based only on the other variables. It is easy to do this using modern econometrics software such as TSP or PcGive, as we illustrate below.

Now we can illustrate the use of the two different packages for conducting this type of analysis. One (TSP) is based on a simple programming language that is used to issue commands. It can be used both in interactive and batch mode, but here I show how to create a program file that can then be executed as a batch job. The other package that is illustrated (PcGive linking up with its "front end", GiveWin) is an example of the "point and click" approach to doing econometrics. There can be advantages and disadvantages in using either approach.

An exercise of this type can be divided into several stages when using econometrics software. The first stage is the construction of the base data set, either via the data entry module within the software or, as I suggest, using a spreadsheet package. Some or all of the data may already be in some kind of electronic form and this can speed things up and prevent transcription errors. Here, since both PcGive and TSP recognize Excel worksheet files (version 2.1), you should first use your spreadsheet software to create such a file containing the data in Table 5.2 (or you could, if you wish, download the file Tansel.xls from my web site). Once the data file is ready you can run your econometrics software.

*Working with TSP*

Let's look first at how to get the results using TSP. (If you have a different version of TSP, or if you use the Through the Looking Glass interface, there may be differences between what is shown here and what you see when you try it.) TSP uses commands to produce results. You can run the program either in interactive mode, so that the results are shown on screen after each instruction is executed, or you can collect together your sequence of commands in a file and run the program as a batch job, sending the results to an output file. Here we adopt the latter approach, but you can type in the commands one at a time if you prefer.

Using any text editor (e.g. the Notepad accessory in Windows) or any word processor, create a text file containing the commands shown in Figure 5.2. Save the file as a pure text file (i.e. with no formatting) and call it something like TANSEL.TSP.

```
FREQ A;
SMPL 1960,1988;
READ(FILE='C:\DATA\TANSEL.XLS');
LQ = LOG(Q);
LY = LOG(Y);
LP = LOG(P);
SMPL 1960,1981;D82_88=0;
SMPL 1982,1988;D82_88=1;
SMPL 1960,1985;D86_88=0;
SMPL 1986,1988;D86_88=1;
SMPL 1961,1988;
LQLAG = LQ(-1);
? Some  descriptive  statistics  and  graph  plots  of  the  series
MSD LQ,LY,LP;
PLOT LQ;
PLOT LY;
PLOT LP;
? Tansel's model 1
OLSQ LQ, C, LY, LP, LQLAG, D82_88, D86_88;
DROP D86_88;
END;
```

**Fig. 5.2**   TSP input file (commands) for the Tansel practical.

Now run the TSP program. You will be asked to enter the batch file name (or to press **Enter** to run in interactive mode). Type in the name of the batch file, including the full path that the computer will need to follow in order to find the file. For example, on my computer I had saved the *input file* on the C drive in a subdirectory of a directory called BOOK. I typed C:\BOOK\CH5\TANSEL.TSP and then pressed the **Enter** key. The computer should start to run the program. It will first inform you that the TSP output will be in a file C:\BOOK\CH5\TANSEL.OUT (or something similar depending upon where you had your input file).

After a little while, if you have prepared the input and data files correctly, TSP will inform you that the batch run has been completed successfully and allow you either to continue in interactive mode (by pressing **Enter**) or to quit the program – just press q and press the **Enter** key. (There are also two other options – you can rerun the same batch file or move to a different batch file.)

If you open the TSP *output file* (TANSEL.OUT) – again you can use Notepad, any word-processor or the Through the Looking Glass interface – you should see the results shown in Figure 5.3. Notice that they begin with the commands from your input file. Before we consider the statistical and graphical output let's briefly review the sequence of commands.

The first two lines prepare the computer for the data file that is to be read in, indicating that the data frequency is annual and that the sample will cover the years 1960 to 1988. The third command gets the computer to read the data file. Here it would have been possible if we had been using a very large data file to select specified variables only from the file by listing their names at the end of the line.

The commands are shown here in upper case letters and with a semi-colon at the end of each line. Neither of these is now strictly necessary, although it was customary for them to be formed in this way with earlier versions of the program. The TSP manual continues to show them and I have become used to producing TSP files that follow this construction.

Lines 4, 5 and 6 are used to generate the derived variables that are the logs of the original series. Then we create the dummy variables. Notice that you can put two commands on one line – although to do this you will need to use the semi-colon to signify the end of a command. The SMPL (sample) keyword is used to specify the time periods for which the dummy variable must take particular values.

On line 16 I have a command to generate a new variable that is the lag of LNQ. This needs to be preceded by a SMPL command to restrict attention to the years 1961 to 1988, since there will be no information available on the lagged value of LNQ for 1960. The sample period will remain 1961 to 1988 for subsequent commands (unless it is changed again).

Line 17 begins with a question mark – so the text on this line is ignored when the program is executed. This is the way that you can add in *remarks* in TSP and is included here to illustrate how it works. The next command – still seen to be line 17 when the program is executed – asks the computer to compute the mean, standard deviation and some other descriptive statistics for the specified series.

Next I ask TSP to plot graphs of each of the series LQ, LY and LP. Tansel has graphs of the original Q, Y and P series but the trend pattern is much the same with or without the transformation. The graphs that are produced will be purely text based with a simple crude look to them – definitely not high resolution. You will also need to turn your head sideways to view them on screen! It is really best to print them out to look at. You can produce higher quality on-screen graphs with TSP but they would have to be viewed and saved separately from the basic results. There can be advantages in having the rough and ready graphs incorporated into the output in this way if you just want to see the general movement of each series.

Now at last we have the command for running the regression, OLSQ, followed by a list of variables to be included in the regression beginning with the dependent variable and including CONSTANT (or C for short) when you want to include a constant intercept in the regression equation. (Here is another label to avoid when naming variables – something you might need to watch out for if you are estimating consumption or cost functions.)

After estimating Tansel's model 1, I wanted to estimate model 2 which is the same except that it omits (or drops) the second dummy variable. Obviously I could have typed in a new OLSQ command with the slightly shorter list of variables. But TSP has a handy facility for situations such as this. If you wish to run a regression similar to the last one, but with some variables missing, you can put in the DROP command, identifying the variables that are to be left out.

The final command ENDs the program.

```
TSP  Version  4.4
                        (10/03/97)  DOS/Win    4MB
                     Copyright  (C)  1997  TSP  International
                            ALL  RIGHTS  RESERVED
                            09/15/99  3:16  PM
              In  case  of  questions  or  problems,  see  your  local  TSP
           consultant  or  send  a  description  of  the  problem  and  the
                         associated  TSP  output  to:
                              TSP  International
                           Palo  Alto,  CA  94306
                                    USA
             PROGRAM


LINE***************************************
|      1      FREQ  A;
|      2      SMPL  1960,1988;
|      3      READ(FILE='C:\DATA\TANSEL.XLS');
|      4      LQ  =  LOG(Q);
|      5      LY  =  LOG(Y);
|      6      LP  =  LOG(P);
|      7      SMPL  1960,1981;D82_88=0;
|      9      SMPL  1982,1988;D82_88=1;
|     11      SMPL  1960,1985;D86_88=0;
|     13      SMPL  1986,1988;D86_88=1;
|     15      SMPL  1961,1988;
|     16      LQLAG  =  LQ(-1);
|     17      ?  Some  descriptive  statistics  and
             graph  plots  of  the  series
|     17      MSD  LQ,LY,LP;
|     18      PLOT  LQ;
|     19      PLOT  LY;
|     20      PLOT  LP;
|     21      ?  Tansel's  model  1
|     21      OLSQ  LQ,  C,  LY,  LP,  LQLAG,  D82_88,
             D86_88;
|     22      DROP  D86_88;
|     23      END;
             EXECUTION


********************************************

Current  sample:        1960  to  1988
Current  sample:        1960  to  1981
Current  sample:        1982  to  1988
Current  sample:        1960  to  1985
Current  sample:        1986  to  1988
Current  sample:        1961  to  1988


                     Univariate  statistics
                     ==================
Number  of  Observations:  28


             Mean         Std Dev       Minimum       Maximum
LQ         0.79087       0.10555       0.65076       1.00173
LY         8.30708       0.24363       7.84776       8.65225
LP         0.70082       0.22997       0.30822       1.37826
```

|    | Sum | Variance | Skewness | Kurtosis |
|----|------|----------|----------|----------|
| LQ | 22.14436 | 0.011141 | 0.36634 | -1.15100 |
| LY | 232.59832 | 0.059354 | -0.46828 | -1.08485 |
| LP | 19.62306 | 0.052888 | 0.77106 | 1.75079 |

### TIME SERIES PLOT
===============

LQ PLOTTED WITH *

```
        MINIMUM                                        MAXIMUM
        0.65076                                        1.00173
        |-+---------------------------------------------+-|
1961 |  *                                                  |  0.65076
1962 |       *                                             |  0.68360
1963 |    *                                                |  0.66114
1964 |    *                                                |  0.65441
1965 |     *                                               |  0.66629
1966 |           *                                         |  0.71246
1967 |        *                                            |  0.68562
1968 |          *                                          |  0.70211
1969 |          *                                          |  0.70112
1970 |               *                                     |  0.74858
1971 |                *                                    |  0.76267
1972 |                   *                                 |  0.79886
1973 |                      *                              |  0.85739
1974 |                             *                       |  0.94546
1975 |                         *                           |  0.87672
1976 |                           *                         |  0.89853
1977 |                              *                      |  0.92307
1978 |                             *                       |  0.95282
1979 |                                             *  |     1.00173
1980 |                       *                             |  0.85314
1981 |                             *                       |  0.92703
1982 |                          *                          |  0.88087
1983 |                        *                            |  0.85271
1984 |                  *                                  |  0.79118
1985 |             *                                       |  0.74527
1986 |          *                                          |  0.70508
1987 |               *                                     |  0.77242
1988 |             *                                       |  0.73333
        |-+---------------------------------------------+-|
        0.65076                                        1.00173
        MINIMUM                                        MAXIMUM
```

### TIME SERIES PLOT
=================

LY PLOTTED WITH *

```
        MINIMUM                                        MAXIMUM
        7.84776                                        8.65225
        |-+---------------------------------------------+-|
1961 |  *                                                  |  7.84776
1962 |     *                                               |  7.88307
1963 |        *                                            |  7.95156
1964 |       *                                             |  7.96624
1965 |        *                                            |  7.97247
1966 |            *                                        |  8.06054
1967 |             *                                       |  8.07714
1968 |               *                                     |  8.11672
```

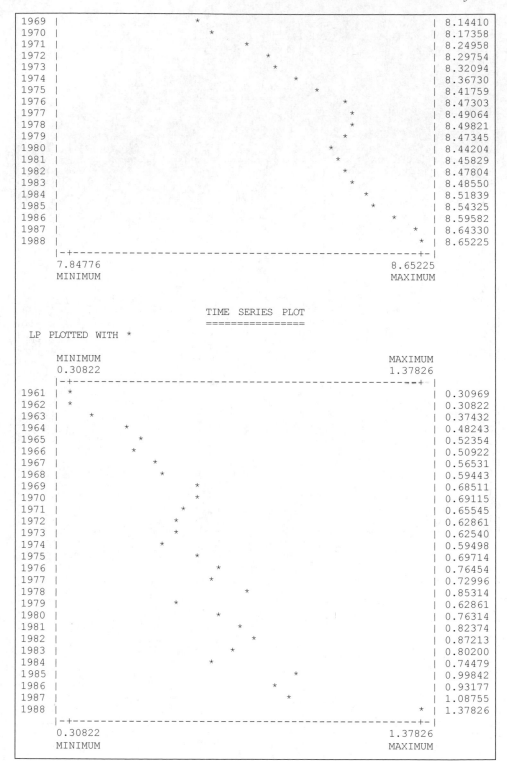

```
1969 |                              *                              | 8.14410
1970 |                               *                             | 8.17358
1971 |                                   *                         | 8.24958
1972 |                                     *                       | 8.29754
1973 |                                     *                       | 8.32094
1974 |                                       *                     | 8.36730
1975 |                                         *                   | 8.41759
1976 |                                          *                  | 8.47303
1977 |                                          *                  | 8.49064
1978 |                                          *                  | 8.49821
1979 |                                          *                  | 8.47345
1980 |                                         *                   | 8.44204
1981 |                                         *                   | 8.45829
1982 |                                          *                  | 8.47804
1983 |                                          *                  | 8.48550
1984 |                                           *                 | 8.51839
1985 |                                            *                | 8.54325
1986 |                                              *              | 8.59582
1987 |                                               *             | 8.64330
1988 |                                                *            | 8.65225
     |-+--------------------------------------------------+-|
       7.84776                                          8.65225
       MINIMUM                                          MAXIMUM


                        TIME  SERIES  PLOT
                        =================

   LP  PLOTTED WITH  *

           MINIMUM                              MAXIMUM
           0.30822                              1.37826
     |-+-----------------------------------------------=-+-|
1961 |  *                                                          | 0.30969
1962 |  *                                                          | 0.30822
1963 |       *                                                     | 0.37432
1964 |           *                                                 | 0.48243
1965 |             *                                               | 0.52354
1966 |           *                                                 | 0.50922
1967 |              *                                              | 0.56531
1968 |               *                                             | 0.59443
1969 |                   *                                         | 0.68511
1970 |                   *                                         | 0.69115
1971 |                 *                                           | 0.65545
1972 |                *                                            | 0.62861
1973 |                *                                            | 0.62540
1974 |              *                                              | 0.59498
1975 |                   *                                         | 0.69714
1976 |                     *                                       | 0.76454
1977 |                    *                                        | 0.72996
1978 |                       *                                     | 0.85314
1979 |                *                                            | 0.62861
1980 |                     *                                       | 0.76314
1981 |                       *                                     | 0.82374
1982 |                        *                                    | 0.87213
1983 |                      *                                      | 0.80200
1984 |                   *                                         | 0.74479
1985 |                          *                                  | 0.99842
1986 |                         *                                   | 0.93177
1987 |                        *                                    | 1.08755
1988 |                                                *            | 1.37826
     |-+--------------------------------------------------+-|
       0.30822                                          1.37826
       MINIMUM                                          MAXIMUM
```

```
                              Equation 1
                              ============
                 Method of estimation = Ordinary Least Squares

Dependent variable: LQ
Current sample: 1961 to 1988
Number of observations: 28

          Mean of dep. var.  = .790870        LM het. test = 6.12833 [.013]
       Std. dev. of dep. var. = .105550       Durbin-Watson = 2.00768
                                                            [.116,.892]
    Sum of squared residuals = .034853        Jarque-Bera test = .714887 [.699]
        Variance of residuals = .158425E-02   Ramsey's RESET2 = .629042 [.437]
    Std. error of regression = .039803        F (zero slopes) = 33.5742 [.000]
                   R-squared = .884132        Schwarz B.I.C. = -5.97476
          Adjusted R-squared = .857798        Log likelihood = 53.9130

                  Estimated     Standard
Variable         Coefficient      Error     t-statistic     P-value
C                 -3.01900       .845574      -3.57036       [.002]
LY                 .446949       .120600       3.70603       [.001]
LP                -.172082       .088138      -1.95242       [.064]
LQLAG              .310979       .173065       1.79689       [.086]
D82_88            -.086711       .026382      -3.28678       [.003]
D86_88            -.050239       .044091      -1.13942       [.267] ·

                              Equation 2
                              ============
                 Method of estimation = Ordinary Least Squares

Dependent variable: LQ
Current sample: 1961 to 1988
Number of observations: 28

          Mean of dep. var.  = .790870        LM het. test = 5.94779 [.015]
       Std. dev. of dep. var. = .105550       Durbin-Watson    = 2.24203
                                                            [.395,.947]
    Sum of squared residuals = .036910        Jarque-Bera test = 1.26620 [.531]
        Variance of residuals = .160479E-02   Ramsey's RESET2 = .040027 [.843]
    Std. error of regression = .040060        F (zero slopes) = 41.1100 [.000]
                   R-squared = .877294        Schwarz B.I.C. = -6.03643
          Adjusted R-squared = .855954        Log likelihood = 53.1103

                  Estimated     Standard
Variable         Coefficient      Error     t-statistic     P-value
C                 -2.67606       .795303      -3.36484       [.003]
LY                 .395432       .112527       3.51410       [.002]
LP                -.191670       .087004      -2.20300       [.038]
LQLAG              .429897       .138947       3.09396       [.005]
D82_88            -.087555       .026542      -3.29876       [.003]

****************************************************************************
END OF OUTPUT.
```

**Fig. 5.3**   The TSP output for Practical 5.1.

When you look at the regression output you can see that you get considerably more information than with Excel. The Durbin–Watson statistic is used to test for (first-order) autocorrelation, although it is biased towards its mean value of 2 when, as here, the regression equation includes a lagged dependent variable. Thus it is better to rely on other autocorrelation tests which can be produced by including additional commands in the program. Several of the other statistics that appear on the right hand side of the regression output are diagnostic statistics that are there to help you assess the suitability of the specification. Tansel's output included a Jarque–Bera test for normality of the residuals, a Lagrange multiplier heteroskedasticity test and a Ramsey RESET test of functional form misspecifiction. However, when we compare the results we have obtained here with those in the original published article we find that, although similar, they are not the same. This is also true of the actual regression results, t-values etc.

Unfortunately this is a far from unusual occurrence when one attempts to replicate published results. Of course, it could be that in copying the data from the article into the spreadsheet I have made a transcription error. Double checking the values here suggests that this is not the problem on this occasion. Or, the results might unintentionally be based on a slightly different specification or time period. Again that would appear not to be the case here. Then one might suspect that the software itself produced errors. Although commercial software is by no means completely free of bugs and errors (as is sometimes revealed by reviewers), one way to check for this kind of problem is to try a different package and see if the results come out the same – as we shall do using PcGive. Finally we are left to draw the conclusion that the data set published in *Applied Economics* was not identical to the one that was actually used to generate Tansel's regression results. Either she used a revised version of the file that was printed in her data appendix, or there was a typo somewhere in the table included in the published article. This may be the problem here.

In any event our results seem to confirm the overall conclusions that are reported by Tansel. "As expected, demand is a negative function of price and a positive function of income. Further, demand is both price and income inelastic." The TSP results shown here do not provide the long-run elasticities but, based on Tansel's preferred Model 2 these can easily be calculated as −0.3362 and 0.6936 (approximately). Again, these are not the same as the values given in the Tansel paper – because they are based on different short-run and speed of adjustment values – but they are in the same ballpark.

The coefficients of the health dummies both have the expected signs in Model 1, although D86_88 is not very significant. Of course the dummies used here are a rather crude attempt to capture an influence that might have varied over the period. If you refer to Tansel's paper you will see that she tried some other formulations that allow the impacts to vary year by year. She also looked at the possible influence of educational attainment on cigarette demand (concluding that it was negatively related to cigarette demand but insignificant except at university level). If you are interested, you may like to search out the Tansel paper to get hold of the full data set and the details of these other models. Then you can investigate them yourself using the econometrics software that is available to you.

*Working with PcGive*

PcGive is a modern interactive econometrics software package which runs under Windows. It can be used by beginners who just want to obtain some basic least squares regression results or by researchers wishing to employ the latest econometric tests and techniques. The program is part of a software suite developed by Jurgen Doornik and David Hendry called *PcGive Professional* which consists of three modules:

- GiveWin – the front end program or module where you load the data, undertake any preliminary data transformations (such as taking logarithms or dividing one series by another), and construct and view any pre-regression graphs. It also contains the results window where the regression results are placed.
- PcGive – the program (or module) for formulating and estimating single equation regression models and for undertaking post-regression diagnostic testing.
- PcFiml – the program (module) for dealing with systems of equations (VAR analysis, cointegration and simultaneous equations modeling). We do not attempt to cover the use of PcFiml in this book – see Harris (1995) for examples of how to use PcFiml for this kind of analysis.

Although you will need to work in the GiveWin window first (to load the data etc.) you need only click on the PcGive icon to open both modules. *Warning*: Although you can minimize one of the modules when working with the other, be very careful not to close down either module until you are ready to finish your session. If you do you may lose your results.

Click on the desktop icon for PcGive (or load the program from the network in any other way that is required on your system). Both the PcGive and GiveWin modules will run, each in their own window. Both programs have menu systems with main menu commands such as **F**ile, **E**dit, **V**iew, **T**ools etc. in GiveWin and **F**ile, **D**ata, **M**odel, **T**est etc. in PcGive. For some commands you can also click on the relevant icon (for example clicking on the little picture of the printer is a quick way to print your results) or you can use a combination of "hot" keys (such as CTRL+P to print).

To call up the TANSEL.XLS file click on **F**ile and then **O**pen in GiveWin. Then move to the directory where the file is stored and double click on the file name to open it (or click once to select the file and then click on the **O**pen button). A spreadsheet information box will appear giving details of the frequency (here it should be annual) and the sample dates (here they should show 1960 1 and 1988 1). If these entries are not shown put them in and then click **OK** to proceed. Another window will open within GiveWin showing the data. Check through the values in the database. If any of them is wrong just go to the cell and double click on it to overwrite the value.

Next you must create the new and derived variables which are to be added to the database. Click **T**ools and then **C**alculator (or ALT+C or click on the little calculator icon on the toolbar). The Calculator window will open, as shown in Figure 5.4.

Highlight the quantity variable Q in the right hand pane (just click on it) and then click the button with the word **l**og on it. The expression log(Q) will appear at the top of the window.

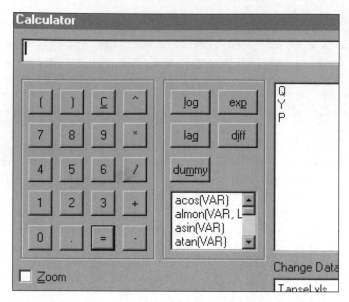

**Fig. 5.4**  The Calculator tool in GiveWin.

Now click on the = (equals) button. Another small box will open labeled "Destination name". In it you will see the variable name LQ being offered to you. If you want to give the variable a different name you can type it in to replace this name. In this case you can just accept the suggested name by clicking the **OK** button. You should notice that the LQ variable has been added to the list of variables in the database.

> **Note**
>
> Although the variable is in the database and available to you to work with during the current session, if you were to quit the program now it would not have been added to the database on disk. To ensure that any new variables are part of the database for use in later sessions you will have to save the database before you exit the program – see below.

Now use the Calculator to create the logs of the other two variables in a similar way. Two further variables, LY and LP, will be added to the current database.

You can use the calculator to apply a whole range of algebraic functions using the +, −, *, / and ^ keys, and also to lag and difference variables or to create dummy variables. We won't actually need to create the lag of LNQ as it can be introduced automatically when we need it in a regression model. We do need to create the two dummy variables, however.

Click on the du**m**my button and the Create a Dummy dialog box will open. Our first dummy needs to be 0 for all years before 1982 and 1 thereafter. So you need to change the first entry in the "Zero before" slot from 1960 to 1982. Click **OK** and you will be returned to the main Calculator box. In the slot at the top you should see `dummy(1982,1, 1988,1)`. Click on the = button (or press **Enter**) and the Destination name box will open. Type in `D82_88` and click **OK**. The dummy variable will be added to the database.

Now create the second dummy in the same way – the only differences are that you need to put 1986 in the "Zero before" slot and give the variable the name `D86_88`. Close the Calculator tool by clicking on the × at the top right hand corner of the box.

At this point you can resave the file. Make sure that the GiveWin window showing the Tansel file is the current window and click on **F**ile and then Save **A**s. The file name showing should still be Tansel and the type XLS [Excel 2.1] (*.xls). Click on the **S**ave button and then **Y**es to confirm that you want to replace the existing file. (Alternatively you can give the augmented file a new name if you wish to keep a "clean" copy of your original file.) The Database Selection box will open. All the variables in the database should be showing in the left hand pane. Just click **OK** to save the file with all the variables in it.

Now you can use GiveWin to create some graphs of the series. Click **T**ools followed by **G**raphics (or ALT+G, or click on the Graphics icon which looks like a pair of intersecting demand and supply curves).

To plot LQ against time click on the variable name (LQ) and then click **OK**. A new (GiveWin Graphics) window will open up within GiveWin showing how the variable LQ moves over the period. You can print or save this graph, or if you wish you can edit it on screen before saving or printing. For example, you could change the Line Attributes setting the Color Type to 1 for black (rather than red) for printing. Or you

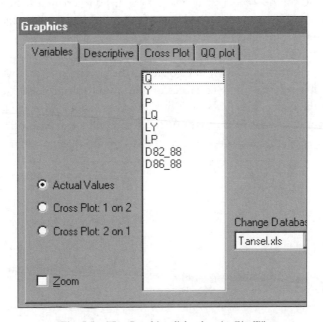

**Fig. 5.5**  The Graphics dialog box in GiveWin.

could add some extra text. Either double click on the graph or click the right mouse button and then choose Edit Graph or Add Text from the options available. If you save the graph remember that only the .GWG format can be reloaded into GiveWin for viewing again at a subsequent session.

Now use the same graphing tool to plot LY against time. Notice that the LQ graph will be reduced in size to take up only half a screen and the new graph will be added underneath. If you want a full screen graph of LY you will have to delete the LQ graph – just select it and press the delete key. You can have a large number of graphs together on screen at once – up to 36 if necessary – although with that many the individual graphs are rather too small to see properly. Each graph has its own Area and you can change the way the graphs are laid out if you wish. You can also create many other different graph types with GiveWin – scatter diagrams (cross-plots), histograms etc. and alter their appearance in a number of ways. Look up Graphics in the GiveWin manual or built-in help system for more information.

You should now have three separate windows within GiveWin. One with the graphs in, another with the Tansel datafile in and one with the results and a log of what you have been doing. To move between them select **W**indow from the GiveWin menu and then pick out the one you want from the drop-down menu. You can also Cascade the windows, move them around, resize them etc. in the usual Windows fashion. Note that if you use the Save **A**s command what you will be saving as a file will be the contents of the current window. So ensure that the file type shown at the bottom of the dialog box corresponds to the type of file that you want (spreadsheet, graphics or plain text for output or results files).

Move now to the Results window. Here you will find a record of what you have done so far, including the *algebra code* that has been used to create the new variables via the Calculator tool. There should also be confirmation that the data file was resaved. It should look something like Figure 5.6 (you may have a later version than the one I have on my laptop).

The code here looks very much like some of the commands that we used in TSP. In fact it is possible to create new variables in GiveWin through the Algebra tool itself rather than via the Calculator (choose **T**ools **A**lgebra, ALT+A or click on the ALG icon). Why might you want to do that? Well, as you will see if you open the Algebra dialog box, it is possible to edit, save and load groups of commands this way –

```
---- PcGive 9.00 session started at 17:43:07 on Thursday 16
September 1999

Algebra code for Tansel.xls:
LQ = log(Q);
LY = log(Y);
LP = log(P);
D82_88 = dummy(1982,1, 1988,1);
D86_88 = dummy(1986,1, 1988,1);
Tansel.xls saved to C:\data\Tansel.xls
```

**Fig. 5.6**  PcGive's log of your work shown in the results window.

something that can be very useful if you have a great many similar transformations to do (where it can be quicker to copy and edit a command than to enter a new one), or if you are likely to want to use the same set of commands with several different files. GiveWin offers you the ease of use of the Calculator with its "point and click" approach but also the power of the Algebra tool.

You are now ready to formulate and estimate Tansel's Model 1. To do this you must move to the PcGive module. Switch to it either by clicking on its window if it is visible on screen or by clicking on its icon on the bar at the bottom of the screen.

Select **M**odel and then **F**ormulate (or use the hot-key combination ALT+Y, or click on the Formulate icon which is on the far left of those available, immediately under **F**ile in the menu). The Formulate Model dialog box should open (Figure 5.7).

In the middle right of the box is a pane showing all the variables in the database. To formulate a regression model you just highlight the variables that you want in the model – here it is all of them from LQ onwards. You should find that the grayed out **OK** button at the top right of the box changes to **Add**. Click on it and the variables you need will be copied into the Model pane on the middle left of the box.

LQ should be the first in the list and there should be a letter E next to it to indicate that this is to be the endogenous (dependent) variable in the regression. If, for some reason, your list doesn't show the correct variable marked as endogenous, you can highlight it in the Model list and then toggle on or off the Endogenous Status using the button to the left of the box. Next a Constant will have been automatically added to the list from the pane containing the "Special " standard variables such as Constant and Trend (if we had been working with quarterly or monthly data this list would have included seasonal dummy variables). After that should come LY, LP and the two dummies.

Tansel's model also includes a lagged dependent variable. To add this in go to the Database pane again and highlight LQ, but before you click **Add** go to the Lag length

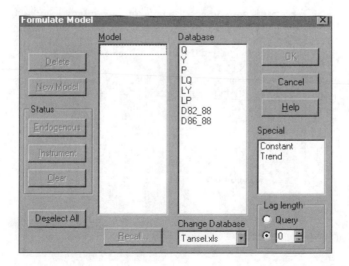

**Fig. 5.7** The Formulate Model dialog box in PcGive.

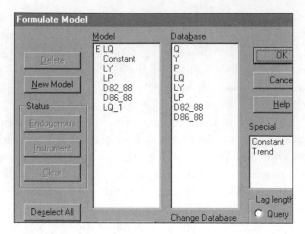

**Fig. 5.8**   The PcGive Formulate Model dialog box showing the formulated model.

spinner at the bottom right of the box and move the setting to 1 rather than zero. Then click **Add** and LQ_1 should be added in to the Model pane.

If by chance the Lag length had been set at something other than zero at the beginning you might find a whole list of lagged variables in the model pane that you don't want. There is no need to worry. Just highlight each in turn and use the delete key to remove unwanted variables from the list.

When the contents of the Formulate Model dialog box are as shown in Figure 5.8 click **OK** to move on.

Next you come to the Estimate Model dialog box (Figure 5.9). Notice that the available sample period has been reduced to 1961 to 1988. The observation for 1960 has been lost due to the inclusion of the lagged dependent variable. For bigger data sets you can select various subsamples to use for estimation, enabling you to test for

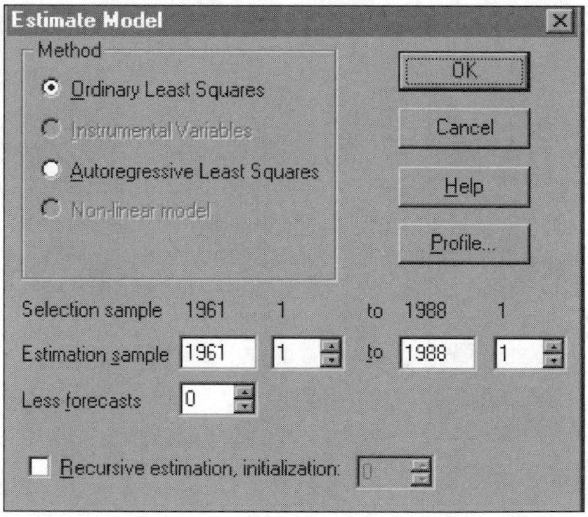

**Fig. 5.9**   PcGive Estimate Model dialog box.

```
EQ( 1) Modeling LQ by OLS (using Tansel.xls)
The present sample is: 1961 to 1988

Variable    Coefficient   Std.Error    t-value     t-prob    PartR^2
Constant       -3.0190      0.84557     -3.570      0.0017    0.3669
LY              0.44695     0.12060      3.706      0.0012    0.3844
LP             -0.17208     0.088138    -1.952      0.0637    0.1477
D82_88         -0.086711    0.026382    -3.287      0.0034    0.3293
D86_88         -0.050239    0.044091    -1.139      0.2668    0.0557
LQ_1            0.31098     0.17307      1.797      0.0861    0.1280

R^2 = 0.884132 F(5,22) = 33.574 [0.0000] \sigma = 0.0398026 DW = 2.01
RSS = 0.03485342758 for 6 variables and 28 observations
```

Fig. 5.10   The basic PcGive regression results for Tansel's Model 1.

parameter stability over time. You can also exclude observations at the end of the sample (through the Less forecasts setting) to be used for post sample predictive testing. This can play an important part in the verification of a model.

A limited number of estimation techniques other than ordinary least squares (OLS) are available in PcGive, although some can only be accessed if appropriate settings have been made in the Model Formulation or Algebra boxes. Here we just want to use OLS so you can click **OK** to move on. (You can use the **P**rofile button to change the default settings for the regression results. For example, you can ensure that a correlation matrix is printed to help you assess whether there might be a problem of multicollinearity.)

Some messages will appear about calculating second moments etc. When things stop you can go to the Results window in GiveWin to look at your regression results. They should be as shown in Figure 5.10.

Reassuringly they are the same as we obtained using TSP (although not as extensive). With PcGive you can get additional diagnostic statistics for a regression, either by changing the Profile before you estimate the model, or afterwards by using the **T**est menu.

Click **T**est and then Test S**u**mmary (alternatively use the ALT+U keys or click on the Test Summary icon – point the mouse at each icon in turn and PcGive will tell you what they represent). Some additional diagnostic statistics will be sent to the Results window, as shown in Figure 5.11.

These are only the basic default set of diagnostic statistics. You can get more details if you click **T**est and then **T**est again. You can then mark various options in the

```
AR 1- 2 F( 2, 20)  =    2.3114     [0.1250]
ARCH 1 F( 1, 20)   =    1.7825     [0.1968]
Normality Chi^2(2) =    0.4045     [0.8169]
Xi^2   F( 8, 13)   =    2.4812     [0.0702]
RESET  F( 1, 21)   =    0.62903    [0.4366]
```

Fig. 5.11   The default diagnostic statistics from PcGive.

Diagnostic Test dialog box to get a more extensive set of test statistics. You will need to consult an econometrics textbook in order to understand the meaning and purpose of each test. (You can also look through PcGive's Help screens as they give quite a lot of information about each test.) As a general principle though you are looking for a model that shows no signs of misspecification, with all the diagnostic statistics taking "low" values so that the probability values are above 0.05. This is what happens with Tansel's Model 1, so there would appear to be no reason to think that the model is unsuitable. (Where diagnostic test statistics are so large that the probability value falls below the significance levels of 5% or 1%, PcGive will draw your attention to the fact by marking them with one or two asterisks.)

PcGive offers a range of post-regression graphics that can enable you to visually judge the performance of the model. We will look at just one such graph here but you should investigate the other options yourself. From the PcGive menu click **T**est and then Graphic Analysis (or press the ALT+G keys or click on the Graphic Analysis icon) (Figure 5.12).

Click on the box next to **A**ctual and fitted values and PcGive will produce the graph shown in Figure 5.13. You will have to go back to GiveWin and look in the PcGive graphics window to find it. (I have slightly modified the appearance of the graph so that the two lines can be distinguished in black and white print.)

The graph shows that the fitted model broadly tracks the actual series quite well, although there are sequences of quite large over- and underpredictions. If you wish you can save or print the graph (with or without editing).

To complete this exercise using PcGive we must go back and estimate Tansel's second model (the one that drops the second dummy variable). Return to PcGive and the Model Formulate box. Highlight and then delete the D86_88 dummy. Click **OK** and then **OK** again to estimate the revised model. The results should be as shown in Figure 5.14.

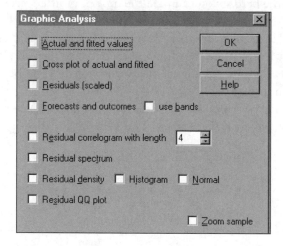

**Fig. 5.12**    PcGive's Graphic Analysis dialog box.

**Fig. 5.13** A graph of the actual and fitted values for Tansel's Model 1.

```
EQ( 2) Modeling LQ by OLS (using Tansel.xls)
The present sample is: 1961 to 1988

Variable    Coefficient   Std.Error    t-value      t-prob    PartR^2
Constant     -2.6761       0.79530     -3.365       0.0027    0.3299
LY            0.39543      0.11253      3.514       0.0019    0.3493
LP           -0.19167      0.087004    -2.203       0.0379    0.1742
D82_88       -0.087555     0.026542    -3.299       0.0031    0.3212
LQ_1          0.42990      0.13895      3.094       0.0051    0.2939

R^2 = 0.877294  F(4,23) = 41.11 [0.0000] \sigma = 0.0400599 DW = 2.24
RSS = 0.03691022722 for 5 variables and 28 observations
```

**Fig. 5.14** The PcGive results for Tansel's Model 2.

You can even get PcGive to work out the long-run solution for you. Select **T**est, **D**ynamic Analysis and then Static long-run solution (and click **OK**). You should get what you see in Figure 5.15 (together with some other results that we shall ignore here). The long-run elasticities are exactly the same as we found with TSP. The values in parentheses are the standard errors.

```
Solved Static Long Run equation
     LQ =  -4.694         +0.6936 LY      -0.3362 LP
(SE)     (  0.8564)       (  0.1115)      (  0.1305)
           -0.1536 D82_88
         (  0.04685)
```

**Fig. 5.15** The Solved Static Long Run equation in PcGive.

This brief introduction to the use of PcGive has only been able to focus on some basic features of the program. However, you should have seen enough to convince you that the package provides a user-friendly framework within which to conduct econometric analysis. It combines the benefits of a modern desktop style (Windows) interface with the tools that are today required for applied econometric modeling. PcGive does not attempt to provide a comprehensive set of procedures for econometric modeling. Rather it focuses principally on the estimation and testing of single equation dynamic models using time series data. It was designed for economists wishing to follow the general to specific modeling methodology advocated by Hendry (see, for example, Hendry, 1995) (The companion program PcFiml should be used when working with models containing more than one equation and endogenous variable.)

If the econometrics software available to you at your institution does not include either TSP or PcGive it is probable that it will nevertheless have some features in common with one or other of the programs covered here so you should be able to work out how to modify the instructions that have been described here. Don't forget to check my web site for further information about other packages. (The contrast between the two packages described here is not quite as great as it used to be. It is possible to set up a PcGive job to run in batch mode. Also you can now run TSP programs with the GiveWin interface.)

## 5.4   More advanced time series analysis with econometrics packages

Although all the packages listed in Table 5.1, including TSP and PcGive, can be used by novices for simple regression work, they are also intended to be used by applied economists and researchers for more advanced types of modeling and testing. In this section we shall see how packages like PcGive incorporate certain tests and procedures that are needed for practical work in modern applied time series econometrics.

### Trends and unit roots

In the last twenty to thirty years econometricians and applied economists have come to realize that the estimation and testing of econometric models based on time series data needs to be approached much more carefully than might be apparent from the examples we have looked at so far. In particular, one needs to have an appreciation of the time series properties of the series themselves. If they are exhibiting *trend* behavior, increasing or decreasing over time rather than fluctuating around a constant mean value, then simple regressions based on the original series (or their logarithms) may give rise to *spurious* regression results (see Granger and Newbold, 1974). Indeed Tansel's study of cigarette consumption in Turkey has been attacked on these very grounds – see Cameron and Collins (1998). To take another example, if one is examining the relationship between consumption and income, if both series are growing over time a high R-squared value may simply reflect this fact, rather than saying anything about the strength of the relationship between the variables. (Remember R-squared tries to account for the observed variation in the dependent variable *about its mean*. If that mean is continually changing the rationale of the statistic is removed.)

Trends can take different forms. One type of trend is purely *deterministic* and it can be removed by including a simple time trend in the regression equation (i.e. a variable whose values go up in steps of one as you move through time). So you could define a variable, call it TREND, and give it values 1, 2, ,3, 4 etc., and then include it in your regression equation. PcGive provides such a variable in its list of "special" (i.e. predefined) variables.

However, upward (or downward) trends that we observe in many time series are *stochastic* in form. For example, suppose the current value of a series ($Z_t$ say) is dependent on its previous value, $Z_{t-1}$ plus a random error $\varepsilon_t$, that is, it follows a stochastic process of the form

$$Z_t = \rho\, Z_{t-1} + \varepsilon_t \qquad\qquad \text{Equation 5.2}$$

where the parameter $\rho$ (rho) can be called the *autoregressive* parameter. We can call this a first-order autoregressive process because our model has Z depending on its own previous value. It is easy to demonstrate that so long as $\rho$ is within the range $-1$ to $+1$ (but not equal to either $-1$ or $+1$) the Z series will not trend upwards or downwards over time. So long as $\rho$ is between $-1$ and $+1$ the series will fluctuate around a constant mean – it will be a *stationary* series.

## Exercise

Why not check this out using your spreadsheet software? Store a starting value of Z ($Z_0$) and the value for $\rho$ in key cells at the top of the spreadsheet. Create a column containing the values for the different time periods t = 0, 1, 2, 3, .... Then generate a set of independent random standard normal values for the $\varepsilon_t$ (using **T**ools/ Data Analysis/ Random Number Generation). Now you can create the column of Z values. The first value simply copies the starting value of $Z_0$ from your key cell. The next value of Z, for t = 1, would make it $\rho$ times $Z_0$ plus the first value of epsilon. You could then copy down the formula and examine the plot of Z against t. Experiment with different values of $\rho$, including $\rho = 1$, to see how the graph plot changes shape. Add a further column showing the first differences of Z and examine its graph in a case where $\rho = 1$. You can find a completed worksheet like this called TSP&DSP.XLS on my web site.

Note that, strictly, stationarity requires not just a constant mean for the series but also a constant variance and autocovariance between terms. In this simple case these will all be guaranteed if $\frac{1}{2}r\frac{1}{2} < 1$. If r is greater than 1 in absolute value the series would show explosive growth or decline. These cases are of limited relevance for economic series. But if $\rho = 1$ the series is what we call a *random walk* and Z will exhibit trend behavior. If $\rho = 1$ the process is said to have a *unit root* and from this simple model we can see that a unit root means that the series cannot be stationary. However, the first difference of the series $Z_t - Z_{t-1} = \Delta Z_t$ will be stationary. A process that does not need to be differenced to achieve stationarity is said to be I(0). If the series has to be differenced (once) to obtain a stationary series it is said to be I(1). In general if a series has to be differenced d times for it to become stationary it would be described as I(d).

The unit root is actually the root of the so-called *characteristic equation* involving the lag operator L. We can define the lag operator L such that $L Z_t = Z_{t-1}$. Then we can write Equation 5.2 as $Z_t = \rho L Z_t + \varepsilon_t$. After taking the $\rho L Z_t$ across to the left hand side of the equation and extracting the factor $(1 - \rho L)$ we get $(1 - \rho L) Z_t = \varepsilon_t$. The characteristic equation $1 - \rho L = 0$ has a unit root for L if $\rho = 1$ (since then $L = 1$). Stationarity requires $L = 1/\rho$ to be *greater* than one in absolute terms – which of course occurs if $\rho$ is less than 1 in absolute terms.

Of course, a real series is likely to be generated by a more complicated process than the simple first-order one described above. However, it is important to establish whether or not the series is stationary, or whether it has a unit root (in which case we should then look at the differenced series to see if that is stationary). A number of unit root tests have been developed, the most widely used one being the *Augmented Dickey–Fuller* (ADF) test and these are implemented in many modern econometrics packages.

The original *Dickey–Fuller* test (Dickey and Fuller, 1979) was based on an examination of a model of the series taking the form

$$\Delta Z_t = \alpha + \phi Z_{t-1} + \varepsilon_t \qquad\qquad \text{Equation 5.3}$$

This is similar to our original Equation 5.2 except that (a) there is an additional constant term $\alpha$, (b) the left hand side of the equation has the first difference of Z rather than Z and (c) the coefficient of $Z_{t-1}$ is $\phi$ rather than $\rho$. However, ignoring for the moment the constant term $\alpha$, the two equations are identical if we let $\phi = \rho - 1$. If you subtract $Z_{t-1}$ from both sides of Equation 5.2 what you have is then identical to Equation 5.3, apart from $\alpha$. Testing to see if $\rho = 1$ is then equivalent to testing to see if $\phi = 0$. Apart from $\alpha$ Equation 5.3 is just a reparameterized version of Equation 5.2. The inclusion of the $\alpha$ term means that when there is a unit root the process is a *random walk with drift*.

So to recap, the null hypothesis for the test is $\rho = 1$ or $\phi = 0$. The series has a unit root and is nonstationary. We would reject this null hypothesis and accept the alternative $\rho < 1$ or $\phi < 0$ if the estimated value of $\phi$ is sufficiently negative. There are a number of problems we must address, however. If the null hypothesis was to be true and the process is nonstationary then we cannot use the ordinary t test. The distribution of the test statistic will not follow the standard t distribution and will not even be symmetrical. However, econometricians, beginning with Dickey and Fuller, have carried out a large number of simulations to see what the distribution would be like for various degrees of freedom. Tables of critical values have been produced but they can also be generated in modern software packages such as TSP, PcGive etc..

A further problem is that a real time series could contain a deterministic trend element as well as a stochastic trend. Furthermore, in modeling the process that generates the series it may be necessary to allow for additional lagged values of the differenced series in the test equation so that one can be satisfied that the remaining error term is free of autocorrelation i.e. it is "white noise". So the test for stationarity that is most frequently used is what is known as the *augmented Dickey–Fuller* test (or the ADF test) and it is based on an equation such as Equation 5.4.

$$\Delta Z_t = \alpha + \beta \text{TREND} + \phi Z_{t-1} + \gamma_1 \Delta Z_{t-1} + \ldots + \gamma_s \Delta Z_{t-s} + \varepsilon_t \qquad \text{Equation 5.4}$$

Since we do not know in advance what maximum lag s will be required, in practice the equation will be estimated for various values of s.

If an ADF test suggests that a series Z is I(1) it is usual to conduct a further ADF test on the differenced series $\Delta Z$ which should, of course, be stationary.

Let's now illustrate unit-root testing with our two packages using data from Tansel's study.

## Practical 5.2 Unit-root tests of Tansel's cigarette consumption data

As we noted above, Cameron and Collins (1998) have cast doubt on the validity of Tansel's results because, after conducting unit-root tests on the series used, they find that the LQ, LY and LP series are all nonstationary.

Modern econometrics software packages such as PcGive incorporate automated unit-root testing procedures. If PcGive is available to you run the program and load the Tansel data.

The unit-root testing routine can be called up in PcGive from the **D**ata menu by selecting Descriptive Statistics (Figure 5.16).

Click on the box next to **U**nit-root tests and highlight the variable in the database that is to be tested (here LQ). As you can see the test can be carried out with or without a constant. Unless you have reason to believe that the variable in question has a zero mean it is best to include the constant intercept as we have done here. It is also possible to include both the constant and a linear trend (you wouldn't want to include the trend but not the constant). Cameron and Collins test both with and without the trend. First let's conduct the test without it.

Next remember that one should add in extra lags of the first differences of the variable to ensure that the residuals are "white noise". In PcGive you enter the maximum number of lags that you want to try in the dialog box. Here a value of 5 has been chosen. PcGive offers two ways of looking at the results from the unit root tests. To

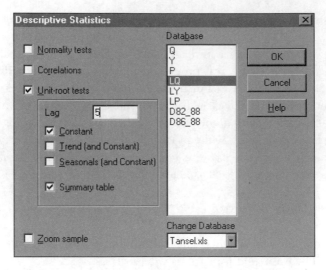

**Fig. 5.16**   The PcGive Descriptive Statistics dialog box.

help with the decision about how many lags to include you can select a S<u>u</u>mmary table. This will show the summary results from a series of tests, beginning with the maximum lag that you have asked for, running down to an equation with no lagged term (Figure 5.17).

The first column is the calculated t-adf value, which is the ADF test statistic. Then comes the estimated value of the parameter $\phi$ (although it is called beta Y_1 here), followed by the standard error. The next three columns give the lag length that has been used, the t-value of the highest lag (of $\gamma_s$, s = 5, 4, 3, 2, 1) followed by the t-probability of that lag. The PcGive manual says that the suggested strategy is to select the highest s with a significant last $\gamma_s$ which here would be a lag of 5. This would imply a t-adf value of −2.3159 which is not far enough below zero for us to reject the null of a unit root. Notice the Critical values at 5% = −2.997 is automatically generated by the program.

Cameron and Collins (who used SHAZAM) say that the number of lagged terms to be included in their ADF test were chosen on the basis of R-squared (adjusted for

```
Unit-root tests 1966 to 1988
Critical values: 5%=-2.997 1%=-3.75; Constant included

     t-adf    beta Y_1   \sigma    lag  t-DY_lag  t-prob    F-prob
LQ  -2.3159   0.71955   0.051677    5   1.8864   0.0775
LQ  -1.8799   0.75960   0.055429    4   1.0948   0.2889    0.0775
LQ  -1.7027   0.78457   0.055734    3   0.61166  0.5484    0.1163
LQ  -1.6335   0.80196   0.054808    2   0.97306  0.3428    0.1894
LQ  -1.5052   0.81987   0.054736    1  -0.89437  0.3818    0.2203
LQ  -1.7099   0.79991   0.054474    0                      0.2549
```

**Fig. 5.17**   A unit-root test summary table from PcGive.

differences in degrees of freedom). Their summary results show that they concluded that no lag needed to be included and so the relevant calculated value of the test statistic is $-1.7099$ or $-1.71$ when rounded to two decimal places. This seems slightly odd as the F-probability given in the final column of the PcGive Summary table indicates the significance level of the F-test on the lags dropped up to that point. While that ought to point to the same lag as the R-squared criterion, it too suggests a maximum lag as high as 5 will be needed.

In fact neither the criterion used by Cameron and Collins nor that suggested in the PcGive manual quite corresponds to the need to ensure "white noise" residuals. Without any further information on them we can't be sure even that 5 lags will be enough. You can, however, get a full set of results from PcGive with a specified maximum lag (Figure 5.18) and the DW statistic of 2.21 suggests that the residuals are free from autocorrelation.

```
Unit-root  tests  for  LQ
The  present  sample  is:  1966  to  1988

Augmented  Dickey-Fuller  test  for  LQ;  DLQ  on
Variable    Coefficient    Std.Error    t-value
Constant     0.22508       0.098326      2.289
LQ_1        -0.28045       0.12110      -2.316
DLQ_1       -0.19757       0.20850      -0.948
DLQ_2        0.15444       0.21760       0.710
DLQ_3        0.17406       0.22186       0.785
DLQ_4        0.39357       0.23173       1.698
DLQ_5        0.44062       0.23357       1.886

\sigma  =  0.0516768  DW  =  2.21  DW(LQ)  =  0.3436 ADF(LQ)  =  -2.316
Critical  values  used  in  ADF  test:  5%=-2.997  1%=-3.75
RSS  =  0.04272780698  for  7  variables  and  23  observations
```

**Fig. 5.18** The full table of results from PcGive for a unit-root test.

However many lags are added here we would still reach the same conclusion, namely that the null hypothesis of a unit root cannot be rejected for this series. It is not stationary (over this period) and consequently the results given in Tansel (1993) are suspect.

## Find out

Does the econometrics package in use at your university have a built-in procedure for testing for unit roots?

If it does try to replicate the unit-root test on LQ shown here.

## Cointegration and error correction mechanisms

Applied economists and econometricians who investigate time series data to see if there is any evidence of a relationship between two or more variables and who find that the individual variables have unit roots (that is they are I(1) series – integrated of order one) do not have to abandon their work. Although the partial adjustment model, as used by Tansel, is invalidated because the variables used in the formulation are nonstationary, it may be possible to obtain satisfactory results by constructing and estimating models based on the related concepts of *cointegration* and *error correction mechanisms (ECMs)*. (Hendry now prefers the term equilibrium correction mechanisms. Because the initials are the same the ECM acronym can still be used.)

The notion of cointegration was originally proposed by Granger (1981) and developed in many other papers, especially Granger (1986) and Engle and Granger (1987).

Suppose we have two series $x_t$ and $y_t$ that have both been found to be I(1). The pair of series is said to be cointegrated if a linear combination of the series is I(0). So if

$$y_t = \alpha + \beta x_t + u_t \qquad\qquad \text{Equation 5.5}$$

and u is I(0) then $x_t$ and $y_t$ are cointegrated. Although the series $x_t$ and $y_t$ may diverge from one another in the short run, in the long run they will be tied together through the behavior of economic agents (perhaps via market forces) so that they follow a common trend and remain in a fixed relationship to each other on average.

The error correction form of dynamic specification has been used extensively in applied econometric modeling since its appearance in the study of UK consumption expenditure in Davidson, Hendry, Srba and Yeo (1978).

A simple form of error correction model involving two variables x and y is shown in Equation 5.6.

$$\Delta y_t = \mu + \delta \Delta x_t - \lambda (y_{t-1} - \beta x_{t-1}) + \varepsilon_t \qquad\qquad \text{Equation 5.6}$$

where $\varepsilon$ is a "white noise" disturbance term and $\mu$, $\delta$, $\lambda$ and $\beta$ are parameters.

$\delta$ measures the short-run impact on y of changes in x, while $\beta$ measures the long-run effect; $\lambda$ measures the extent to which agents correct for any disequilibrium of the system in the previous period; $\mu$ is a constant intercept which may, or may not, be needed. Most actual error correction models are likely to involve slightly more complex short-run dynamics with sufficient lagged values of $\Delta x$ and $\Delta y$ appearing on the right hand side of the equation to ensure that the disturbance is "white noise".

Engle and Granger (1987) showed that when two series are cointegrated there will also be an error correction representation of the relationship between the series. They proposed a two-stage procedure for estimating the parameters of the model. First, the static equation relating the variables (Equation 5.5) is estimated. (This is also known as the *cointegrating regression*.) If the two variables are cointegrated then the OLS estimators for this regression will be "super consistent" (a result due to Stock (1987)) so that, *provided the sample is large enough*, the estimates obtained from this regression can be regarded as suitable estimates of the long-run (equilibrium) relationship between the variables.

Thus the residual from this regression ($\hat{u}_t = \hat{y}_t - \hat{\alpha} - \hat{\beta}x_t$) is a measure of the disequilibrium in the relationship in period t. So in the second stage of the Engle–Granger procedure its lagged value can be used in the short-run error correction equation in place of $y_{t-1} - \beta x_{t-1}$.

## Practical 5.3  Cointegration analysis of the advertising–sales relationship

To provide a practical illustration of these ideas, and see how they can be implemented in modern econometrics software such as PcGive, we look at a study of the advertising–sales relationship by Baghestani (1991).

Baghestani applied the Engle–Granger two-step procedure to a well-known set of data that has frequently been used in studies of the advertising–sales relationship. The data, given in full in Table 5.3 and shown graphically in Figure 5.19, consist of annual observations for the period 1907–1960 of the sales revenue and advertising expenditure of the Lydia Pinkham Company (both series in \$US

**Table 5.3**  The Lydia Pinkham sales and advertising data.

| Date | Sales (S) | Advertising (A) | Date | Sales (S) | Advertising (A) | Date | Sales (S) | Advertising (A) |
|------|-----------|-----------------|------|-----------|-----------------|------|-----------|-----------------|
| 1907 | 1016 | 608 | 1925 | 3438 | 1800 | 1943 | 2602 | 1164 |
| 1908 | 921 | 451 | 1926 | 2917 | 1941 | 1944 | 2518 | 1102 |
| 1909 | 934 | 529 | 1927 | 2359 | 1229 | 1945 | 2637 | 1145 |
| 1910 | 976 | 543 | 1928 | 2240 | 1373 | 1946 | 2177 | 1012 |
| 1911 | 930 | 525 | 1929 | 2196 | 1611 | 1947 | 1920 | 836 |
| 1912 | 1052 | 549 | 1930 | 2111 | 1568 | 1948 | 1910 | 941 |
| 1913 | 1184 | 525 | 1931 | 1806 | 983 | 1949 | 1984 | 981 |
| 1914 | 1089 | 578 | 1932 | 1644 | 1046 | 1950 | 1787 | 974 |
| 1915 | 1087 | 609 | 1933 | 1814 | 1453 | 1951 | 1689 | 766 |
| 1916 | 1154 | 504 | 1934 | 1770 | 1504 | 1952 | 1866 | 920 |
| 1917 | 1330 | 752 | 1935 | 1518 | 807 | 1953 | 1896 | 964 |
| 1918 | 1980 | 613 | 1936 | 1103 | 339 | 1954 | 1684 | 811 |
| 1919 | 2223 | 862 | 1937 | 1266 | 562 | 1955 | 1633 | 789 |
| 1920 | 2203 | 866 | 1938 | 1473 | 745 | 1956 | 1657 | 802 |
| 1921 | 2514 | 1016 | 1939 | 1423 | 749 | 1957 | 1569 | 770 |
| 1922 | 2726 | 1360 | 1940 | 1767 | 862 | 1958 | 1390 | 639 |
| 1923 | 3185 | 1482 | 1941 | 2161 | 1034 | 1959 | 1387 | 644 |
| 1924 | 3351 | 1608 | 1942 | 2336 | 1054 | 1960 | 1289 | 564 |

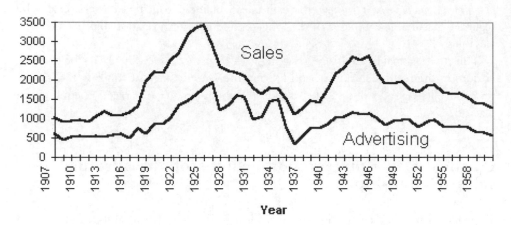

**Fig. 5.19** Time series plot of the Lydia Pinkham Company sales and advertising data.

thousands). The graph suggests that the series maintain a close relationship with each other over time. (The Lydia Pinkham Company was a family owned company that produced a single product, a herbal remedy. There were no close substitutes available on the market. The data came into the public domain as the result of a court case following a family argument. The data have been most recently published in Zanias, 1994).

Baghestani first examines the time series properties of each series using Dickey–Fuller and Augmented Dickey–Fuller tests. He concludes that both series are I(1). Use your econometrics software to confirm these results. Examine A, S, ΔA and ΔS. Use up to five lagged differences for the ADF tests.

> **Note**
>
> Baghestani conducted both his DF and his ADF tests without a constant term. Confirm that although the computed and critical t-values are different when one includes a constant term in the tests, the overall conclusions are unaffected.

Next, Baghestani estimated two cointegrating regressions. In one regression A was treated as the dependent variable and S as the independent variable, while in the other regression the roles were reversed.

Use your software to replicate these results. Figure 5.20 shows the results I obtained using PcGive. Before you run the regressions note that you need to save the residuals from each regression. Adopt the same names used by Baghestani, EA and ES respectively.

**Note**

In PcGive you can store the residuals immediately after running a regression by going to the test menu and selecting Store in Database. If you are using a different package find out how to do this with your software.

```
EQ( 1) Modeling ads by OLS (using Pinkham.wk1)
The present sample is: 1907 to 1960

Variable   Coefficient   Std.Error   t-value   t-prob    PartR^2
Constant        27.930      84.748     0.330    0.7430     0.0021
sales          0.49554     0.043823   11.308    0.0000     0.7109

R^2 = 0.710901 F(1,52) = 127.87 [0.0000] \sigma = 201.865 DW =
0.793
RSS = 2118973.962 for 2 variables and 54 observations

EQ( 2) Modeling sales by OLS (using Pinkham.wk1)
The present sample is: 1907 to 1960

Variable   Coefficient   Std.Error   t-value   t-prob    PartR^2
Constant        488.83     127.44      3.836    0.0003     0.2205
ads            1.4346      0.12687    11.308    0.0000     0.7109

R^2 = 0.710901 F(1,52) = 127.87 [0.0000] \sigma = 343.466 DW =
0.582
RSS = 6134380.667 for 2 variables and 54 observations
```

**Fig. 5.20** The cointegrating regression results for the sales and advertising series.

The next step is to use DF and ADF tests on these residuals to check that they are stationary. Use your software to try to replicate the test results shown in Figure 5.21. Note that the additional regressions (3) and (5) which use DEA and DES as the dependent variable are equivalent to the ADF tests. If your software does not include a specific routine for conducting ADF tests you can still formulate the regression model on which it is based as shown here. However, in this case you will have to refer to tables for the critical values of the t-statistic as they will not be generated for you by the software. The other reason why they have been estimated separately here is so that we can check whether some intermediate lagged augmentation terms could be eliminated. Regressions (4) and (6) omit such terms and it is interesting to note that this results in insignificant modified ADF statistics for both variables. Thus the results suggest that the sales and advertising series are cointegrated.

Having satisfied himself that sales and advertising are cointegrated, Baghestani was then in a position to examine the short-run dynamics of the relationship by estimating a pair of error correction mechanism (ECM) models (one for each variable) each of which contains, amongst other terms, the lagged residuals from the relevant cointegrating regression (the ECM term).

**Tests of the EA residuals**
Unit-root tests for EA
The present sample is: 1908 to 1960
Dickey-Fuller test for EA; DEA on
Variable    Coefficient    Std.Error    t-value
EA_1            -0.39751      0.11087      -3.585

\sigma = 160.992 DW = 1.94 DW(EA) = 0.7898 DF(EA) = -3.585**
Critical values used in DF test: 5%=-1.947 1%=-2.606
RSS = 1347749.831 for 1 variables and 53 observations

Unit-root tests for EA
The present sample is: 1913 to 1960

Augmented Dickey-Fuller test for EA; DEA on
Variable    Coefficient    Std.Error    t-value
EA_1           -0.35695       0.15823     -2.256
DEA_1          -0.041728      0.18426     -0.226
DEA_2          -0.10727       0.18408     -0.583
DEA_3          -0.034846      0.17417     -0.200
DEA_4           0.29031       0.15853      1.831
DEA_5           0.16512       0.15188      1.087

\sigma = 162.887 DW = 2.01 DW(EA) = 0.7849 ADF(EA) = -2.256*
Critical values used in ADF test: 5%=-1.948 1%=-2.611
RSS = 1114348.843 for 6 variables and 48 observations

Unit-root tests for ES
The present sample is: 1908 to 1960

Dickey-Fuller test for ES; DES on
Variable    Coefficient    Std.Error    t-value
ES_1            -0.30050      0.097201     -3.092

\sigma = 240.743 DW = 2.02 DW(ES) = 0.5905 DF(ES) = -3.092**
Critical values used in DF test: 5%=-1.947 1%=-2.606
RSS = 3013786.469 for 1 variables and 53 observations

Unit-root tests for ES
The present sample is: 1913 to 1960

Augmented Dickey-Fuller test for ES; DES on
Variable    Coefficient    Std.Error    t-value
ES_1           -0.39791       0.13813     -2.881
DES_1           0.031037      0.16339      0.257
DES_3           0.087791      0.15726      0.558
DES_4           0.32519       0.14980      2.171
DES_5           0.21966       0.14794      1.485

\sigma = 248.231 DW = 2.07 DW(ES) = 0.6284 ADF(ES) = -2.881**
Critical values used in ADF test: 5%=-1.948 1%=-2.611
RSS = 2587982.69 for 6 variables and 48 observations

EQ( 3) Modeling DEA by OLS (using Pinkham.wk1)
The present sample is: 1913 to 1960

Variable    Coefficient    Std.Error    t-value    t-prob    PartR^2
DEA_1          -0.041728      0.18426     -0.226    0.8219    0.0012
DEA_2          -0.10727       0.18408     -0.583    0.5632    0.0080
DEA_3          -0.034846      0.17417     -0.200    0.8424    0.0010
DEA_4           0.29031       0.15853      1.831    0.0742    0.0739

```
DEA_5          0.16512     0.15188      1.087      0.2832     0.0274
EA_1          -0.35695     0.15823     -2.256      0.0293     0.1081


R^2 = 0.329636 \sigma = 162.887 DW = 2.01
* R^2 does NOT allow for the mean *
RSS = 1114348.843 for 6 variables and 48 observations


AR 1- 2 F( 2, 40)   =      0.8196      [0.4479]
ARCH 1 F( 1, 40)    =      1.0586      [0.3097]
Normality Chi^2(2)  =      3.5464      [0.1698]
Xi^2   F(12, 29)    =      0.98497     [0.4853]
Xi*Xj  F(27, 14)    =      1.4708      [0.2266]
RESET  F( 1, 41)    =      3.9866      [0.0525]


EQ( 4) Modeling DEA by OLS (using Pinkham.wk1)
The present sample is: 1913 to 1960

Variable   Coefficient  Std.Error    t-value     t-prob    PartR^2
DEA_4          0.33568     0.12444      2.698      0.0098     0.1392
DEA_5          0.19267     0.12646      1.524      0.1346     0.0491
EA_1          -0.40389     0.11192     -3.609      0.0008     0.2244


R^2 = 0.323835 \sigma = 158.043 DW = 2.01
* R^2 does NOT allow for the mean *
RSS = 1123991.376 for 3 variables and 48 observations


AR 1- 2 F( 2, 43)   =      0.59418     [0.5565]
ARCH 1 F( 1, 43)    =      1.3271      [0.2557]
Normality Chi^2(2)  =      2.9861      [0.2247]
Xi^2  F( 6, 38)     =      1.2465      [0.3049]
Xi*Xj F( 9, 35)     =      0.90269     [0.5335]
RESET F( 1, 44)     =      2.5947      [0.1144]


EQ( 5) Modeling DES by OLS (using Pinkham.wk1)
The present sample is: 1913 to 1960

Variable   Coefficient  Std.Error    t-value     t-prob    PartR^2
DES_1          0.031037    0.16391      0.189      0.8507     0.0009
DES_2          0.041987    0.16339      0.257      0.7985     0.0016
DES_3          0.087791    0.15726      0.558      0.5796     0.0074
DES_4          0.32519     0.14980      2.171      0.0356     0.1009
DES_5          0.21966     0.14794      1.485      0.1451     0.0499
ES_1          -0.39791     0.13813     -2.881      0.0062     0.1650


R^2 = 0.267361 \sigma = 248.231 DW = 2.07
* R^2 does NOT allow for the mean *
RSS = 2587982.69 for 6 variables and 48 observations


AR 1- 2 F( 2, 40)   =      1.8509      [0.1703]
ARCH 1 F( 1, 40)    =      0.24861     [0.6208]
Normality Chi^2(2)  =      5.8535      [0.0536]
Xi^2   F(12, 29)    =      0.22153     [0.9958]
Xi*Xj  F(27, 14)    =      1.1004      [0.4395]
RESET  F( 1, 41)    =      0.72977     [0.3979]


EQ( 6) Modeling DES by OLS (using Pinkham.wk1)
The present sample is: 1913 to 1960

Variable   Coefficient  Std.Error    t-value     t-prob    PartR^2
DES_4          0.29451     0.13017      2.262      0.0285     0.1021
```

```
DES_5            0.19316      0.13350      1.447      0.1548      0.0445
ES_1            -0.36555      0.10450     -3.498      0.0011      0.2138

R^2  =  0.261892 \sigma  =  240.707  DW =  2.05
*  R^2  does  NOT  allow  for  the  mean  *
RSS  =  2607302.968  for  3  variables  and  48  observations

AR 1- 2 F( 2,  43)    =        0.36938      [0.6933]
ARCH 1 F( 1,  43)    =        0.30016      [0.5866]
Normality Chi^2(2)   =        6.1887       [0.0453]  *
Xi^2    F( 6,  38)    =        0.30111      [0.9325]
Xi*Xj   F( 9,  35)    =        0.40668      [0.9230]
RESET   F( 1,  44)    =        1.6867       [0.2008]
```

Fig. 5.21   Unit-root tests of the residuals from the cointegratimg regressions.

The modeling strategy followed was to include sufficient lagged differences of each variable to ensure that the residual is free of autocorrelation. Then, he sought to remove any terms that appeared not to contribute to the relationship as indicated by very low t-values, provided that the restrictions implied by omitting these variables could be accepted (one can conduct an F-test) and the resulting restricted model is also free of diagnostic problems (this is the so-called *General to Specific* modeling strategy).

So, looking first at the equation for advertising, Baghestani's general ECM model takes the form

$$\Delta A_t = \text{CONSTANT} + g_{1i} \sum_{i=1}^{5} \Delta A_{t-i} + g_{2j} \sum_{i=0}^{5} \Delta S_{t-j} + h_1 \hat{u}_{t-1} + w_{1t} \qquad \text{Equation 5.7}$$

where $w_{1t}$ is the disturbance term for this equation and $\hat{u}_{t-1}$ is the lagged residual from the cointegrating regression of advertising on sales. Baghestani chose to include the current period DS term on the grounds that, with annual data, some of the short-run effect on advertising of a change in sales might begin to be felt within the first year.

A similar model form was adopted for the equation with $\Delta S$ on the left hand side, i.e.

$$\Delta S_t = \text{CONSTANT} + g_{3i} \sum_{i=1}^{5} \Delta S_{t-i} + g_{4j} \sum_{i=0}^{5} \Delta A_{t-j} + h_2 \hat{v}_{t-1} + w_{2t} \qquad \text{Equation 5.8}$$

Here $w_{2t}$ is the disturbance term for this equation and $\hat{v}_{t-1}$ is the lagged residual from the cointegrating regression of sales on advertising.

Attempting to replicate Baghestani's regressions using PcGive I obtained the results in Figure 5.22.

The coefficient estimates, t-values etc. are the same as those found by Baghestani. He gives some diagnostic statistics which show that there are no problems of autocorrelation – something which is confirmed by my results. However, the other diagnostic statistics given by PcGive suggest that the models may not be entirely free of misspecification problems.

```
EQ( 7) Modeling Dads by OLS (using Pinkham.wk1)
The present sample is: 1913 to 1960

Variable   Coefficient  Std.Error   t-value    t-prob    PartR^2
Constant     -2.8794      23.368     -0.123     0.9026    0.0004
Dads_1     -0.012019      0.22258    -0.054     0.9572    0.0001
Dads_2      -0.16051      0.20879    -0.769     0.4472    0.0166
Dads_3     -0.062653      0.18413    -0.340     0.7357    0.0033
Dads_4       0.19946      0.16734     1.192     0.2413    0.0390
Dads_5    -0.0017481      0.16420    -0.011     0.9916    0.0000
Dsales       0.31594      0.12097     2.612     0.0132    0.1631
Dsales_1     0.18584      0.17295     1.075     0.2899    0.0319
Dsales_2  -  0.19853      0.16383    -1.212     0.2337    0.0403
Dsales_3    0.013656      0.16636     0.082     0.9350    0.0002
Dsales_4   -0.044287      0.16050    -0.276     0.7842    0.0022
Dsales_5    0.071587      0.15118     0.474     0.6388    0.0064
EA_1        -0.37879      0.21527    -1.760     0.0872    0.0813


R^2 = 0.642218 F(12,35) = 5.2354 [0.0001] \sigma = 160.332 DW = 1.93
RSS = 899717.9046 for 13 variables and 48 observations


AR 1- 2 F( 2, 33)   =     1.2449    [0.3011]
ARCH 1 F( 1, 33)    =     2.1222    [0.1546]
Normality Chi^2(2)  =     0.75553   [0.6854]
Xi^2   F(24, 10)    =     1.4379    [0.2809]
RESET  F( 1, 34)    =    14.988     [0.0005]  **

EQ(8) Modeling Dsales by OLS (using Pinkham.wk1)
The present sample is: 1913 to 1960

Variable   Coefficient  Std.Error   t-value    t-prob    PartR^2
Constant      5.2675      28.727      0.183     0.8556    0.0010
Dsales_1     0.33129      0.19662     1.685     0.1009    0.0750
Dsales_2     0.17845      0.19692     0.906     0.3710    0.0229
Dsales_3     0.17413      0.19482     0.894     0.3775    0.0223
Dsales_4     0.11517      0.19171     0.601     0.5519    0.0102
Dsales_5     0.16773      0.18548     0.904     0.3720    0.0228
Dads         0.63063      0.19419     3.247     0.0026    0.2315
Dads_1     -0.013588      0.22899    -0.059     0.9530    0.0001
Dads_2      -0.19617      0.22086    -0.888     0.3805    0.0220
Dads_3      -0.12224      0.20815    -0.587     0.5608    0.0098
Dads_4      -0.12506      0.19403    -0.645     0.5234    0.0117
Dads_5      -0.34838      0.18823    -1.851     0.0727    0.0891
ES_1        -0.26409      0.16302    -1.620     0.1142    0.0698

R^2 = 0.52041 F(12,35) = 3.1649 [0.0039] \sigma = 197.672 DW = 2.13
RSS = 1367600.143 for 13 variables and 48 observations

AR 1- 2 F( 2, 33)   =     2.2253    [0.1240]
ARCH 1 F( 1, 33)    =     0.59429   [0.4463]
Normality Chi^2(2)  =    27.941     [0.0000]  **
Xi^2   F(24, 10)    =     0.58968   [0.8603]
RESET  F( 1, 34)    =     0.51171   [0.4793]
```

**Fig. 5.22** Estimates of the general error correction model of advertising and sales.

Use your own econometrics software to replicate these results.

Lastly Baghestani eliminated a number of insignificant terms, namely $\Delta A_{t-1}$, $\Delta A_{t-2}$, $\Delta A_{t-3}$ and $\Delta A_{t-5}$ together with $\Delta S_{t-3}$, $\Delta S_{t-4}$ and $\Delta S_{t-5}$ in the advertising equation and $\Delta S_{t-3}$, $\Delta S_{t-4}$ and $\Delta S_{t-5}$ together with $\Delta A_{t-1}$, $\Delta A_{t-2}$, $\Delta A_{t-3}$ and $\Delta A_{t-4}$ in the sales equation. OLS estimates from PcGive of these final ECM models are given in Figure 5.23. Use your software to see if you can replicate them. (Baghestani actually used two stage least squares (TSLS) rather than OLS for these final regressions in an effort to reduce any bias that might result from measurement errors in the variables. Although the actual numerical values of the two sets of estimates are different, the general pattern of the results is much the same.)

```
EQ( 9) Modeling Dads by OLS (using Pinkham.wk1)
The present sample is: 1913 to 1960

Variable    Coefficient   Std.Error    t-value     t-prob    PartR^2
Constant      -2.7691       21.682      -0.128      0.8990    0.0004
Dads_4         0.24162      0.10323      2.341      0.0241    0.1154
Dsales         0.33329      0.10421      3.198      0.0026    0.1958
Dsales_1       0.19545      0.11098      1.761      0.0855    0.0688
Dsales_2      -0.29769      0.10095     -2.949      0.0052    0.1715
EA_1          -0.38840      0.11988     -3.240      0.0023    0.2000

R^2 = 0.62461 F(5,42) = 13.977 [0.0000] \sigma = 149.92 DW = 1.96
RSS = 943995.4833 for 6 variables and 48 observations

AR 1- 2 F( 2, 40)   =       0.77742        [0.4664]
ARCH 1 F( 1, 40)    =       2.4446         [0.1258]
Normality Chi^2(2)  =       0.59894        [0.7412]
Xi^2    F(10, 31)   =       3.2373         [0.0058]  **
Xi*Xj   F(20, 21)   =       3.7717         [0.0019]  **
RESET   F( 1, 41)   =      12.634          [0.0010]  **


EQ(10) Modeling Dsales by OLS (using Pinkham.wk1)
The present sample is: 1913 to 1960

Variable    Coefficient   Std.Error    t-value     t-prob    PartR^2
Constant       6.9051       27.038       0.255      0.7997    0.0016
Dsales_1       0.27649      0.13893      1.990      0.0531    0.0862
Dsales_2       0.15278      0.14845      1.029      0.3093    0.0246
Dads           0.68938      0.15911      4.333      0.0001    0.3089
Dads_5        -0.19546      0.12126     -1.612      0.1145    0.0583
ES_1          -0.17426      0.10400     -1.676      0.1012    0.0627

R^2 = 0.489107 F(5,42) = 8.0418 [0.0000] \sigma = 186.245 DW = 2.15
RSS = 1456865.189 for 6 variables and 48 observations

AR 1- 2 F( 2, 40)   =       0.68323        [0.5108]
ARCH 1 F( 1, 40)    =       0.6816         [0.4139]
Normality Chi^2(2)  =      30.42           [0.0000]  **
Xi^2    F(10, 31)   =       0.17088        [0.9972]
Xi*Xj   F(20, 21)   =       0.15426        [1.0000]
RESET   F( 1, 41)   =       0.1476         [0.7028]
```

**Fig. 5.23**   OLS estimates of the restricted error correction model of advertising and sales.

As Baghestani remarks, these results provide information on the short-run dynamic adjustment of the advertising–sales relationship. For example, looking at EQ (9) in Figure 5.23, the response of advertising to departures from the long-run equilibrium relationship of EA = A – 27.93 – 0.49S (from EQ (1), Figure 5.20) is indicated by the coefficient of –0.388 for the ECM term. This suggests that less than 40% of the adjustment towards the long-run equilibrium position occurred within the first year through changes in the company's advertising expenditure. The results from EQ (10) (Figure 5.23) suggest that in the short run sales responded to departures from the long-run equilibrium relationship of ES = S – 488.83 – 1.43 (from EQ(2) in Figure 5.20) with a coefficient estimate of below 0.2 in absolute value. However in the long run it appears that the Pinkham company sought to maintain a relationship between advertising expenditure and sales with a slope of just under a half (0.49 from EQ(1)).

*Note:* It has recently been argued by Gerrard and Godfrey (1998), following an earlier contribution from Wickens and Breusch (1988), that rather than using the Engle–Granger two-step procedure when estimating single-equation ECMs, one should follow an approach that is based on the estimation of a restricted autoregressive distributed lag (ADL) model. The long-run parameters can then be deduced from the final version of the estimating equation. Although the two methods are asymptotically equivalent, *in small samples* they can give quite different results. Monte Carlo simulation results show that "the ADL approach provides not only better estimators of long-run coefficients, but also more reliable diagnostic procedures for the derived ECM".

# Summary

This chapter has provided information about some of the best known statistics and econometrics software packages used by economists in their applied work. It has highlighted some key features to look out for whether the software available to you is operated in a Windows environment via the mouse and menu and icon choices or by providing a set of commands based on the use of keywords.

We have illustrated the use of two packages, TSP and PcGive, attempting to replicate the results obtained in a number of published studies. By working through these examples you should become familiar with the way that the software operates. Even if neither of these packages is available to you, you should be able to modify the instructions given here so that they work with your software. (For example, both RATS and SHAZAM have command languages very similar to TSP. Microfit incorporates procedures like those in PcGive which are operated by pointing and clicking the mouse.)

If you wish to use a procedure that has not been built-in to the software you might still be able to program it using the commands that are available within the packages like TSP that give you a programming language to work with. If you are likely to do this kind of work on a regular basis it may pay you to learn how to use one of the specialist matrix programming systems such as Ox or GAUSS.

If you are dealing with very large cross-section data sets you may be better off working with a statistical package such as SPSS or SAS. If the variable that you wish to explain is a dummy variable or is limited to just a few values that correspond to different categories, you will probably need to use a package such as LIMDEP.

More information about different statistics and econometrics software is available on the book's web site. Other good sources of information and links on the web can be found at the CTI Economics site at Bristol (http://www.ilrt.bris.ac.uk/ctiecon/software/), the MIMAS web site at Manchester (http://www.mimas.ac.uk/stats/), Bill Goffe's Resources for Economists web site (http://rfe.wustl.edu/Software/) and the web site for Timberlake Consultants (http://www.timberlake.co.uk/software/).

# Exercises and mini-projects

1. Take Gujarati's data on roses (Figure 5.1) and use your statistics or econometrics package to fit the following two models. (If your statistics or econometrics package can read in spreadsheet files use the one that you produced in the Exercise in section 5.2. If it does not use the package's own data entry module.)
   Model A:
   $$\text{roses} = \text{constant} + \beta_1 \text{ price} + \beta_2 \text{ pcarn} + \beta_3 \text{ income} + u$$
   Model B:
   $$\ln(\text{roses}) = \text{constant} \, \beta_1 \ln(\text{price}) + \beta_2 \ln(\text{pcarn}) + \beta_3 \ln(\text{income}) + u$$
   Analyze the results, including any diagnostic statistics that you can get from your software. If you can, use the software to plot actual and fitted values of roses together for each model.

2. Use your econometrics software to reestimate the demand for beef in Greece based on the data in Exercise 5 at the end of Chapter 4. Get the computer to generate a range of diagnostic statistics and interpret what they show. Produce also post-regression plots of actual and fitted series, the residuals and, if the software allows, a histogram showing the distribution of residuals.

   Now rerun the regression, this time including an *impulse dummy* variable that takes the value 1 in 1981 when there was an unusually sharp fall in the demand for beef. Is this dummy significant? How does its inclusion affect the results?

3. In another study of the effects of an anti-smoking campaign on cigarette consumption (this time for Greece) Vasilios Stavrinos (1987) estimated a model of the form

$$\ln Q_t = \alpha + \beta_1 \ln P_t + \beta_2 \ln Y_t + \beta_3 \ln Q_{t-1} + \alpha_1 D1_t + \alpha_1 D2_t + u_t$$

where Q = annual consumption of cigarettes per person over 15, P = the relative cigarette price index (1970 = 100), Y = undeflated per capita personal disposable income, D1 = a dummy variable to allow for the possible effects of TV advertising on consumption, (= 0 for 1961–1969; = 1 for 1970–1978; =0 for 1979–1982), and D2 = a dummy variable to allow for the possible effects of an anti-smoking health campaign, (= 0 for 1961–1978; = 1 for the campaign years 1979–1982).

Stavrinos's data set is given below. Use your econometrics package to estimate the model for the period 1961–1982 (using the 1960 value of Q to give you the first value of the lagged dependent variable). Compare your estimates of the long-run price and income elasticities with those found by Stavrinos (–0.079 and 0.176 respectively). What do the results suggest about the effectiveness of the anti-smoking health campaign?

*Note:* Don't be concerned if your results are not exactly the same as those given by Stavrinos. Again there appears to be a discrepancy between the published data set and that used to obtain the published results.

|      | Q    | Y       | P     |
|------|------|---------|-------|
| 1960 | 1717 |         |       |
| 1961 | 1748 | 11 668  | 75.6  |
| 1962 | 1785 | 12 230  | 77.0  |
| 1963 | 1859 | 13 716  | 78.5  |
| 1964 | 1879 | 15 261  | 82.9  |
| 1965 | 1954 | 17 503  | 91.8  |
| 1966 | 2034 | 19 158  | 93.8  |
| 1967 | 2094 | 20 448  | 100.0 |
| 1968 | 2119 | 21 682  | 100.0 |
| 1969 | 2168 | 24 032  | 100.0 |
| 1970 | 2261 | 26 616  | 100.0 |
| 1971 | 2311 | 30 226  | 100.0 |
| 1972 | 2411 | 34 261  | 100.0 |
| 1973 | 2522 | 43 436  | 100.0 |
| 1974 | 2678 | 51 152  | 108.6 |
| 1975 | 2743 | 61 660  | 134.4 |
| 1976 | 2866 | 73 371  | 168.5 |
| 1977 | 2955 | 84 731  | 176.0 |
| 1978 | 3061 | 100 383 | 200.0 |
| 1979 | 2989 | 120 302 | 231.9 |
| 1980 | 2943 | 142 911 | 277.7 |
| 1981 | 2961 | 176 436 | 340.7 |
| 1982 | 3172 | 213 261 | 368.2 |

Source: Stavrinos (1987).

**4.** Use your econometrics software to conduct unit-root tests for the Stavrinos data. What conclusions do you draw about the validity of his results?

# CHAPTER 6

# The Internet for economists

## Objectives

The objectives of this chapter are

- to extend your knowledge of the use of the Internet by economists
- to develop your skills in locating data and other information relevant to economists on the World Wide Web
- to introduce you to the main bibliographic databases used by economists via the World Wide Web
- to help you familiarize yourself with how to access the economics journals that are available on-line
- to help you keep up to date with new articles and working papers
- to alert you to some of the on-line learning material that is available on the web for economics
- to help you to begin to build a home page of your own on the web

By now you should be familiar with the process of sending and receiving e-mail messages (perhaps even with file attachments). If you worked through section 3.4 of Chapter 3 you might also now belong to a mail discussion list such as cti-econ. You will probably also feel quite adept at using your web browser to connect to web sites of interest to economists. The purpose of this chapter is to extend your knowledge of the Internet, particularly as it relates to the work of economists, and to equip you with further skills that will enable you to exploit its tools and resources in your everyday work.

# 6.1  Introduction: the ever changing Internet – expansion, evolution and revolution

The use of the Internet is growing all the time and at an ever increasing rate. According to the Online section of *The Guardian* newspaper (20 May 1999), 22% of the population of the UK over the age of 15 are now connected to the Internet (the figure is, of course, much higher in the US). The introduction of "free" Internet access by companies such as Dixons, with their Freeserve facility, has further stimulated the spread of Internet use in the UK. Professor Ray Wild, Principal of Henley Management College, writing in *The Guardian* on 25 September 1999, says that around 30% of the UK adult population now have Internet access.

More and more people are using the Internet to send e-mail and to access the World Wide Web in their work and at home for leisure and household management purposes. They are using the web for electronic banking, to trade in stocks and shares, to order and pay for goods and services (especially books via Amazon.co.uk and Amazon.com), to take part in on-line auctions and to track down last minute holiday bargains. Most big companies (and quite a few small and medium sized ones) have their own web sites, and TV and newspaper advertisements for their products carry their web page URLs. Although e-commerce is still in its infancy it is set to make the Internet a medium for transactions as well as one for communications and publishing.

Web pages are becoming more colorful, dynamic and lively. In the beginning web pages consisted of mostly static text and graphics. Now they contain sound, moving images and video clips, with real audio, streaming video and live broadcasts. With the upgrading of telephone lines from copper to optical fiber, more cable connections, and the extension of broadband communications, the infrastructure of the Internet is being transformed to allow more of us to have access to Internet delivered entertainment. (Optical fiber links allow one to download a VHS quality video in less than a second.)

Chat rooms, web cams and video conferencing are becoming part of today's culture. The convergence of telecom and Internet technology can provide Internet access via mobile phones, or with suitable equipment worldwide telephone calls can be made via computers at local rates.

All of these developments make the Internet a topic of great interest for economists. (See, for example, *Internet Economics* (1998) edited by Lee McKnight and Joseph Bailey.) However, already the Internet has had a substantial impact on the way that many economists work. In this chapter we shall see how it has affected the way that economists find information and keep up to date, the way that they prepare and deliver material for their courses and even how it is influencing professional journal and book publishing.

## A brief history of the Internet

The origins of the Internet go back to the late 1960s and the creation of *ARPANET* (Advanced Research Projects Agency Network) by the Department of Defense Advanced Research Projects Agency in the US. ARPANET originally connected four universities and enabled scientists to exchange information and resources across long distances. It was intended to provide a test-bed for new developments in network technology. Military interest lay in the fact that the network provided a means of ensuring that vital information could be shared across a network so that if any one computer connected to the system was, for any reason, to go down the information stored on it could be recovered from another part of the network. Two crucial features of the design of the network were that it should be *distributed* (there would be no headquarters) and that it should be *platform independent* – computers made by different manufacturers should be able to link up to the network.

Some of the researchers working on the ARPANET project started to exchange messages with each other across the network. *Electronic mail* or *e-mail* had been invented. A man called Ray Tomlinson is credited with setting up the first ever e-mail system (see `http://www.zinezone.com/zones/digital/internet/tomlinson/interview.html`).

Through the 1970s various networking tools and protocols were developed, including *telnet* (which enables you to log-in to a remote computer somewhere else on the network from the machine in your office) and *FTP* (file transfer protocol, which standardized the method of transferring files between networked computers). In the 1980s further developments led to the acceptance of a standard set of *TCP/IP internet protocols* (or rules). Each computer was given a unique IP address and the protocols provided a reliable method for establishing connections between computers across the network.

A decision was made to separate the military part of the network from the nonmilitary part and further investment in the US by the National Science Foundation (NSF) connected up the country's six supercomputing centers to form *NSFNET*, which provided a "backbone" national network. Other countries too were developing their own networks. For example, in the UK the government provided funds to connect together university computing systems through *JANET* (the Joint Academic Network). When these networks were linked together they formed the Internet, an international interconnection of computer networks. The development of the computer operating system *UNIX*, which included networking utilities, allowed many more universities and individuals to connect up to the Internet.

One of the next important steps forward was the creation of the *gopher* system, developed at the University of Minnesota. This provided a hierarchical menu-based method for locating and accessing information on the Internet and it made working on the Internet much easier.

But the real breakthrough came with the creation of the *World Wide Web (WWW)* and *hypertext transfer protocol (http)* by Tim Berners-Lee, working at CERN, the European Laboratory for Particle Physics in Geneva. This changed the way that information on the Internet can be organized, presented and accessed. Instead of having to type in text-based commands, a graphical user interface was provided. Hypertext "hot-links" between files meant that users needed only to double click on a link to connect up with another file.

The term *hypertext* had been coined by Ted Nelson during the mid 1960s when he set up a project known as *XANADU*. Building on the even earlier ideas of Vannevar Bush, Nelson envisaged a worldwide library of information held on computers across the globe and accessible to everyone. (See Bush (1945), Nelson (1981) and Nelson (1990).)

Hypertext principles were initially developed across documents but essentially on individual computers and depended on specific software packages for their implementation. Packages such as *HyperCard* (for Apple Macintosh computers only) and *Guide* enabled practitioners in a wide variety of subject areas to develop hypertext and hypermedia applications for their students (see, amongst others, Judge (1991) and McAlleese (1989)).

But it was the establishment of the World Wide Web, and the creation of user-friendly browsers such as *Mosaic* (developed in the early 1990s at the National Center for Supercomputing Applications – NCSA) which enabled users to navigate the web, that finally provided the breakthrough to make the ideas of Bush and Nelson a reality. As well as working with the new hypertext protocol, browsers such as Mosaic and later Netscape were able to incorporate gopher and FTP protocols, so material that was already on servers attached to the Internet could still be accessed but via a more user-friendly interface.

During the 1990s a variety of *helper-applications* and *plug-ins* were developed which enabled users (who possessed the necessary hardware) to access graphics, sound and video material via their web browser. RealPlayer (`http://www.real.com`), Apple QuickTime (`http://www.apple.com/quicktime`) and Macromedia Shockwave (`http://macromedia.com/software/downloads`) are three of the best known plug-ins for dealing with graphics and video material. Often the plug-in software that enables you to view files created by these programs is free and downloadable via the Web; the companies charge only for the programs needed to create these special graphics, audio and video files. Some economists have produced multimedia material for viewing on the web using one or other of these file types.

Even more common, though, is the use of *Adobe Acrobat PDF* (Portable Document Files) files. By using the full Adobe software it is possible to create view-only versions of files from programs such as MS Word and Excel. With the PDF reader plug-in other users can then display documents on-screen, via their browsers, exactly as they appear on paper. One can then print these files, but not edit them. This gives authors some additional copyright security. Because PDF files are so much smaller than the original files created using Word and other packages they are much more economical to use for downloading over the web (see `http://www.adobe.com/`).

*Warning*: To get plug-ins and helper applications to work it is usually necessary for the browser software to be configured so that it can recognize them. If you are working on your university's network computer (rather than your home PC) *DO NOT CHANGE ANY OF THE BROWSER SETTINGS YOURSELF.* Consult your local computer network manager if you are not sure whether certain types of file can be dealt with by the browser on your network.

## 6.2   Finding information on the web

With literally millions of web pages now accessible, how do you find the information you are looking for? There are five main ways of finding out where to locate the material you want on the web (or of discovering whether the information you are looking for is on the web): (1) personal recommendation; (2) hypertext links; (3) intelligent guesswork; (4) search tools; and (5) subject gateways and specialist directories.

### Personal recommendation

Your lecturer might suggest that you go to a web site such as *CTI Economics* (`http://www.ilrt.bris.ac.uk/ctiecon`), *Biz/ed* (`http://www.bized.ac.uk`) or *Resources for Economists on the Internet* (`http://rfe.org/` or `http://econwpa.wustl.edu/EconFAQ/EconFAQ.html` or in the UK `http://netec.mcc.ac.uk/EconFAQ/EconFAQ.html`).

You might even be provided with a URL to take you directly to the exact page on the web site that holds the specific information that your lecturer wants you to look at. For example, you could be asked to look at *Virtual Economy*, the on-line model of the UK economy that allows users to run potential economic policies through the Treasury model, just as the Chancellor of the Exchequer might do before he introduces a new policy measure. (Go to `http://www.bized.co.uk/virtual/economy/` – see also the article in *CHEER* (Beharrell, Church, Paine and Stark, 1999) that gives some background information on the project.)

You might also be recommended to look at a web site in a book, newspaper or magazine. I hope that you find most of my suggestions in this book worthwhile!

## Hypertext links

You might also discover a useful site *indirectly* by coming across a hypertext link to it while examining material at another web site. For example, suppose you have gone to the CTI Economics web site to look at the on-line version of *CHEER* (http://www.ilrt.bris.ac.uk/ctiecon/cheer.htm). While reading the report in Volume 13 Issue 1 on the CAI (Computer Assisted Instruction) sessions at the New York meetings of the ASSA (Allied Social Sciences Association) by Betty Blecha and Tod Porter, you notice that the slide show prepared by Bill Goffe and Bob Parks for their talk "What's on the Internet for Economists? A Demonstration and Update" can be viewed at http://wuecon.wustl.edu/~goffe/ASSA.99.html. Because you are reading *CHEER* on-line you can just click on the hypertext link to go straight to the Goffe and Parks presentation.

## Intelligent guesswork

Now suppose that you are trying to find a particular web site – say you half remember hearing about it. Or perhaps you are wondering if a particular company or organization that interests you has a web site. Maybe in conversation someone has mentioned to you that the booksellers Waterstones has a web site where you can order books on-line. Or possibly you want find out the latest information on Microsoft products. Or you wonder whether CNN has a web site with all the latest news from around the world. Many organizations, including these three, keep to a standard format in constructing their URLs: www.<organization name>.<type of organization>.<country code>. So, for example, the URL for Waterstones is http://www.waterstones.co.uk. The home page for Microsoft is at http://www.microsoft.com, while you can find CNN at http://www.cnn.com. Remember US based organizations don't need to include the country code. It's always worth quickly trying what you think might be the URL since, if you guess correctly, it can save you time by avoiding the need to call up a search tool (see below). However, not every company and organization adheres to this standard format when deciding on the URL for its web site.

Rather than simply finding a particular home page, you may want to find all the home pages with information on a particular topic. For this you need to turn to either a *search tool*, a *specialist subject directory* or a *subject gateway*.

## Search tools

There are now a great many search tools connected to the World Wide Web that can look for web pages containing a key word or phrase. There are three main types of search tool that you can use when searching for information on the web: *search engines*, *meta search agents* or *searchbots* and specialist *subject directories* or guides.

## Exercise

All the following companies have standard looking URLs. See if you can guess what they are. Check your guesses next time you connect up to the World Wide Web. (Hint: Organizations are sometimes known by their initials.)

1. *Financial Times*
2. *Wall Street Journal*
3. MasterCard
4. Visa
5. IBM
6. Apple
7. Sainsbury's
8. Tesco
9. Disney
10. MTV

*Search engines*

Search engines use automated tools and programs (variously referred to as *worms*, *spiders*, *crawlers* or *bots*) to roam around the web collecting information on different topics and adding the information to their databases. Then when you submit a query via an interactive form on the web, the search engine will check its database for relevant entries and return them to you in the form of a list of results (or "hits"). The list will be "clickable", so if the brief description that is provided with one of the entries on your list looks promising you can go straight to the web page. Some search engines will rank the entries using a scoring system based on how often the keyword has been found in the web pages that it has located. Some of the best known search engines and where to find them are listed, in alphabetical order, in Figure 6.1. Figures 6.2 and 6.3 show the screen layouts for two of the search engines.

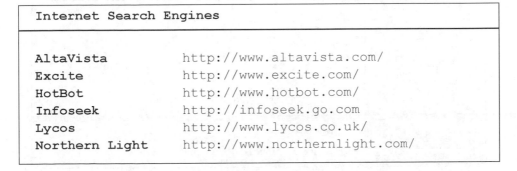

| Internet Search Engines | |
|---|---|
| AltaVista | http://www.altavista.com/ |
| Excite | http://www.excite.com/ |
| HotBot | http://www.hotbot.com/ |
| Infoseek | http://infoseek.go.com |
| Lycos | http://www.lycos.co.uk/ |
| Northern Light | http://www.northernlight.com/ |

**Fig. 6.1** A list of the main search engines and where to find them.

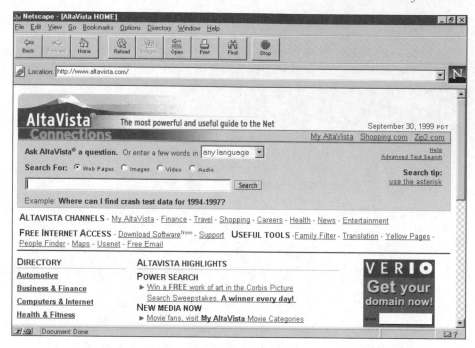

**Fig. 6.2**    The AltaVista home page.

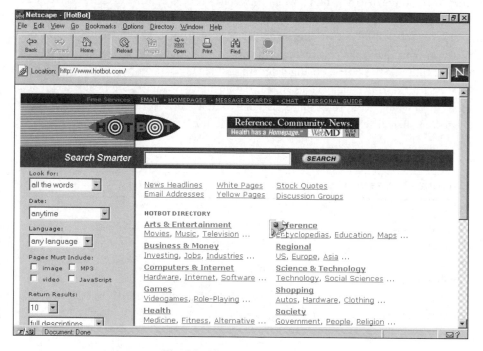

**Fig. 6.3**    The HotBot home page.

Each of the search tools in the above list can have its advantages and disadvantages, according to the circumstances. AltaVista appears to have the biggest database, but many people find HotBot easier to use. Keep in mind that for some keywords the search tool may return a list with literally thousands of hits. You will need to formulate your search thoughtfully so that you find only the most relevant web sites (see the text box, "Successful search strategies", below).

### Meta search agents

These are not search engines as such, but tools for looking through a number of search engines from a single site. For example, `http://www.locate.com/` provides an all in one search covering most of the search tools listed in Figure 6.1.

### Subject directories

To the user these might appear to be just the same as search engines. You enter a keyword or key phrase and get a list of places to look. But the database in the subject directory has been compiled by a human being and you tend to start with a general subject category. You can then search for topics within the category. Yahoo (`http://www.yahoo.com` or `http://www.yahoo.co.uk`) probably has the best general set of subject directories, but more specific economics subject directories may give better results if you know the type of information you are looking for (see below).

### Inomics – a dedicated search engine for economics information
`http://www.inomics.com`

In 1998 Thorsten Wichmann from Berlecon Research in Berlin established a new search tool on the web, especially for economists. Because the well-known Internet search engines described above cover the whole of the web they will tend to return many irrelevant and unwanted references if a search is based on a word that can have many meanings other than the one used in economics. For example searching for "game" will produce references to football games, poker games and game theory. The Inomics index, because it only covers economics pages, will limit the references that it provides to those in the area of game theory (Figure 6.4). It is possible to restrict your query by type of resource (information from individual scholars or economics departments, government agencies, professional organizations etc.). Inomics has two other main sections that are likely to be of interest to professional economists: Job Openings for Economists and Conference Announcements. I have found this relatively new site to be a most valuable addition to the on-line resources available to economists.

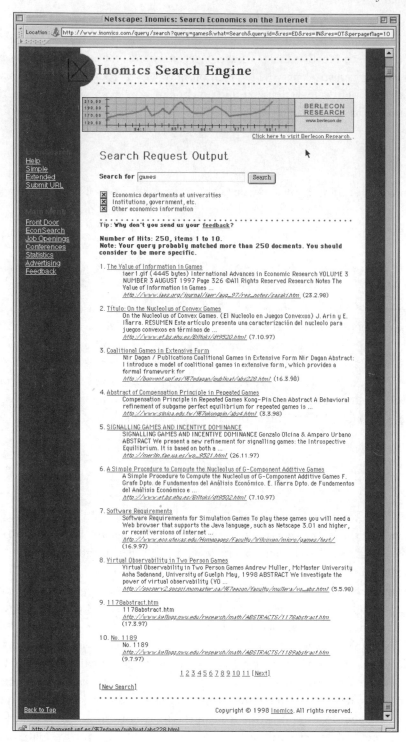

**Fig. 6.4**    Inomics – the special search engine for economics.

## Successful search strategies

First, think carefully about the *type of resource* that you are seeking. Is it some data, a list of bibliographic references, information on some computer software or some on-line learning resources? If it is one of these you may be better off beginning at a recognized specialist site (such as MIMAS or the Penn World Tables for data; EconLit or BIDS for bibliographic information; the CTI Economics or Timberlake web pages for software information).

If you do use a search engine, identify a number of keywords that might be relevant for your search before you start. You can *narrow the scope* of your search by providing several keywords that must all be found in the database entry. For example, you could look for unemployment AND inflation. This will only return pages with both terms in them. If you ask for information on unemployment OR inflation this will *broaden the search* and return pages with either term. If you specify that your search should look for references with unemployment NOT inflation this will exclude any pages that include any reference to inflation.

Other techniques that can be used to be more or less specific are to enclose a phrase in inverted commas (e.g. "Unemployment and inflation" – to list only documents containing this exact phrase) and to truncate (shorten) the text string and add an asterisk to pick up all words that begin with a particular set of characters (e.g. unemp* will find references to unemployment, unemployed, unemployable etc.).

*Note*: Different search tools have slightly different ways of narrowing or expanding searches. Those that allow you to check boxes specifying that you want references with all or any of the words submitted are probably the easiest to use.

Check whether the search engine offers additional tools such as a thesaurus or further facilities for narrowing or expanding the scope of a search. For example, you might be able to limit a search to web pages in a particular country or those that have been updated within a recent time period. It is also worth checking whether the search engine that you are using has a regional version. This can help to overcome the US bias that pervades the databases of search engines – which arises from the fact that most of the main search engines belong to US companies and of course the majority of web pages are on computers in the US. It can also keep down the cost and the time that it takes you to find items (because you will be searching databases on servers in your own country rather than having to connect with computers in the US – see also the following text box on caches and mirrors.)

Don't just limit yourself to a single search engine. If your usual favorite fails to find what you want then try one of the others, or maybe use a meta search tool.

When you have your list of potential sites, examine the URL carefully before you click on it. Can you tell what organization and country the web page comes from? As you look down the list you may be able immediately to reject or prioritize certain items. (See also the text box 'Assessing the quality of web resources' later in this chapter.)

## Caches and mirrors

Caches come in many types but essentially they all work in the same way – they store information where you can get to it quickly. When you use your browser to link up to a web site the pages, graphics and other files that you call up will be stored in a folder or subdirectory (called cache) on your PC. Then when you go back to the web page the files don't all have to be reloaded from the remote server as they can be picked up straightaway from your disk cache. Your university might also operate a network-wide cache, storing files on a central server. So sometimes even when you visit a web page for the first time you may be able to load it quite quickly if the files needed have been stored in the network cache as the result of an earlier visit to the site by someone else on the network.

The cache on your PC will be automatically emptied when it reaches full capacity, but it can be helpful to know where it is so that you can empty it manually if need be (you can do this from the browser menu). The reason for this is that if the remote site has been updated since you last visited it you may be looking at the old version stored in your cache, rather than the new version at the web site.

There is also a UK-wide mirror system for universities, based at the universities of Kent and Lancaster. Many important US web sites are mirrored there so that when you call up an American web site you may get redirected to the UK mirror (go to `http://www.mirror.ac.uk/` for more information).

## Subject gateways and specialist directories

The five key economics web sites listed here have already been mentioned in Chapter 2. Now we provide a little more information about each of them.

*CTI Economics*
`http://www.ilrt.bristol.ac.uk/ctiecon/`

CTI Economics is one of more than twenty subject based centers, funded by the UK government under the *Computers in Teaching Initiative*, which were established to encourage the use of computers and learning technologies in UK higher education. CTI Economics is based at the University of Bristol, within the Institute for Learning and Research Technology (ILRT) which also includes *SOSIG* and *Biz/ed* amongst its projects – see below. As part of the service, CTI Economics has a web site providing links to key economics resources on the Internet, teaching material, a searchable software catalog, news and advice (Figure 6.5). It is also the home of the on-line version of *CHEER (Computers in Higher Education Economics Review)* the twice yearly journal of CTI Economics and the CALECO Research Group at the University of Portsmouth.

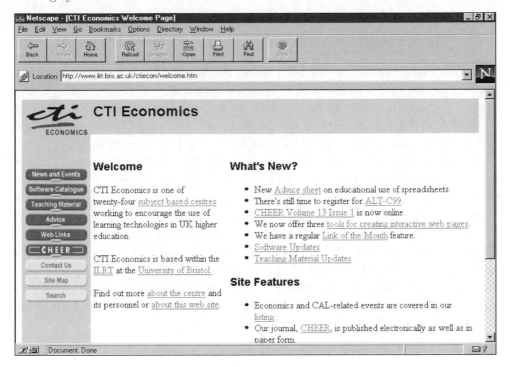

**Fig. 6.5** The CTI Economics home page.

*Note*: Under the UK government's new *Learning and Teaching Support Network (LTSN)* initiative the current CTI subject centers will be replaced by a new set of subject centers, including one in economics based at the University of Bristol. By the time this book is published, the new center will have its own web site and users accessing the CTI Econ web site will be redirected.

## SOSIG
http://sosig.ac.uk/

In the UK, as part of the Electronic Libraries Programme (eLib), and in conjunction with the Joint Information Systems Committee (JISC), the government has funded a number of specialist subject gateways.

The teams working on each project include both subject specialists and library staff with expertise in electronic library resources. The aim of each gateway is to provide links to useful resources on the Internet, where the resources covered have been fully cataloged and have been carefully vetted for quality and reliability. This means that you can save yourself time by reading the description of the site at the gateway and only visiting those that appear to be most relevant to your needs. You also have some guarantee that what you find there will be of suitable quality.

The subject gateway with the greatest relevance to economists is *SOSIG (Social Science Information Gateway)* (Figure 6.6). SOSIG (pronounced "sausage" ) was established in 1994 and is based in the ILRT at the University of Bristol. SOSIG has a specific economics section which points to thousands of Internet resources of value to economists. The items are collected together in further subsections corresponding to areas such as Agricultural Economics, Finance, Development Studies etc. The SOSIG catalog can be searched via a simple form using single keywords or more complex search procedures that can refine or broaden the scope of the search. Or you can just browse through the entries in any section or subsection of the catalog that interests you. A particularly valuable feature is the thesaurus, which can provide alternative words to search under if your initial submission fails to track down what you want. In 1996 SOSIG became involved with the European Union's DESIRE (Development of a European Service for Information on Research and Education) project. This is a large project involving 22 partners across Europe with the aim of providing a pan-European catalog of high quality resources for the social sciences, with multilingual access. SOSIG has recently (August 1999) expanded the service that it provides. It has close links with its sister projects at the ILRT such as CTI Economics and Biz/ed.

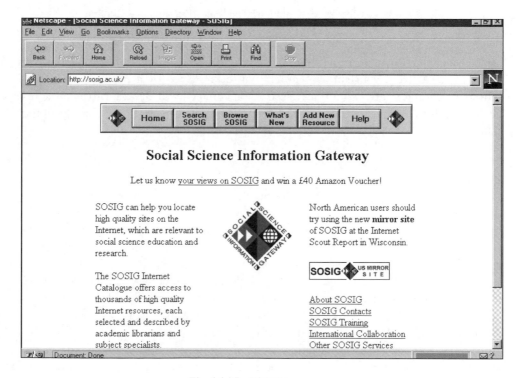

**Fig. 6.6** The SOSIG home page.

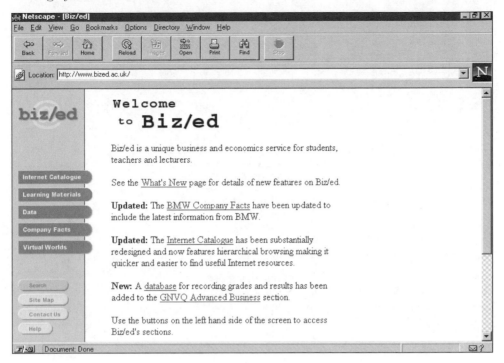

**Fig. 6.7** The Biz/ed home page.

*Biz/ed*
`http://www.bized.ac.uk/`

Biz/ed is a specialist site for Business and Economics on the Internet, funded under eLib (Figure 6.7). It provides a gateway to peer-reviewed Internet resources for economics and business studies students and staff in the UK. Its focus is slightly more towards teaching and learning material than SOSIG, which has a greater proportion of material relevant to researchers and practitioners. As a consequence Biz/ed has special sections devoted to Learning Materials and Data for use in class (it incorporates data from the Office for National Statistics, Extel, the Penn World tables and the US Census Bureau).

*Resources for Economists on the Internet (RFE)*

If you are in the US go to either
`http://rfe.org/`
or
`http://econwpa.wustl.edu/EconFAQ/EconFAQ.html`
   If you are in the UK go to
`http://netec.mcc.ac.uk/EconFAQ/EconFAQ.html`

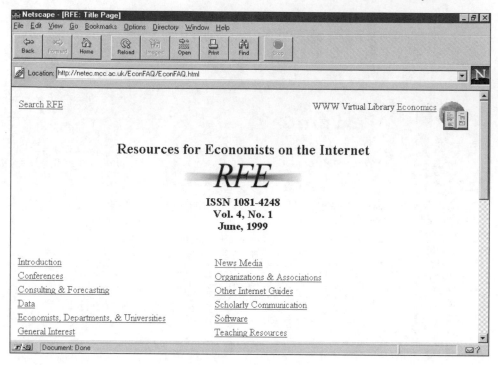

**Fig. 6.8**   The RFE home page.

RFE is also mirrored at
`http://www.general.uwa.edu.au/EconFAQ/EconFAQ.html`
and
`http://netec.ier.hit-u.jp/EconFAQ/EconFAQ.html`

Resources for Economists on the Internet, as its name suggests, is an on-line guide to economics resources on the Internet (Figure 6.8). Edited by Bill Goffe, of the University of Southern Mississippi, it is sponsored by the American Economic Association and is probably the most used starting place for economists looking for material on the web. It lists more than 900 resources on the Internet of interest to academic and practicing economists, and gives brief but informative descriptions of almost all the resources that are covered. There is a table of contents providing links to resources that can be categorized under specific headings (such as Data, Software, Teaching Resources etc.). Alternatively you can search the guide for links to material using specified keywords.

The original version of Bill Goffe's guide was published in the *Journal of Economic Perspectives* and a revised version of it is to be published in the *Journal of Economic Education*. In addition, it will be kept up to date and published on the web with periodic revisions. At the time of writing the current version is Vol. 4, No. 1 (June 1999).

*WebEc*

The original site is in Finland at
`http://www.helsinki.fi/WebEc/`
   In the UK go to
`http://netec.mcc.ac.uk/WebEc.html`
   In the US go to
`http://netec.wustl.edu/WebEc.html`
   WebEc is also mirrored at
`http://netec.ier.hit-u.jp/WebEc/WebEc.html`

WebEc provides links to a wide range of economics resources on the web, categorized according to the *Journal of Economics Literature* (JEL) classification (Figure 6.9). It is edited by Lauri Saarinen from the Helsinki School of Economics in Finland. It originated as Lauri's personal collection of economics links. Later it became known as the "Helsinki Economics page" before it finally joined up with the NetEc project (see section 6.5), where it became WebEc.

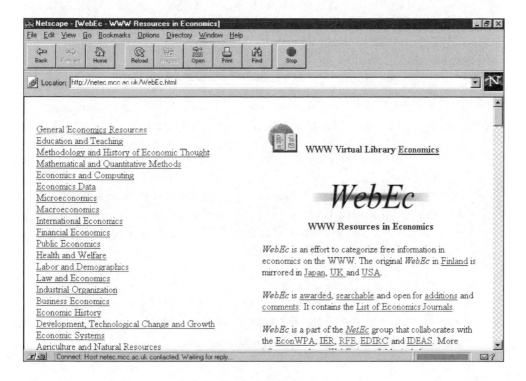

**Fig 6.9**  The WebEc home page.

## Assessing the quality of web resources

Because all kinds of individuals and organizations now maintain web sites it is crucial that you develop some critical faculties to help you assess the quality and reliability of web sites and the information you find on them. If you have arrived at a web site via a recognized gateway such as SOSIG, where subject specialists have personally vetted all the material that is displayed, you may have greater confidence that the material you have reached is reliable and up to date than if you have just picked up one of the "hits" from an automated search tool.

In the latter circumstance some key points to look out for are:

1.  Are the aims of the web site clear? Is its primary function just to give you links to other places, to support an educational program or to sell you something?

2.  Is it clear who is the author of the web site? (It may be an individual or an organization.) Do you feel that they can be trusted to provide reliable, up-to-date and unbiased information? Is there an e-mail address given for the author so that you can contact them if you want to ask about a particular point on the web site, or indeed to help you verify that they are who they say they are?

3.  How up-to-date is the information on the web site? Does the web site show when the site was last updated? Of course old information isn't necessarily out of date, but for some types of information it can be very important that you have only the most recently available information.

Two excellent sites with tutorial material on how to assess the quality and reliability of web resources are:

*   *The Internet Detective*
    `http://www.sosig.ac.uk/desire/internet-detective.html`
    A web-based tutorial on evaluating the quality of information found on the Internet written by staff at the ILRT in Bristol, funded by the European Union as part of the DESIRE project.
*   *QUICK   The Quality Information Checklist*
    `http://www.quick.org.uk/`
    A teacher's guide, produced by the Centre for Health Information Quality in association with the Health Education Authority and Showme Multimedia Ltd.

# Practical 6.1   Using search engines

Use at least *three* of the search tools listed in Figure 6.1 to search the web for information on *one* of the following topics:

(a) e-commerce
(b) Economic convergence
(c) Economic forecasting
(d) Energy economics
(e) Transport economics

Compare the results that you get from the different search engines and subject directories.

Suppose you had been asked to prepare a report on "Recent developments in …<topic (a)…(e)>". List the ten web sites from those that you have found that would be most useful to you.

Spend some time evaluating the way that the different search tools enable you to formulate your search (including any advanced searching features) and the way that the results are presented to you. If you have time, take a look at the Review of Search Engines that can be found on the University of Strathclyde's web site at `http://www.dis.strath.ac.uk/business/search.html`.

> **Tip**
>
> You can locate a word you might be looking for within a particular web page using **E**dit and then **F**ind from the browser's main menu where you type in the word you are trying to match. This can be particularly helpful for finding where a topic is covered in a long web page.

# Practical 6.2   Using SOSIG

Go to the SOSIG web site and click the Search SOSIG button on the bar at the top of the screen. Search for information on transport economics. If necessary, narrow or widen your search, or follow related threads, to see if you can find information on road pricing and the environment.

When you have time, click on the Browse SOSIG button and look through the Economics section of the catalog, following any leads that you find interesting. Browsing in this way is not an efficient way of locating information on a particular topic that you are searching for, but it can be interesting and you might stumble across something that is really useful.

You might also like to look at the SOSIG Subject Guide for Economics (at `http://sosig.ac.uk/subject-guides/economics.html` or click on the link at the top right of the Economics Index screen), to check the What's New section or see what advice is offered when you click the Help button.

## 6.3 Finding specific types of economics information on the web

### Data

There is a huge amount of data now available directly on the web. It includes official data provided by national and international government agencies, data provided by private sector organizations such as banks, data to go with textbook exercises and for teaching, and data used for research and journal articles.

In some cases you will need to register before you can use a site, access being restricted by user name and password. There are also some sites where you must pay to use the data. Data can be downloaded in a variety of formats. Sometimes it will be put into a suitable form to be loaded straight into a statistics or econometrics package. Alternatively it may be easiest just to copy and paste from the screen. Some useful sites are listed below. For further sources see the sections on data at the CTI Economics, Biz/ed and RFE web sites.

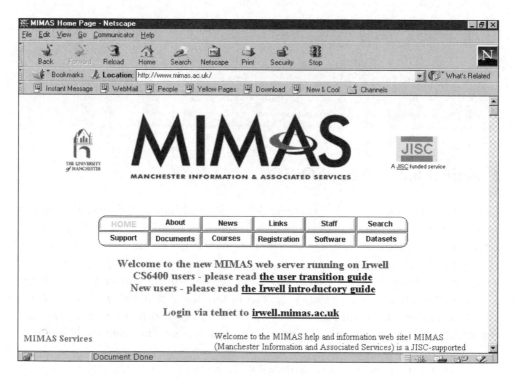

**Fig. 6.10**   The MIMAS home page.

*MIMAS (Manchester Information and Associated Services)*
`http://www.mimas.ac.uk/`

Formerly known as MIDAS, this site contains a huge selection of economics and other data, including the Office for National Statistics Time Series databank, Census Data, World Bank data and data from surveys such as the Family Expenditure survey (Figure 6.10). You will need to register and access is restricted to members of UK higher education (HE) institutions by user name and password.

---

**Find out**

If you are a student at a UK university or other HE institution find out about how to register to use MIMAS. (Ask your lecturer or Information Services Officer.)

---

*The Penn World Tables*
`http://arcadia.chass.utoronto.ca/pwt/`
Also available at `http://www.nber.org/pwt56.html` and `http://bized.ac.uk/dataserv/pennhome.htm`.

The Penn World Tables (PWT) are described in Summers and Heston (1991). A revised and updated version 5.6 was released in January 1995. The tables contain data for 152 countries and 28 subjects. This is a well-known and well-used data set, especially for teaching, despite the fact that it only includes information up to 1992. The Biz/ed site includes an exercise to help you to get to know the Penn World Data that you might like to try (`http://bized.ac.uk/dataserv/pennknow.htm`).

*Economic Report of the President*
`http://www.access.gpo.gov/usbudget/fy2000/erp.html`

The statistical tables from the United States Council of Economic Advisers "Economic Report of the President" are available on the web in spreadsheet form (in either .wk4 or .xls format), or you can download the full set of tables as a "zip" file. The tables cover all the areas listed below as annual series since 1959, with quarterly and some monthly information from 1993 until the end of 1998. For those people who are investigating the performance of the US economy this is an extremely useful resource (Figure 6.11).

Spreadsheets are available for the following categories:

- National income or expenditure
- Population, employment, wages and productivity
- Production and business activity
- Prices

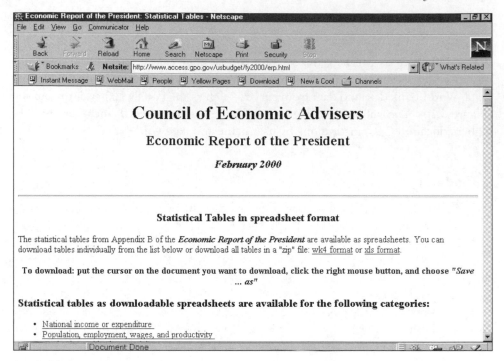

**Fig. 6.11**   Accessing data from the tables in the Economic Report of the President.

- Money stock, credit and finance
- Government finance
- Corporate profits and finance
- Agriculture
- International statistics

*Other sites*

Other sites worth looking at for UK data are *Statbase* http://www.statistics.gov.uk/, the *Bank of England* http://www.BankofEngland.co.uk and *HM Treasury* http://www.hm-treasury.gov.uk/.

Other useful sites for US data are *STAT-USA* http://www.stat-usa.gov/, which gives "taster" pages to some of the many data series available to subscribers, *FRED* (Federal Reserve Economic Data) http://www.stls.frb.org/fred/datindx.html and the *Statistical Abstract of the United States* http://www.census.gov/statlab/www/, which is an on-line edition of the widely used Census Bureau document that contains many economic statistics. You might also like to look at *The Dismal Scientist* http://www.dismal.com and *Economagic* http://www.economagic.com/, which belongs to Ted Bos of the University of Alabama at Birmingham.

Other useful sites for multi-country comparative data are:

- *Eurostat* (the European Union Statistical Office)
  `http://europa.eu.int/en/comm/eurostat/`
- the *IMF* `http://www.imf.org/` (look especially for the World Economic Outlook database)
- the *OECD* `http://www.oecd.org/`
- the *United Nations FAO* (Food and Agricultural Organization)
  `http://www.fao.org/`
- the *World Trade Organization* `http://www.wto.org/`
- the *World Bank* `http://www.worldbank.org/data/` (look especially for the World Development Indicators database).

Two important web sites for economics researchers in the UK are the *ESRC Data Archive* at the University of Essex `http://dawww.essex.ac.uk/` and *r.cade* at the University of Durham `http://www-rcade.dur.ac.uk/`. The Data Archive is a specialist national resource containing the largest collection of accessible computer-readable data in the social sciences and humanities in the UK. Through these web pages it is also possible to search the catalogs of other national archives for computer readable data and to use the services of the Data Archive to acquire these data on your behalf. *r.cade* provides efficient access to key statistical data about Europe and covers not only official statistics from the European Union Statistical Office (Eurostat), but also the United Nations Educational Scientific and Cultural Organization (UNESCO), the International Labour Organization (ILO) and the United Nations Industrial Development Organization (UNIDO). Both these services are aimed at researchers rather than students and they require registration and user name/ password access. They may involve a (small) payment.

A few *journals* are now providing access to the data sets used by authors whose articles they have published. At present it appears to be limited to the following archives:

- *The Economic Journal* `http://www.res.org.uk/datasets/`
- the *Journal of Applied Econometrics* `http://qed.econ.queensu.ca/jae/`
- the *Journal of Business and Economic Statistics* `ftp://www.amstat.org/jbes/View/`
- the *Journal of Money, Credit and Banking*
  `http://economics.sbs.ohio-state.edu/jmcb/volumes.html`

# Practical 6.3 Downloading and using data from the web

Obtain annual data, covering at least twenty years, on real consumption and income for a country of your choice from one of the web sites described above. (*Note:* You may have to download additional price deflators or other series so that you can derive the series you require from the data series available.) Next, load the data into a spreadsheet or statistics/econometrics package and plot both time series graphs of the series and a scatter diagram of consumption against income. Run a simple least squares regression. Now prepare a brief report on your findings, incorporating the graphs and including the regression output and a table of the data as appendices. Don't forget to state very clearly the source(s) of your data and exact definitions of the series used.

## Bibliographic databases

Searchable bibliographic databases in electronic form are now well established. The most important ones for economists are *EconLit*, the *Social Sciences Citation Index* and *ABI-Inform*. They are all available both on CD-ROM (from a variety of different vendors) and via the web. Your university may have installed one or more of these databases on its Intranet to give you access from workstations that are connected to the university network. Or you may be able to connect to the database on a remote server with user access restricted by user name and password (or you might be screened on the basis of your IP address). You can search the databases by author, title or subject, restricting if you wish the years to be covered by the search. You can mark records that you want to keep and then download and save the file for future reference or printing.

### *EconLit*

Produced by the American Economic Association (AEA), EconLit is the primary bibliographical search tool for economists. EconLit uses the *Journal of Economic Literature* (JEL) classification and the database covers the international economics literature since 1969. It provides citations, with selected abstracts, of articles in more than 400 journals, as well as books, conference papers, dissertations and working papers. Access is via libraries and university computer networks or on CD-ROM. Depending on your subscription the database is updated on a monthly or quarterly basis. AEA members may subscribe to EconLit-AEA, a personal CD-ROM version of EconLit, which contains the most recent fifteen years of EconLit records. AEA members who also subscribe to the JEL can also obtain e-JEL, an electronic edition of the JEL containing the full text (in Acrobat PDF format) of articles that have appeared in the JEL since December 1994.

For further information, and hints on how to search EconLit, visit the EconLit web site at http://www.econlit.org.

See also http://www.aeaweb.org and http://www.e-jel.org.

### *Social Sciences Citation Index*

The Social Sciences Citation Index (SSCI), published by the Institute for Scientific Information (ISI), is a multidisciplinary index with searchable author abstracts to the international literature of the social sciences. SSCI provides references from 1988 (and from 1992 onwards, abstracts) to articles in over 1700 journals in the social sciences, plus items relevant to the social sciences from a number of additional science journals. Subject areas cover all the social sciences including economics, business, management, environmental studies, health, urban studies and women's studies. It is updated monthly and is available on CD-ROM from a number of vendors, and can be accessed from many university networks. (In the UK it can also be accessed from BIDS and MIMAS – see below.)

SSCI can locate sources that may be missed by EconLit, particularly those relating to interdisciplinary research topics. For more information go to `http://www.isinet.com/products/citation/citssci.html`.

## *ABI/INFORM Global and ABI/INFORM Global Full Text*

ABI/INFORM from the UMI company is a searchable bibliographic database covering business (and related subjects such as economics, accounting and management). It has over half a million citations (with abstracts) to articles appearing in approximately 1000 periodicals. With the Full Text version subscribers can view the full text (in ASCII form) of over 500 of the indexed publications. Full text coverage begins in 1991 with abstracts and indexes going back to 1985 (and for some journals to 1971). ABI/INFORM is available on CD-ROM and over the Internet (payment can be by subscription or pay-as-you-go). The database is updated monthly.

### Find out

Find out how you can access *EconLit*, the *Social Sciences Citation Index* and *ABI-Inform* from your university web site. If you need a user name and password, make sure that you know what they are.

## *IBSS Online*

The International Bibliography of the Social Sciences (IBSS) database is produced by a group at the British Library of Political and Economic Science (BLPES) at the London School of Economics, with additional funding from the Economic and Social Research Council (ESRC) and JISC. The information in the database covers journal articles, book reviews and book chapters in four social science disciplines: Anthropology, Economics, Political Science and Sociology. Entries in the database go back as far as 1951, giving IBSS a unique chronological coverage with over 1 600 000 records. IBSS is global in its coverage with around 50% of the source journals being published outside the UK and US. There are English language title translations for all foreign language articles. The database is updated weekly, with about 2000 new records being added each week. The full text of some articles in the IBSS database is available from the *ingentaJournals* service that runs under BIDS (formerly known as the *BIDS JournalsOnline* service).

IBSS Online is available via BIDS (see below) but can also be obtained on CD-ROM. For further information go to `http://www.lse.ac.uk/ibss/` (see also Shaw, 1998).

*BIDS (Bath Information and Data Services)*
`http://www.bids.ac.uk/`

BIDS is probably the best known and the most used on-line bibliographic service for the academic community in the UK (Figure 6.12). BIDS is funded by JISC and located at the University of Bath, and it provides network access to a number of important bibliographic databases, including IBSS and SSCI. To use the service you must be a member of an HEFC (Higher Education Funding Council)-funded HE institution and have a valid user name and password. To connect to IBSS or SSCI at BIDS go to the general BIDS URL, log-in and then select the service you require.

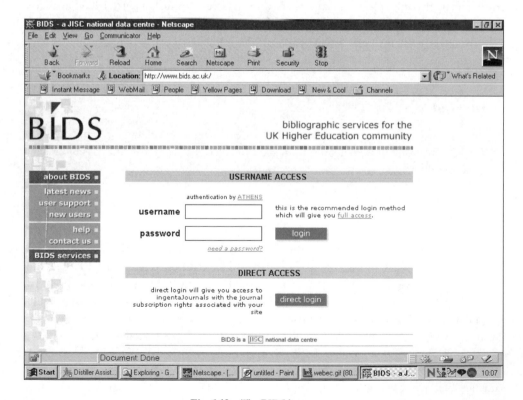

**Fig. 6.12**   The BIDS home page.

**Note**

During the year 2000 the SSCI service at BIDS will be replaced by a new service based on the ISI's "Web of Science Interface" which will be accessible from the MIMAS web site in Manchester (go to `http://wos.mimas.ac.uk`). It is planned that the services will overlap until July 2000, after which time the SSCI service at BIDS will be discontinued.

**Find out**

If you are a student at a British university or other HE institution you should find out your BIDS (or MIMAS) user name and password (ask your lecturer, the university librarian or Information Services Officer).

*COPAC*

One other bibliographic service on the web that you might find useful is COPAC (`http://copac.ac.uk/copac/`). This provides free access to the unified on-line catalogs of some of the largest university research libraries in the UK and Ireland. The COPAC database currently contains over 5.5 million records and you can search using title, author, subject, organization name, publisher, date, language and library. It can be useful if you are trying to track down the full details of a publication that is not in your own library.

**Note**

Don't forget to find out about your own university's on-line library catalog service. There will probably be direct links from the library's web page to many of the services described in this chapter.

## Practical 6.4    Conducting a bibliographical search

Using one of the databases described above (whichever you have access to but preferably EconLit, SSCI or IBSS) conduct a search for recent journal articles on any of the topics mentioned in Practical 6.1. If you are able to access more than one database compare the results that you get. If you get a very long list mark the six articles that look most interesting and save the information for later use.

Pick one of the articles from the list that you have generated and copy down the author's name – or better still copy it to the clipboard so that you can paste it back in on your next search. (If the article has more than one author just select one name.)

Now search for other journal articles by this author. Look at the abstracts and full details of the articles. Does the author tend to write mainly on one topic or for one journal or does he or she contribute across a number of areas and journals?

## 6.4 Economics journals available on-line

Once you have tracked down an article that appears (from its title and abstract) to be relevant to your current research or study, you will want to read it. This can mean a trip to your university library, or if your library doesn't stock the journal in question, an inter-library loan. It would be much more convenient if you could simply click on the title of the paper and call up the full text on-line on your desktop computer. Gradually, as a result of a number of schemes and deals between publishers, libraries and funding bodies, this is becoming possible.

Academic Press were amongst the pioneers in on-line publishing of journals with their IDEAL service (International Digital Electronic Access Library), which began in 1996. Today Academic Press publishes nearly 200 journals, although only a handful are of interest to economists (*Journal of Comparative Economics, Journal of Economic Theory, Journal of Environmental Economics and Management, Journal of Housing Economics, Journal of Urban Economics, Games and Economic Behavior, Research in Economics, Review of Economic*

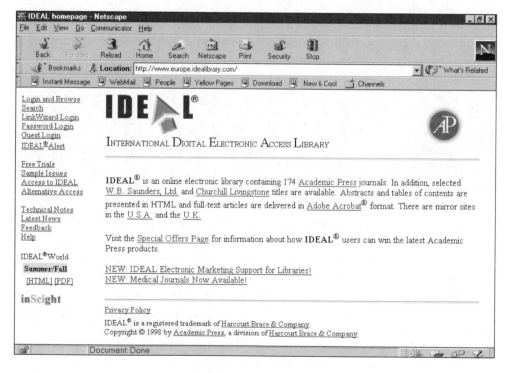

**Fig. 6.13**   The European mirror of the IDEAL home page.

*Dynamics, Explorations in Economic History*). The articles are displayed in Acrobat PDF form, although the journal contents and abstracts are viewable in HTML without charge to anyone with Internet access (Figure 6.13). For full access you will need a user name and password. In the UK the Higher Education Funding Council has negotiated a three year license for all UK universities and HE institutions. Many other individual universities and consortia worldwide have paid for licenses for their members to use IDEAL. According to a recent news release from Academic Press there are nearly 8 million authorized users at over 1000 institutions in 15 countries. You can find out if your university is covered at `http://www.apnet.com/www.ap/conslist.com`.

IDEAL is available at both the following places:

`http://www.idealibrary.com`
`http://www.europe.idealibrary.com`

---

**Find out**

Does your university have a license arrangement for its members to use IDEAL, and if so, what are the user name and password that you need to use? Look at the contents of a recent issue of one of the economics journals and, if you can, view on screen an article that looks interesting.

---

*Note*: Academic Press is joining with several other publishers (including John Wiley & Sons) to work with the newly formed *ingentaJournals* company. In future people at UK universities will be able to access the journals covered by this service via BIDS. More details can be found at `http://www.ingenta.co.uk`. This approach makes it easier for users – there is only one place to go and there is a common interface and set of instructions to work with. It also assists publishers by removing from them the need to create their own systems or collect charges directly from users.

Members of the Royal Economic Society are now entitled to access the contents of the *Economic Journal* on-line. You will need to register to get your password, providing information about your customer number. *The Economic Journal Book Notes* are now available in a searchable on-line database and, as has been mentioned before, the datasets used for papers published in the *Economic Journal* since January 1995 are also available on the web. The Royal Economic Society, together with Blackwell Publishers, has also created a completely new journal for its members, *The Econometrics Journal*, which is available on-line. For access to all the services and for more information go to `http://www.res.org.uk/econ.html`.

The publishers of the *Journal of Economic Education*, in addition to providing an on-line version of the journal, have also initiated a new section called "Online" to provide an outlet for more interactive material. Rather than simply writing about new developments in learning technology and their use in economics, authors can demonstrate their work providing links to their web sites. Go to `http://www.indiana.edu/~econed/`.

Another publisher to provide on-line access to journal articles is Routledge. Some of their journals that will be of interest to economists are *Applied Economics*, *Applied Economics Letters*, *Applied Financial Economics*, *Feminist Economics* and the *Review of International Political Economy*. Institutions that subscribe to these journals get free on-line access for no extra charge. Even if your university doesn't subscribe you will still be able to view the contents, title and abstracts of all the papers published in these journals and look at a sample issue on-line. Go to `http://www.thomson.com/routledge/journal/onpub.html`.

Routledge is also one of the participants in the *SuperJournal* project. This is a major collaboration between publishers, universities, libraries and government agencies (through eLib) to develop electronic journals. The project is designed to explore both the technical issues and practical problems from the point of view of authors, readers, publishers and libraries. Economics journals are not included in this pilot project, but the lessons learned from it will undoubtedly influence the future shape of electronic journal provision in all subjects.

A further important development in the provision of on-line access to journals is the *JSTOR* (Journal Storage) project. Old issues of key journals, in some cases dating back to the nineteenth century, have been scanned in so that they are now available in electronic form. This not only helps to reduce the long-term cost of storing these materials but also provides new research opportunities because the electronic format can speed up searches and widen access to articles. Thirteen important economics journals are covered: *American Economic Review*, *Econometrica*, *The Economic Journal*, the *Journal of Applied Econometrics*,

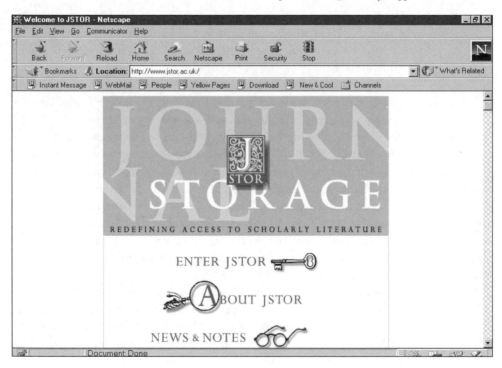

**Fig. 6.14**  The UK mirror of the JSTOR home page at MIMAS.

*The Journal of Economic History*, the *Journal of Economic Literature*, *The Journal of Economic Perspectives*, *The Journal of Industrial Economics*, the *Journal of Money, Credit and Banking*, the *Journal of Political Economy*, *The Quarterly Journal of Economics*, the *Review of Economics and Statistics* and the *Review of Economic Studies*. *The Journal of the Royal Statistical Society* (Series A and B) and the *Statistician* are also covered. The service provides complete runs of these journals from their very first issue up to a "moving wall" which is set at five years before the date of the current issue. You can search for an author, a title, a word or phrase, and then retrieve the full text of the article.

The home site is at `http://www.jstor.org/` but the service is mirrored on the MIMAS site in the UK at `http://www.jstor.ac.uk/`. MIMAS provides a demonstration of how the service works at `http://www.jstor.ac.uk/demo/` (Figure 6.14).

Even though relatively few journals so far provide on-line access to the articles published in them, many now have web sites where you can check the contents pages. WebEc provides a list of on-line journal information with links to home pages at `http://netec.mcc.ac.uk/` and with mirrors at:

`http://netec.wustl.edu/WebEc/journals.html`
`http://netec.ier.hit-u.ac.jp/WebEc/journals.html`
`http://www.helsinki.fi/WebEc/journals.html`

For an interesting discussion of possible developments in on-line journal publication from the perspective of economics, see Goffe and Parks (1997) (this paper can also be viewed at `http://econwpa.wustl.edu/eprints/mic/papers/9704/9704001.abs`).

## 6.5 Working papers and pre-prints

Traditionally economists, in common with researchers in many other disciplines, have produced working papers and discussion papers with pre-publication drafts of their articles. Many departments, including the Department of Economics at Portsmouth, have discussion paper series. Authors can get helpful (usually!) comments from other economists that can lead to improvements in a paper before it is submitted to a journal. Getting hold of working papers by other people working in your area can help to speed up the research process, alerting you to new concepts and techniques. (Sometimes the journal publication lag can be several years, by which time things can have moved on.)

With the advent of the World Wide Web many departments, research institutes and individuals are now making their working papers available via the Internet. A very small subset of those currently available follows (go to the RePEc pages on the web – see below – for a more complete list):

Duke University (Department of Economics)
`http://www.econ.duke.edu/Papers/wpindex.html`

Brown University (Economics)
  `http://econ.pstc.brown.edu/wp99/list99.html`
Brookings Institution
  `http://www.brook.edu/ES/discussion/defaults.htm`
National Bureau of Economic Research
  `http://www.nber.org/new.html`
London School of Economics
  `http://econ.lse.ac.uk/papers/`
University of York (Department of Economics)
  `http://www_users.york.ac.uk/~econ32/dp.htm`
The European University Institute
  `http://www.iue.it/PUB/eco_fm.html`
Econometric Institute, Erasmus University, Rotterdam
  `http://www.few.eur.nl/few/research/pubs/ei/1999/reports.htm`
The Australian National University (Department of Economics)
  `http://ecocomm.anu.edu.au/Departments/ecoh/misc/work1999.html`
University of Wollongong, Australia
  `http://www.uow.edu.au/commerce/econ/wplist.html`
Queen's University, Kingston, Ontario
  `http://qed.econ.queensu.ca/pub/papers/abstracts/download.html`

Usually an abstract will be provided on screen (HTML) with an opportunity for you to view or download the full paper in PDF form, or occasionally as a PostScript or zipped file.

## PostScript

PostScript is a "page description language" that is used to communicate with laser printers. Files can be saved in PostScript format for later printing or viewing. Because PostScript files are compact and self-contained they have frequently been used for transferring documents over the Internet, although today Acrobat PDF files are more likely to be used for this purpose. If you want to see a PostScript file on screen you will need to have a suitable PostScript viewer installed on your system.

## Working paper archives

There have been a number of initiatives to collect economics working papers together into central (or distributed) archives and/or to provide searchable databases of on-line (and printed) working papers. The owners of these different services have mostly tried hard to work in harmony with each other and to agree a common set of standards.

## Economics Working Paper archive (EconWPA)

The Economics Working Paper archive is run by Bob Parks and Larry Blume at Washington University in St Louis and has been in operation since July 1993 (Figure 6.15). It is an automated system for archiving and distributing working papers in all areas of economics, based on the earlier and very successful pre-print archive for physics. Most of the working papers stored in the archive are available in both PostScript and Acrobat PDF form. Papers are grouped under the JEL category headings and you can browse through a section or subsection of interest, or you can search by author, title, subject or keyword. Parks and Blume work closely with WoPEc so that papers submitted to the EconWPA are covered by RePEc (see below).

## NetEc

NetEc is a collection of projects intended to improve access to scholarly economics material on the Internet. We focus here on three of the projects: *BibEc*, *WoPEc* and *RePEc*. BibEc is a collection of bibliographic information about printed working papers. It originated with a collection put together by Fethy Mili of the Université de Montréal, but this has now been supplemented by material from

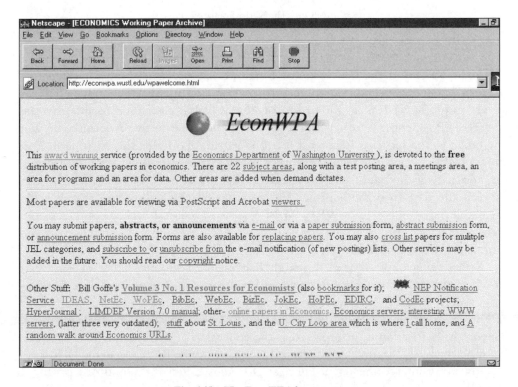

**Fig. 6.15** The EconWPA home page.

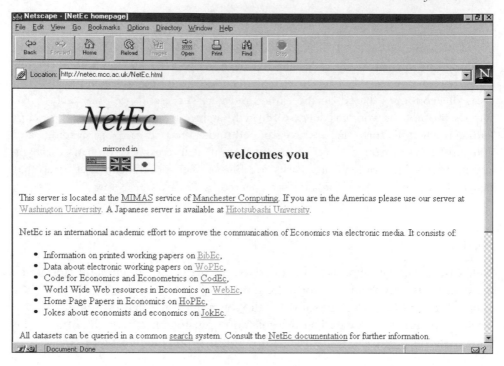

**Fig. 6.16**   The NetEc home page.

some other sources. The sister project WoPEc, which is under the supervision of Thomas Krichel at the University of Surrey, does the same thing for electronic papers and contains bibliographic information (author, title, abstract etc.) for every entry, as well as an indication of the available electronic form(s) of the papers – PostScript, Acrobat PDF etc. When you click on the hyperlink you will be taken to the server, wherever it is in the world, that holds the document. You may be able to view the paper on screen, or save it for later viewing and printing. In some cases the papers are not freely available but must be paid for. You can search the data from both projects at once using any one of the search tools available. (So, unlike EconWPA, WoPEc is not a central archive of electronic working papers but a system linked to papers on computers attached to the Internet wherever they may be.)

*RePEc* (which stands for "Research Papers in Economics") has at least two interpretations. First, it may be considered as the group of people who are working together to provide a standard system (ReDIF) for economics working paper archives and databases. Both BibEc and WoPEc conform with the RePEc protocol. Secondly, RePEc can be interpreted as the collection of archives themselves (now numbering over 100) that are structured according to the RePEc system. All RePEc archives are interconnected using a set of rules called the Guildford protocol (GuilP).

The NetEc services are available in the UK at `http://netec.ac.uk/` and are mirrored at `http://netec.wustl.edu/NetEc.html` and `http://netec.ier.hit-u.ac.jp/NetEc.html` (Figure 6.16).

See also Krichel (1997), which may be viewed at: `http://www.ilrt.bris.ac.uk/ctiecon/cheer/ch11_1/ch11_1p19.htm`.

---

### Other NetEc projects

In addition to BibEc, WoPEc, RePEc and WebEc (all discussed in this chapter) there are three further NetEc projects that may be of interest. HoPEc is a directory of home pages in Economics, CodEc is a directory of computing code for Economics and Econometrics and JokEc is a warehouse for jokes about economics and economists.

---

## IDEAS
`http://ideas.uqam.ca/`

Another valuable service for economists trying to locate working papers (whether in electronic or printed form) is *IDEAS* (Internet Documents in Economics Access Service), which is run by Christian Zimmermann at the Université du Québec à Montréal (UQAM). Papers are classified by JEL codes and you can search through the database with the Excite search engine. IDEAS uses the complete RePEc database so if you search there you will pick up papers that are held in EconWPA and the many other working paper archives, together with all the references covered by WoPEc and BibEc.

## Practical 6.5   Tracking down working papers by Hal Varian

Using one of the services described above, conduct a search for working papers by Hal Varian. What topics has he been working on during the 1990s? Find a link to one of his papers that is available in electronic form and download it so that you can read it later.

---

### Find out

Does your economics department makes its working papers available in electronic form via the web? Even if it does not, are printed versions of the papers sent to BibEc? What research topics are lecturers at your university currently pursuing?

## 6.6   Current awareness services

As we have seen, whether you are trying to track down working papers or published journal articles on a particular topic of interest there are databases on the web with information about the stock of past papers. Increasingly there are also sites to give you direct on-line access to some of these papers. But there are also other services that can help you to keep up to date with the flow of new additions to this stock of papers. These *current awareness services* (some commercial, some free) can alert you to new work in areas of interest to you. When you subscribe to these services you will receive regular e-mails informing you about the contents of the latest issue of a journal or a list of recently available working papers that relate to a particular topic.

### ERN Economics Research Network

ERN, which is a division of SSRN (the Social Science Research Network), is a commercial fee-based service. It disseminates information about economics research in the form of an e-mail newsletter, which also contains news about meetings, jobs and calls for conference papers. SSRN also has a separate service called the Financial Economics Network (FEN). For further details go to `http://www.SSRN.com/`.

### UnCover Reveal (CARL)

This is a fee-based subscription service that will send you (by e-mail) weekly updates of the contents tables of journals covered by the UnCover database (around 1700 journals including most of the main economics journals). Subscribers can also set up as many as 25 different "search strategies" to look for new articles on specified topics. You can arrange (by e-mail or fax) for articles of interest to be faxed to you.

More information can be found at `http://uncweb.carl.org/reveal/`.

### ContentsAlert and ContentsDirect

The publishers Elsevier/ North Holland offer a free e-mail notification service covering all their economics journals called Contents Alert. They have also introduced a slightly more extensive service giving information about books as well as journals called ContentsDirect. For more information go to:

`http://www.elsevier.com/locate/ContentsDirect`
`http://www.elsevier.nl/locate/ContentsDirect`
`http://www.elsevier.co.jp/locate/ContentsDirect`

# IDEAL Alert

Information about recent papers published in the journals covered by IDEAL can be delivered, free of charge, via e-mail. See `http://www.academicpress.com/ideal_alert`.

# SARA Scholarly Articles Research Alerting

This is a free service provided by Carfax Publishing Limited, which publishes over 200 academic peer-reviewed journals across a variety of disciplines including economics. Subscribers receive regular e-mails containing the contents pages with the journal title, volume/issue number, authors and paper titles with page numbers, of any of the journals covered that they have requested. For more information go to `http://www.carfax.co.uk`.

# Springer's LINK ALERT

This is a free service provided by the Springer publishing company. You can automatically receive (by e-mail) the table of contents and abstracts of new articles published in recent issues of journals published by Springer.

Users can also retrieve a complete article if they or the institution to which they are affiliated have a subscription to the relevant journal. Go to `http://link.springer.de/alert/`.

# NEP New Economics Papers

NEP is an announcement service that provides subscribers with free up-to-date information about new working papers that have been added to the RePEc database. There are over 30 different NEP subject groups covering areas such as Microeconomics, Econometrics, Health Economics etc. Each subject group has an editor who is responsible for papers in his or her area. Information is circulated by e-mail. If you subscribe to more than one subject group there may, of course, be some overlap in the papers included in the reports. The service was started by Thomas Krichel at the University of Surrey but is now managed by John Irons of MIT. For more information and details about how to subscribe go to one of the following:
`http://netec.mcc.ac.uk/NEP/`
`http://netec.wustl.edu/NEP/`
`http://netec.ier.hit-u.ac.jp/NEP/`

## 6.7  On-line learning and interactive tools on the web

Increasingly the World Wide Web is becoming the focus for active and interactive learning in economics, as in other subjects. It is not just that lecturers are using the web to post information about their courses, lecture notes and other course material (such as PowerPoint slides, data sets, past exam questions etc.), although this of course does mark a significant break from the previous era of printed paper handouts.

Lecturers are getting students to undertake projects in which they make full use of the resources of the web as they conduct a literature review on a topic, obtain data and other relevant information and perhaps even publish their findings on their own web pages (see section 6.8). During the process they will communicate with their lecturer and other members of the class via e-mail and class bulletin boards. Many accounts of pioneering work of this type can be found in *CHEER*, the *Journal of Economic Education* and the *Social Science Computer Review*.

What is also happening is that lecturers and others are making use of Java applets and other tools to construct web pages with interactive features to assist learning by exploration and experimentation with models. Here we highlight just a couple of the many interesting economics learning resources that can now be found on the web (look at the Teaching Materials sections of the CTI Economics, Resources for Economists and WebEc pages for links to other examples).

### oo_Micro!

http://medusa.be.udel.edu/oo_Micro!.htm

Joseph Daniel has developed a web site called oo_Micro! which provides an on-line multimedia world for teaching, learning and applying microeconomic theory. The "oo" in the title stands for "Object-Oriented"; Daniel has used object-oriented programming techniques in Java to represent economic models as graphical objects that can be drawn, manipulated and animated directly on the web page by pointing and clicking with the mouse.

The project has its origins in a HyperCard stack produced by Daniel, but in early 1996 he began work on preparing a web version using Java. There are four parts to oo_Micro!

1. *oo_MicroModels!* An electronic textbook with all the standard intermediate micro models of consumer theory, producer theory and market structures. There are over seventy Java applets that control preconstructed animated graphical models. Each model is accompanied by a brief commentary in text form, and in many cases (eventually all) by a RealAudio mini lecture.
2. *oo_MicroGraphs!* An application program that integrates a graphical calculator, drawing program, spreadsheet and basic mathematics and regression tools. It contains a large variety of pre-programmed functional forms that can be drawn or modified

on screen. Related functions can share parameters so that interrelationships can be maintained if a parameter is changed. This application can be used in the classroom as an electronic blackboard for presenting mathematically accurate graphs (Figure 6.17).

3. *oo_Micro Lessons!* A set of audio lessons that talk the student through the construction of standard intermediate micromodels (which can be used with oo_MicroGraphs!).

4. *oo_MicroExercises!* A set of exercises to give students experience in applying the models to real world policy problems and to test their understanding of these models.

oo_Micro! has many attractive features. The graphs that you see are real graphs of actual functions, not drawings. You can change the parameters, click the animate button and watch the curves move to their new equilibrium position. Having the instructions and mini lectures in audio form provides a convenient alternative to the text (although the text can still be read on screen or printed/saved for reference later). Because the audio clips operate through RealAudio a user has complete control over them; you can start, stop, rewind and replay as required. oo_Micro! is pretty well exhaustive as far as intermediate micro goes – there is a full table of contents which you can use to take you to the models you want to work with.

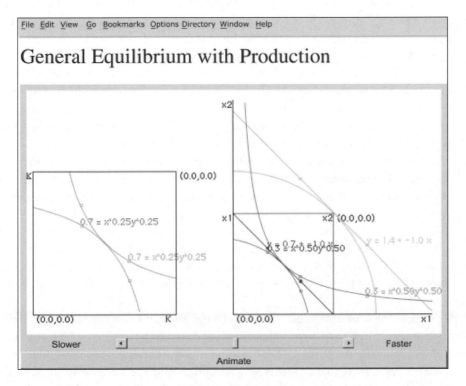

Fig. 6.17   An example of an oo_Micro! graph.

## Interactive resources for intermediate microeconomics
`http://www.pbs.port.ac.uk/~murphy/mcad/resource.mcd`

As part of the ongoing CALECO Group research program on computer-based learning at the University of Portsmouth, Barry Murphy has been investigating the use of symbolic algebra packages such as Mathcad, Mathematica and Scientific Notebook for creating interactive quantitative economics material (see Chapter 7).

For one of his courses, Intermediate Microeconomics, he has developed an extensive set of interactive material using Mathcad. One of the reasons for using Mathcad is that it was the first of the symbolic algebra packages to have the capability of working as a helper application with a browser. Consequently, provided that you have a Mathcad Reader on your computer, you can interact with the material over the web. This offers an alternative route to the HTML/ Java applets approach to the authoring of documents for the web which contain interactive mathematical and graphical elements. It is more powerful (in that it can handle symbolic algebra as well as ordinary numerical equations) and, Murphy believes, is easier to program.

The Mathcad Resource Site contains a set of approximately ninety interactive linked Mathcad worksheet files written by Barry Murphy containing lecture material and exercises for the entire course. The files covering the individual topics consist of a combination of explanatory text and separate regions containing equations and parameter settings and associated graphs. Each is quite short with an interactive exploratory experiment at its heart where the user is invited to alter the settings of one or more key parameter values (highlighted in yellow) and to observe the effect on the graph. Typically the user should respond to a message such as "Make (small, sensible) changes in the parameter highlighted above and observe the results in the diagram. Make a note of your results."

The material builds up gradually, with users first visually exploring what happens when parameter settings are changed and then learning more about the theory that underlies the models. There are hot-links to files containing associated material (underlined text indicates a hypertext link) and each section ends with a summary of the points covered and suggested further reading. Users are not required to work through the mathematical manipulations themselves (although they should attempt to understand the essential structure of each model). The Maple engine that is built into Mathcad handles that. However, students with above average mathematical ability are encouraged to try to work things through themselves by the use of messages such as "If you are feeling adventurous you can confirm your results algebraically".

Because the files are accessible via the web students can work through the material as many times as they wish, experimenting with different parameter values until they have understood the properties of each of the models and the lessons to be learned from them. The aim is that students should understand the underlying logic of the models, not just be able to reproduce sketched diagrams. Figure 6.18 shows the use

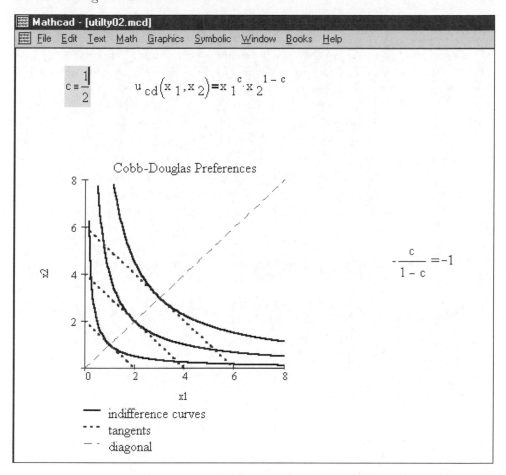

**Fig. 6.18** A screen from Barry Murphy's Mathcad resource site.

of Mathcad over the web in an example to illustrate the nature of Cobb–Douglas preferences.

Don't forget also to look at *Virtual Economy*, mentioned earlier. It has a large collection of introductory learning resources as well as a version of the HM Treasury model which can be used for simulations (`http://www.bized.ac.uk/virtual/economy`).

Finally I must mention Roger McCains' pioneering on-line principles text *Essential Principles of Economics: A Hypermedia Text*. There are more than thirty chapters covering an equal balance of macro- and microeconomics (`http://william-king.www.drexel.edu/top/prin/txt/Ecotoc.html`).

*Note*: The Economics Consortium, who produced the WinEcon software, are working on its web-based successor *WebEcon: Interactive Economics on the Web*. It will provide a complete interactive learning resource for introductory economics through Java on the web (details at `http://www.webecon.bris.ac.uk`).

## Other tools on the web

Students, and lecturers, might want to make use of some of the quantitative tools that are beginning to appear on the web which have been constructed using Java applets. For example:

Basic spreadsheet (Robert Lunn)
    `http://www.intrepid.com/~robertl/spreadsheet1.html`
Simple regression (R. Webster)
    `http://www.stat.sc.edu/~west/javahtml/Regression.html`
Linear programming (Optimization Technology Center)
    `http://www.mcs.anl.gov/home/otc/Guide/CaseStudies/`
    `simplex/`

Links to further examples will be found on this book's web site.

## Warning

Do not become so fixated with the Internet that you neglect other sources of information, both electronic (CD-ROM) and printed (books, journals, databooks etc.). Also don't forget to talk to your lecturers, your librarian and other students!

## 6.8   Building your own web page

At some point, having visited many pages on the web, you might think it would be good to create a web page of your own. Many service providers now throw in a few free megabytes of web space on their servers when you sign up with them for e-mail and other services. Or it could be that your lecturer has asked you to create a web page to present the results of a project that you have been working on, rather than asking for a word-processed document or PowerPoint presentation. Whatever the reason, being able to create a simple web page is another skill that more and more economists like to have.

Web pages come in all sizes and styles. Some make use of frames, or are part of a huge interlinked site. Some web pages are very graphics intensive – others have on-line forms to be filled in by users. Whatever your ultimate goal, when you first start working on web pages it is best to begin with a fairly simple structure. Once you understand the basics you can develop your skills just as you have done in other areas of computer use such as word processing and spreadsheeting. It may be that later on if you need to create a very elaborate web site you will be better off working with a professional web page designer rather than attempting to do it all yourself (don't forget the benefits of specialization). But even in that case it can help if you are aware of some basic concepts and principles of web page construction.

There are four stages in constructing a web site:

1. Planning and designing the web site.
2. Creating and formatting the material for your web site.
3. Testing the files.
4. Uploading the files to the server.

(Plus stage 5 – keeping it up to date!)

## Planning and designing the web site

Before you start you should think carefully about what it is you are trying to achieve. Will it be a small construction, created to convey a few key points for a presentation – perhaps with the odd graphic and a few links to other sites? Or will it be a more extensive affair with new material created by you and with a large number of cross-references both to other parts of the document and to other pages on the web? Perhaps your pages will be intended to interlink with other parts of your organization's site. If so they may need to conform in terms of style and structure the company layout.

Begin with a pencil and paper and try to sketch out what the site will look like in terms of separate pages, what is on each page and how the pages will be linked together. This is called "storyboarding". Of course, like any plan that you make at the start of a project, the actual end product may be rather different from how you initially imagined it because your ideas will develop once you have got to work. But you should at least have a plan that can be modified if necessary. Try not to make individual pages bigger than they need to be. It is better to have more pages and links between them than one large scrolling document. Remember, the people who look at your page won't be able to view it until the contents have been loaded onto their computers. So avoid having really large images that take a long time to download, especially on the first page. Keep to plain backgrounds with well-organized content and clear links so that users can easily navigate their way around. Include links at the bottom of each page to take you back to the top of the first page or to the department's home page.

> **Tip**
>
> When planning your own web site look at other sites on the web. What do you find most appealing about their design and structure? You may be able to modify the code used to create someone else's web site (see below). But don't forget the content must be your own!

**Creating and formatting the material for your web site**

There are now a variety of ways of creating web sites. For example, you can

- handcraft the material using HTML in a simple text editor
- use special web page creation software such as Front Page or Hot Metal Pro
- use the Composer component in Netscape Communicator
- use the wizards in programs like Word and PowerPoint to save your material in HTML form

If you use any of the last three approaches you will be able to format your document automatically, "marking up" sections of text using automated built-in tools. We will begin, however, by showing you how to create a simple web page with nothing more than a text editor since an appreciation of some basic elements of HTML can be valuable, even if you subsequently use another tool to construct your web pages.

# Practical 6.6   Creating a simple web page

Using either your word processor or just the Notepad text editor, type in the text shown in Figure 6.19. Save it with the name LINKS.HTM. Make sure that you save it as a pure text (ASCII) file.

Now run your browser software (e.g. Netscape Navigator or Internet Explorer) and open the file you have just saved (choose either Open File or Open Page from the File menu, depending on your browser, or press the CTRL+O keys). You should see on screen something that resembles what is shown in Figure 6.20 – if not go back and check for any typing errors. You can amend the file and reload it until it is as you require it to be (thus completing Stage 3, Testing the files).

*Note*: You always test the files off-line on your local computer. They should only be uploaded onto the server when you are sure that they are working correctly.

The text in Figure 6.19 makes use of *HTML tags*. These tags are part of the *hypertext mark-up language* or HTML and they control the display of the HTML document on your screen via your browser. These are the codes enclosed between the < > brackets. Some tags always come in pairs – for example <TITLE> and </TITLE> to signify the beginning and the end of a block of text to be interpreted in a particular way. There are certain tags that must appear in any HTML document (Figure 6.21).

Every HTML document must begin with <HTML> and end with </HTML>. In between these two tags will be the *Head* and *Body* of the document. The Head includes the *Title* of the document. As you will see if you compare Figures 6.19 and 6.20, this will be shown not on the web page itself but above the menu bar at the top of the screen. It will also be shown if you print out the page. It enables you to identify the document.

```
<HTML>
<HEAD>
<TITLE> Links to key sites for economists </TITLE>
</HEAD>
<BODY>
<H2> Economics Links </H2>
<HR>
Five key web sites for economists
<UL>
<LI> <A href="http://www.ilrt.bristol.ac.uk/ctiecon/">
CTI Economics </A>
<LI> <A href="http://sosig.ac.uk/">
SOSIG </A>
<LI> <A href="http://www.bized.ac.uk">
Biz/ed</A>
<LI> <A href="http://rfe.org/">
Resources for Economists </A>
<LI> <A href="http://netec.mcc.ac.uk WebEc.html">
WebEc</A>
</UL>
<HR>
This page authored by <A HREF="mailto:Guy.Judge@port.ac.uk">
<I>Guy Judge</I></A><BR>
Page Last Updated <B> 1st January 2000 </B>
<HR>
</BODY>
</HTML>
```

**Fig. 6.19**   The contents of the HTML file for Practical 6.6.

The body contains the content that you want to be shown on the screen. Here we begin with a *header* for the document enclosing the text Economics Links between the tags <H2> and </H2>. The header tags range from H1 to H6; the bigger the number the bigger the text size.

Next comes the horizontal rule <HR> tag. This appears on its own and is not essential but helps to break up the blocks of text on screen. When you become more experienced you can replace this simple horizontal rule with more interesting graphics images if you wish.

Then there is a bit of text: Five key web sites for economists. I have kept it short here in this illustration, but you can type as much or as little text as you wish. The text will automatically wrap around to the next line when it gets to the right hand end of the window showing with the browser. If you want to move on to the next line before you reach the end you can put in the line break tag <BR>. If you want to begin a new paragraph use <P>. Blocks of text to be shown in bold are enclosed between the tabs <B> and </B> while <I> and </I> are used if you want the text to be shown in italics. (There are examples of all these towards the end of the document.)

Many web documents include lists. Here we have an unordered list of five items so we use <UL> to signify the beginning of the list and </UL> to show the end of the list. Each list item then begins with <LI>. Ordered lists replace <UL> and </UL> with <OL> and </OL>.

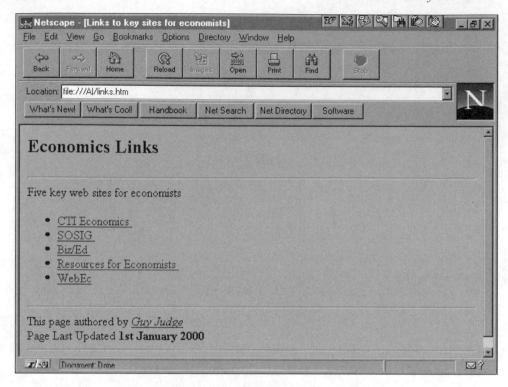

**Fig. 6.20**    What the browser shows for LINKS.HTM.

```
< H T M L >
< H E A D >
< T I T L E >  y o u r   t i t l e   g o e s   h e r e   < / T I T L E >
< / H E A D >
< B O D Y >
y o u r   c o n t e n t   g o e s   h e r e
< / B O D Y >
< / H T M L >
```

**Fig. 6.21**    A minimalist set of HTML tags.

If I had only wanted to display the names of the sites my list would have appeared as follows:

```
< U L >
< L I >  C T I   E c o n o m i c s
< L I >  S O S I G
< L I >  B i z / e d
< L I >  R e s o u r c e s   f o r   E c o n o m i s t s
< L I >  W e b E c
< / U L >
```

But I can put in hyperlinks to the web sites using the format:

```
<LI>   <A   href="URL">
name   of   web   site   </A>
```

To connect to other documents or files, whether on the same server or elsewhere on the web, you need a *hypertext reference* or *href*. The href is used to identify the address or URL of the document to go to. By including the information about the address of the web site next to the text in this way the text becomes a "hot-link". If you click on to it (provided your computer is connected to the Internet) you will be taken straight to the web site in question. Try it now with any one of the items in the list.

At the end of my list I have another horizontal rule and then some information about me as the author and the date when the document was prepared. Look at how the text is marked up and how it appears in the browser. If you were to click on the text showing my name a web e-mail box would open up (provided your browser had been configured to do this) so that you could send me an e-mail message. Even if the web mailer isn't set up you can still see what the e-mail address is by pointing your mouse at my name.

The HTML document that you have produced here is pretty simple. There are no graphics files in it, certainly no fancy backgrounds or colors, let alone frames, tables, video clips or Java applets. However, once you have understood the basics of HTML you can gradually add bells and whistles (literally if you like!) to your web pages as you build up your understanding of the features of other web pages.

One way to develop your understanding of HTML is to look at the HTML source code behind a web page. To do this you can select **V**iew and then Document **S**ource in your web browser. Do this now for the document you prepared for this practical. The code should be shown on screen just as you typed it in when you copied Figure 6.19. When you look at other web pages you can view the source code behind the document in the same way. If you want to save the source code from a web site so that you can edit it, all you need to do is to select **F**ile and Save **A**s in your browser. The text and HTML tags (but not any graphics or other files that they call upon) will then be saved in whichever folder you place them.

## Meta data tags

If you look at the source code of some web pages you may find that they include in the head part of the file a number of meta tags. For example, the WebEc pages produced by Lauri Saarinen have a whole series of lines beginning `<meta name="Keywords"` followed by a language identifier and then a list of keywords. He has one for each of seven different languages! These are included so as to maximize the chances of his page being located by a search engine when any one of these keywords, in any one of these languages, has been entered.

Web pages are often constructed from a number of files. If there is more than one HTML file in the folder, the first page – the one that should be loaded up first – is usually called INDEX.HTM or INDEX.HTML So if a URL takes you just to a folder rather than to a specific HTM or HTML file the index file will be loaded. (The extension .HTML usually means that the file was created on a UNIX server while PCs have .HTM files. You needn't worry too much about the difference.)

### Graphics

Graphics of various types are often used to enhance web pages. The graphic might have been created using a graphics package or come from a photograph, either directly from a digital camera or indirectly using a scanner. The graphics image will need to be converted to JPEG (JPG) or GIF form. Many of the graphics used in this book come from screen grabs that were first saved as bitmap files and then converted to GIF files using the graphics software LView Pro. Find out if this software is available on your system. If not, you can download it from the Internet (`http://www.lview.com`).

---

**Hint**

You can save graphics images from web pages by pointing at them and right clicking on your mouse. Follow the instructions to save the file. Don't forget that copyright applies to images as well as text. Most people won't mind you using images picked up in this way to practice your HTML skills, but before you put web pages with "borrowed" images up onto the web you should check the copyright position with the originator.

---

My web page provides some further examples of simple web documents that you can copy, edit and experiment with. The following web sites are some of the many that can help you build up your expertise:

`http://www.ilrt.bris.ac.uk/ctiecon/advice/authoring.htm`
`http://www.wesleyan.edu/its/web/html`
`http://www.southgate.ac.uk/stan/donnelly/html/`
`http://www.dtp-aus.com/firstpage/frstpage.htm`

You might also like to look at the article by Jane Leuthold in the *Journal of Economic Education*, Leuthold (1998) (available on-line at `http://www.indiana.edu/~econed/pdffiles/summer98/leuthold.pdf`).

### Uploading the files to the server

So far you have created an HTML file but it will still be on your computer and not on the World Wide Web, available for other people to view. For this to happen the

> **Tip**
>
> If you are planning to create a number of web pages, all with a similar structure, it makes sense first to create a template which has all the common features required. Save it and you can reuse and edit it each time.

HTML file (and any related files) must be saved on a server that is connected to the web. You can only do this if you have reserved space on a server and permission to transfer files to the server. (An intermediate situation that might apply is that space could be reserved on the server for you but you don't have permission to transfer the file(s) yourself. In this case you will probably be asked to put your files in a particular folder on the local network and then someone from your network team will move the files to the server for you.)

The usual way to transfer files to a server is using *File Transfer Protocol (FTP)* software. However, if you are using Netscape Composer you may be able to save your files directly onto a server, provided that you know the host name for the server (its address on the Internet) and have a user name and password to give you access to the relevant computer.

In fact FTP software can be used to transfer files between any *local system* and a *remote system* on the Internet (provided that you have permission to use the system that you are transferring to). Older methods of working with FTP involved typing in UNIX commands at the system prompt. Fortunately we now have FTP software such as WS_FTP which can exploit the point and click capabilities of the Windows environment.

Figure 6.22 illustrates the WS_FTP software that I use at Portsmouth to place files held on my local system (the C drive of the computer in my office) and the server for the Portsmouth Business School (called "thoth" for reasons best known to the Support Staff who look after the server). Before you can get to a window like this not only do you need the FTP software on your computer (or somewhere on the local network from where you can access it), but you must have a user name and a password and you must know the name of the server you want to connect to (the host name – here it is thoth.pbs.port.ac.uk). (If you have been given space on a server belonging to an Internet service provider, such as Yahoo!, they should be able to let you know the host name and how to upload files to the server. If you don't have your own FTP software there are plenty of freeware FTP packages available on the web.)

> **FTP (File Transfer Protocol)**
>
> The protocol or set of rules that enables files to be transferred from one computer on the Internet to another. It is part of the TCP/IP protocol. FTP client software is the interface that allows users to locate the files to be downloaded (or uploaded) and to initiate the process.

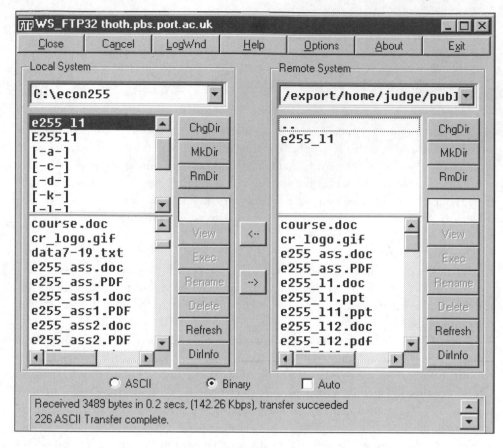

**Fig. 6.22**   Using FTP software.

As you can see, the local system files are shown in the pane on the left side of the window while the remote server files appear in the pane on the right hand side of the window. You can move between directories in a similar way to how you do it with Windows Explorer. Between the left and right panes you will see two buttons with arrows indicating which way the transfer is to take place. To transfer a file from the local system simply select it and click on the button marked --> (make sure that the correct folder where you want to place the file has been selected in the right hand pane). To transfer a file from the remote system to a local system you would work in the opposite way, clicking on the <-- button. You can select more than one file to move at a time. You can also undertake routine file maintenance on the remote system, deleting and renaming file etc.

The files that were being transferred here all relate to my course ECON255 (Introduction to Econometrics). You can see the web page that I have created with them if you go to http://www.pbs.port.ac.uk/econ/~judge/econ255/.

*Note*: Sometimes when you are connected to the web you will come across links to files that can be downloaded to your system by FTP (their address begins ftp://

rather than `http://`). You should be able to do this using the browser software itself since the FTP protocol is recognized by browsers.

*Anonymous FTP* sites are sites that have been set up for outside users to access information without the need for a user name. However, sometimes such sites require users to log-in with the name "anonymous" and their e-mail address as the password.

> ### Warning
>
> It is a good idea to have current virus-checking software on your computer before files are downloaded onto it. If you are uploading files to a server using FTP, makes sure that you have checked that they are virus-free first.

Once you have placed files on a server to set up your web page you should check them once more. You might find that for some reason some of the files were not copied across for example. Don't forget to keep them up to date. You can edit the files on your local system and then just upload the new versions to the server to overwrite the existing files. (You may note that, despite my good intentions, I don't always practice what I preach!)

## Summary

This chapter has helped you to extend your knowledge of the use of the Internet by economists, informing you about specialist directories, subject gateways and other tools for locating relevant information on the web including data sources, bibliographic databases, on-line journals and economics working papers. By working through the practicals you will have developed your skills in using these tools and in assessing the quality and relevance of what you find. You have also had the chance to see how to construct a simple web page of your own.

## Exercises and mini-projects

1. Use one of the main search engines to locate web pages with information on *one* of the following:
   (a) economic indicators
   (b) house prices
   (c) the recent economic performance of China
   (d) small business enterprises
   (e) women in the labor market
   (f) the minumum wage

(g) any other economics topic of your choice
Pick several sites from the list of hits returned to you and evaluate the information they provide.

**2.** Repeat the exercise but this time use SOSIG or the Inomics search engine.

**3.** Use one of the bibliographic databases to conduct a search for recent journal articles that relate to the topic you chose from the list in Practical 6.1.

**4.** Search for any working papers on the topic. If you can, view or download and print two or three that look interesting.

**5.** Attempt to locate relevant data to help you provide empirical evidence on the topic of your choice. If appropriate, use a spreadsheet or a statistics or econometrics package to undertake any analysis of the data that you think fit.

**6.** Prepare a brief report on your topic. Then construct a web page identifying key points with links to source material.

# CHAPTER 7

# More advanced computing skills for economists

## Objective

The objective of this chapter is to suggest to you how you can build on the skills you have already developed by:

- extending your knowledge of and facility with the tools that you already know about from earlier chapters
- indicating to you some of the computing tools used by economists that have not been covered in this book, but which could be an important part of the toolkit of economists working in particular areas of the discipline
- anticipating future developments in computing and IT and how they may affect the way that economists work

## 7.1 Introduction

If you have read the first six chapters of this book and worked through the practicals you should have a good grounding in the use of many of the computing tools now regarded as standard by economists for assisting them with the tasks that they wish to undertake. The more that you work with these tools the more skilled you will become in their use.

The role of this chapter is not to provide any more detailed descriptions of computing tools and how to use them but to indicate to you three directions that you might take from here in extending your computing skills as an economist. The first is to extend your knowledge of and facility with the tools that you have already know about. For example, in section 7.2 we look at how you can control your spreadsheet using macros and your econometrics software by writing programs with loops, conditional statements etc. The second is to indicate some of the computing tools used by economists that have not been covered in this book, but which could become part of the toolkit of economists working in particular areas of the discipline. In section 7.3 we take a brief look at matrix programming languages such as GAUSS, Ox and MATLAB which econometricians and others use to write their own computational procedures. In section 7.4 we look at scientific word processors; that is, specialist software that is designed for use in heavy mathematical applications where the basic equation editors of Word and similar packages are inadequate (and we also briefly discuss the use of TeX and LaTeX in computerized typesetting). In section 7.5 we look at a related type of software that will actually assist you with the mathematical analysis as you go – symbolic algebra software such as Mathematica and Maple.

Finally, in section 7.6 we look towards the future and consider where some current developments in computing and related technologies might be taking us.

## 7.2   More advanced use of spreadsheets and econometrics software: controlling your software with macros and procedures

### Spreadsheet macros

Suppose you regularly use your spreadsheet software to undertake similar tasks. For example, perhaps you might obtain the latest daily values for the stock prices of a small set of companies that you have been tracking. You might add these prices into a worksheet that already contains the company names and previous price observations, with the stock prices plotted against time. Now you want to get the software to replot the time series graph of the prices, extending the graphs to include the extra last observation, and to update calculations of the mean and standard deviation of the series and of correlations between them.

Essentially the procedure that you will follow each day will be the same. Add in the extra values and then redraw the graphs and recompute the statistics. It may even be that you wish to hand over this tiresome task to an assistant who neither has nor needs the advanced computing skills that you possess. What you can do is to write a *macro* – that is a program that will automate the procedure that must be followed every time. Packages like Excel incorporate a simple programming language (in Excel it is called Visual Basic) that can allow you to do this. A simple program (not unlike those that we saw in use with TSP in Chapter 5) can be written and stored, either as a separate worksheet in the same workbook or in a special workbook where you store all your macros. Then it can be invoked by selecting **T**ools and then **M**acro from the main menu, after which you would choose from the available list the macro to be executed and then click on the Run button. Alternatively you can set it up so that the macro is invoked by the selection of specified hot-key combinations (e.g. CTRL+E), or by clicking on a special item that you can add to the Toolbar menu, or even by clicking on a special custom-built toolbar that you have created for the purpose.

Rather than actually writing a program, for some fairly straightforward procedures it is possible to record the steps that you take and then the package will create the macro that will automate the procedure. All you need to do is select **T**ools **R**ecord Macro and then **R**ecord New Macro, give a name for the macro and indicate where to store the instructions. Step through the key strokes and mouse clicks that accomplish the task and then turn off the macro by clicking the Stop Macro button. It will then be ready to run. Because you can edit macros, sometimes it can be helpful to record subroutines that form part of a larger set of commands that can then be copied and pasted into your bigger programs.

For more information users of Excel can go to the Help menu and look up "macro" in the index or run the Visual Basic demos (select **H**elp and then **E**xamples and Demos).

## Programs for TSP and other econometrics software

We saw in Chapter 5 that TSP has a command language based on keywords and a simple syntax that is used to issue instructions to the computer to get it to undertake the various estimation and testing routines that it has available. Many other econometrics software packages such as RATS, EViews and SHAZAM have similar sets of commands which can either be issued interactively, one at a time, or in the form of a program to operate the software in batch mode.

You may find yourself wishing to execute a group of TSP commands (or statements as they are also called) but using a different set of data or parameter values each time. The steps to be followed may even need to be conditional on values obtained at a previous stage in the program. You can program TSP to loop back over a series of statements and to check whether specified *conditions* apply before moving to the next step.

The following example (Figure 7.1), from the TSP Version 4.4 User's Guide, p. 103, Hall and Cummins (1997), gets the computer to run a least squares regression of Y on X (including a constant intercept C). Then, if the value of the Durbin–Watson statistic is less than or equal to 1.5, it gets the computer to generate a new set of transformed series XT, YT and CT and run the regression based on the transformed series. I am not advocating this as a way of dealing with models with autoregressive residuals, merely using it to illustrate the control that TSP can give you over what is done.

```
OLSQ Y, C, X;
    IF @DW ,= 1.5; THEN; DO;
    SET RHO = 1.0-@DW/2;
    GENR YT = Y - RHO*Y(-1);
    GENR XT = X - RHO*X(-1);
    GENR CT = 1-RHO;
    OLSQ YT CT, XT;
ENDDO;
```

**Fig. 7.1**   A simple TSP program with a DO loop.

In the example shown in Figure 7.1 the DO loop is executed only once but one can also get the statements between DO and ENDDO to be executed several times according to the value of a counter variable. For example, the statement DO I=1 TO 10; would cause the computer to go back to the beginning of a block of statements and work all through them again ten times until the counter variable I reaches 10. One might, for example, link the start or end date of a sample to the value of I to get the computer to estimate a model for a moving window of observations. You can also program the computer to select different variables each time it passes through the loop (it reads the series names one by one from a list of names in a vector) or to vary the number of lags that it allows for in a model.

As you become an advanced user of this type of software you will probably find it useful to construct and save blocks of code that can be reused by copying and pasting. Or you can give a group of statements a name and store them as a *procedure* that can be called up within a longer program. A group of statements like this will begin with the keyword PROCEDURE (or PROC for short), followed by the name you want to give to the procedure, and end with ENDPROC or ENDP for short. For example, the procedure shown in Figure 7.2 (also taken from the User's Guide) computes Y as the percentage rate change of X.

```
PROC PCNTCH X, Y;
    GENR Y = 100*(X - X(-1))/(X(-1);
ENDPROC;
```

**Fig. 7.2**   A simple TSP procedure.

Then, if you want to invoke the procedure and use it to compute the percentage change of GNP and call the result GNPPCH, you could add to your program the statement:

```
PCNTCH GNP, GNPPCH;
```

TSP, like several similar econometrics software packages, also includes a set of *matrix handling* commands. In addition to commands for adding, subtracting, multiplying and inverting matrices (MADD, MSU, MMULT and INV) there are further useful commands for splitting a matrix into its constituent columns or a vector into its scalar elements (UNMAKE) and for dealing with triangular and symmetric matrices, computing eigenvalues and eigenvectors etc. With these commands users can program estimators or test procedures of their own in an efficient and compact way.

## 7.3  Other computing tools for programming in econometrics

As we have seen, programs like TSP offer users extensive sets of commands, including matrix handling commands, so that they may supplement the built-in "canned" procedures with those of their own. However, some econometricians still find the facilities offered by these packages too restrictive for their needs (especially those who are working on large, complicated or computationally intensive problems). In such cases one possibility might be to program from scratch using a standard programming language such as FORTRAN, C or C++. However, for the many economists who do not have the time or expertise to do this there is a middle way, which is to work with one of the *matrix programming systems* such as *GAUSS*, *Ox* or *MATLAB* that have been created to provide powerful yet flexible frameworks for the development of mathematical and statistical procedures.

### GAUSS

The *GAUSS Mathematical and Statistical System,* produced by Aptech Sytems, Inc. of Maple Valley, Washington, USA (http://www.aptech.com), was introduced as long ago as 1984 and it has set the standard for this class of software. It is widely used, not only by econometricians but also by scientists from many other mathematically based disciplines. It is a versatile yet powerful tool for numerical analysis and computation of all kinds. If an equation or solution can be expressed in matrix form then it can be programmed in GAUSS. In addition, the package itself contains a large number of built-in mathematical and statistical routines that can be called upon.

The GAUSS system can produce a wide range of high resolution 2D and 3D graphs, including XY plots, XYZ plots, bar charts, histograms and surface plots. You can use GAUSS interactively (in command mode) or with batch files (edit mode). The package includes a debugger to help users track down errors as they are developing their programs. Programs can be compiled and saved to disk so that they can be run under a special Run-Time Module as stand-alone applications. There are versions for DOS, Windows and UNIX operating systems – also a cut down version called GAUSS Light (for DOS and UNIX only).

You can find many web sites established by GAUSS users providing helpful introductory guides, examples and applications. There is also an active "Gaussians" mailing list (run from the University of Texas at Austin mail to `gaussians@econ.utexas.edu`) where you can find discussions of GAUSS problems. A searchable archive of earlier threads is stored at the University of Groningen in the Netherlands (`http://www.eco.rug.nl/gauss/gauss96/threads.html`).

There are also many free and commercially available GAUSS applications that have been created for use with the program by third-party developers. For example, Sam Ouliaris and Peter Phillips have written a suite of routines for the analysis of Co-Integrated systems to run under GAUSS. See also the software archive at the American University (`http://gurukul.ucc.american.edu/econ/gaussres/GAUSSIDX.HTM`).

## Ox

Ox is an object-oriented matrix programming language developed by Jurgen Doornik of the University of Oxford. As Jurgen explains in the Preface to the Ox manual, it grew out of his dissatisfaction with other matrix programming languages while he was working on some simulations required for his doctoral thesis. The syntax of Ox is rather similar to C and C++ but Doornik has developed Ox as a language that is specifically designed to deal with matrices. It has a comprehensive library of mathematical and statistical functions which may be called upon. Because Ox is object-oriented it is possible to use pre-programmed *classes* for data management, simulation etc. This approach means that there can be a considerable reduction in the programming effort once the base class has been written. (*Note*: A class is a group of variables (the data) and functions (the actions) that are packaged together.)

Ox is available in a number of forms to run under various operating systems – Windows, MS-DOS and Linux. (Linux is a free, open-source UNIX-type operating system originally developed by Linus Torvalds. Go to `http://www.linux.org/` for more information.) If you have the Windows version you can use GiveWin (which was also programmed by Doornik) as a front-end to hold databases and to receive graphical and text output. Ox is therefore particularly attractive to regular users of the PcGive family of products. OxEdit can be used when you are developing an Ox program and its use of coloring to distinguish keywords, constants and comments makes the code more readable and errors easier to find.

In the years since its introduction (1994 and then more widely in 1995) Ox has built up an enthusiastic band of users. There is a mail list by which they exchange ideas (`ox-users@mailbase.ac.uk`). A number of Ox packages have been developed (e.g. *DPD* for dynamic panel data, *Arfima* for Arfima and Arima models) and more are in the pipeline.

For further information on Ox go to Doornik's web site at `http://www.nuff.ox.ac.uk/Users/Doornik/` or visit the Timberlake Consultants Ltd web site at `http://www.timberlake.co.uk`.

Another matrix programming language that is widely used is *Matlab*, produced by The MathWorks Inc. (`http://www.mathworks.com`).

We won't attempt to give any details here, but you can find an on-line tutorial for Matlab at `http://www.math.montana.edu/~umsfjdoc/matlab.html`.

## 7.4 More advanced word processing for mathematical documents

If you need to include a lot of mathematics in your documents you may soon become frustrated by the equation editors that are available in most of the best known word-processing packages. Although the Equation Editor toolbar in Word, for example, is much easier to use than the equivalent tools in older systems which were based on the use of control keys and special formatting codes, it can still be rather fiddly. It is clearly a supplementary tool, something added on to the main system rather than a central feature for everyday repetitive use. If you are writing mainly mathematical documents it would be a big help to have a more specialized tool at your disposal. A number of such packages are now available.

### Scientific Word

Scientific Word, from TCI Software Research, Inc. (a division of Brooks/Cole Publishing Company, which in turn is part of International Thomson Publishing), is a complete word-processing system that has been designed for preparing technical documents, especially those containing considerable numbers of, possibly complicated, mathematical expressions and equations. The system provides free form editing of mathematics within the document itself and it uses correct "natural" mathematical notation. The latest version (3.0) also makes publishing with LaTeX easier (see the following text box) by providing the option of saving documents in LaTeX format and so can produce typeset-quality mathematical documents. The approach taken is what TCI refer to as *logical design* rather than the WYSIWIG – you concentrate on properly constructing the mathematical elements and you leave the software to take care of all the styling and layout decisions. Of course you can still preview the prepared document before printing.

In addition, Scientific Word has built-in web functions – so you can publish your document on the web and let anyone with Scientific Word (or Scientific WorkPlace or Scientific Notebook – see below) work with it. There are PC (Windows) and Macintosh versions of the program. For more information go to `http://www.tcisoft.com/tcisoft.html`.

### Scientific Workplace

Scientific Workplace combines the processing of text and mathematical expressions provided by Scientific Word with functions that permit you to perform numerical and symbolic computations, or to plot graphs directly in a document while you are working on it. Scientific Workplace can do this because it has embedded in it the Maple computer algebra engine (see section 7.5). As Barry Murphy says in his review of Scientific Workplace version 2.5 in *CHEER* (Murphy, 1996) "How often has one the task of separating a symbolic derivation into steps and inputting the necessary equations, even when one knows the answer? With SWP this is not a problem. It can be done as one works, virtually without any input after the initial steps." (See also Shone, 1995.)

The latest version of the software, Scientific Workplace Version 3.0, is available for both Windows PCs and Macintosh computers. With version 3.0, you can produce your document with or without LaTeX typesetting. When you need the elegant document formatting that LaTeX provides you can typeset the document using the commands on the Typeset menu. This will give hyphenation, kerning, and many other precise typesetting features. (Kerning refers to the amount of space left between characters.) With the typesetting approach the document will automatically generate footnotes, tables of contents and indexes. If such fine formatting doesn't matter and you don't need automatically generated document elements, you can just print from the File menu. The program prints your document using the page setup specifications and the same routines it uses to display the document in the program window.

## Scientific Notebook

Scientific Notebook is another package from TCI Software Research, Inc., but with slightly different features to Scientific Workplace (also it is not available for the Mac). The Style Editor for formatting typeset documents which is available in Scientific Workplace is missing, but Scientific Notebook gives direct Internet access so you can create dynamic documents and materials with hypertext links. You can also read input from graphing calculators.

### TeX and LaTeX

TeX is a powerful text-processing language which was specifically designed to typeset mathematical expressions (although it is reckoned by many to provide the best approach to computerized typesetting even for documents which contain no mathematics). The American Mathematical Society (AMS) commissioned Donald Knuth to design the language and to write a program that could be used in book and journal publishing. LaTeX is a collection of TeX macros written by Leslie Lamport to be used as a markup language. There are a number of programs that can generate LaTeX formatted documents, including, as we have seen, Scientific Word and Scientific Workplace.

*Note*: The X in TeX and LaTeX is pronounced as a k, not an x.

See Knuth (1986a,1986b) and Diller (1999), or go to `http://www.ams.org` (the American Mathematical Society web site); `http://www.cs.stir.ac.uk/ guides/latex/guide.html` (an on-line guide to document preparation with LaTeX written by members of the Department of Computing Science at the University of Stirling); `http://tug2.cs.umb.edu/` (TeX user group information).

## 7.5  Symbolic algebra software

In the previous section we mentioned that Scientific Workplace and Scientific Notebook both incorporate the Maple computer algebra engine. This means that as well as typing in mathematics expressions to display them in a document you can actually do the mathematics within the software too. If your work is likely to involve you doing a lot of mathematics it may be worthwhile learning to work with a fully functioned symbolic algebra package such as Maple or Mathematica.

Packages of this type provide a comprehensive set of tools for doing mathematics. You can do numerically based computations – so, for example, you could solve a particular set of equations with known coefficient values or search for the values of a set of choice variables that maximize a particular objective function. But as their name suggests symbolic algebra packages can also do symbolic or analytical mathematics for you. So, for example, they will be able to work out the determinant and inverse of a matrix whose elements are unspecified quantities $a_{11}$, $a_{12}$, etc., rather than specific numerical values. So you could deal with a macroeconomics model such as the one we looked at in Chapter 4, section 4.6 when working with a spreadsheet, but without the need to specify numerical values for the coefficients and exogenous variables, which could just be given symbolic values.

Symbolic algebra software will find derivatives and integrals of functions for you, factorize expressions, find roots of equations as expressions based on unspecified parameters – all kinds of analytical mathematics can be undertaken. And on top of all of this they will be able to produce clear 2D, and where appropriate 3D, graphics. You can mix text in with your maths and your graphs and copy and paste these objects into ordinary word processors (so an alternative to having Scientific Workplace could be to have Mathematica or Maple and a word processor to copy and paste into).

It is hard, in a few short lines, to convey the full potential of having available to you on your desktop such a versatile and powerful computing environment. You can use one of these packages for relatively mundane tasks, such as checking your "proofs"

```
In[1]:= Solve[{y == c + i, c == 100 + .75*y, i == 50}, {c, y}]

Out[1]= {{c → 550., y → 600.}}
```

**Fig. 7.3**  Solving numerical systems of equations with Mathematica.

In[2]:= **Solve[{Q == a + b \* P, Q == e + d \* P}, {Q, P}]**

Out[2]= $\left\{ \left\{ Q \rightarrow -\dfrac{ad - be}{b - d} ,\ P \rightarrow -\dfrac{a - e}{b - d} \right\} \right\}$

**Fig. 7.4**   Solving systems of equations analytically with Mathematica.

(it can check that the ratio of two expressions is 1 and the difference between them is 0), or you can use the package constructively, for example to solve a system of equations for you (Figures 7.3 and 7.4).

The high quality graphics that these programs possess make them an attractive environment for plotting contour plots or 3D plots. For example you could plot 3D graphs of production functions (Figure 7.5).

You can use a package like this as the environment for doing all your quantitative and analytical work, either utilizing the built-in procedures or writing your own using the package's programming language. (As with some of the other packages we have looked at, users tend to share the applications they have developed either freely or on a commercial basis.)

A number of economists now make extensive use of symbolic algebra software in their research, in their teaching and in their preparation of textbook material. Reference has already been made to Barry Murphy's Mathcad web site which contains a full set of interactive lecture notes for intermediate microeconomics. Another exceptionally good resource is the set of Mathematica and Maple files produced by Ronald Shone to go with his book *Economic Dynamics* (Shone, 1997). This shows to good effect the

In[11]:= **Plot3D[L^0.2 \* K^0.8, {L, 0, 500}, {K, 0, 500}]**

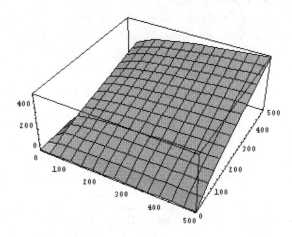

Out[11]= - SurfaceGraphics -

**Fig. 7.5**   3D plot produced by Mathematica.

graph plotting capabilities of these packages (`http://www.cup.cam.ac.uk/ Scripts/webbook.asp?isbn=0521474469`).

Belsley (1999) – available at `http://136.167.24.33/ec-p/wp364.pdf` – makes a case for *all* students of economics being taught to work with a symbolic algebra package from an early stage. In fact he recommends that you "pick one [symbolic algebra package], learn it early and well, and use it often and productively".

Belsley is a devotee of Mathematica, but the argument is similar even if you happen to prefer one of the other packages (perhaps your department has a site license for it, for example). Whilst he recognizes that Mathematica has a long learning curve – one has to work with it for some time to become a proficient user with an appreciation of the full power of its programming language (although even the novice can exploit some of the program's features right away) – he believes that in the long run it really pays off. Because "Mathematica is integrated, full-featured, powerful, versatile, extensible and effective" it allows the user "within a single environment, to do almost everything".

## Mathematica

The latest version is *Mathematica 4*. There is also a special *Mathematica for Students* program. The program runs on a variety of platforms (Windows 95/98/NT, Mac, UNIX, Linux etc.). Mathematica is available from the developers, Wolfram Research Inc. (`http://www.wolfram.com/`) or in the UK from Timberlake Consultants Ltd (`http://www.timberlake.co.uk`).

## Maple

The latest version is *Maple V Release 5.1*. There is also a special student edition. Maple provides a complete mathematical environment for accurate numerical computation, the manipulation of algebraic expressions and equations and stunning 2D and 3D graphics. It has its own programming language and is available for many platforms. Maple V is available from the developers Maplesoft of Ontario, Canada (`http://www.maplesoft.com`) or in the UK from Timberlake Consultants Ltd (`http://www.timberlake.co.uk`).

Like the latest version of Mathematica, Maple is now much more web-oriented, allowing users to jump straight to web sites by clicking on hot-links in a document. This is the way that all these packages are going.

## Mathcad

Several versions of Mathcad are currently available including: *Mathcad 2000 Professional*, *Mathcad 8 Professional Academic Edition* (for Windows), and *Mathcad 6 Plus* (for Macintosh). Visit the developer's site for details and comparisons of the features of the different versions (`http://www.mathsoft.com/`). A nice feature that has already been mentioned is the fact that you can use Mathcad with your browser to interact with Mathcad files anywhere on the Internet. There is also a Mathcad mailing list with searchable archives at the Adeptscience web site (`http://lists.adeptscience.co.uk/listindex/mathcad/`).

## Macsyma

*Macsyma 2.4* (for Windows) and *Macsyma 422* (for UNIX and Linux) both use the same mathematics engine. Some nice features include: the use of color coding to denote matching parentheses, brackets and braces; the ability to query coordinates in 2D and 3D graphics with a mouse; many executable demos and examples; and the export of notebooks as TeX, LaTeX or HTML documents. It has been developed by Macsyma Inc., who have a web site at `http://www.macsyma.com/`.

## Others

Another useful but slightly less extensive (and expensive!) package from this group that many people like to work with is *DERIVE*. Go to `http://www.chartwellyorke.com/` for information. A little known program that can be very useful for working with numerical simultaneous equation systems, whether linear or nonlinear, is *TK Solver* – see the review by Shone (1999).

## 7.6 Getting ready for the future

In this book I have tried to give an introduction to the computing and information technology tools that presently exist together with the services that are based around them, and to suggest ways in which economists can use these tools and services to undertake the everyday tasks that face them as they do their work. Because this is an introductory book some areas have only been touched upon, and I am conscious that there are others that I have left out completely because they require more knowledge of economics or econometrics than an introductory reader is likely to possess (e.g. software for exploring game theory applications and tools for computable general equilibrium models or for dealing with panel data in econometrics).

To close the book, especially because it comes out at the beginning of the new millennium, I think it is appropriate to speculate a little bit about the future. What further changes will technology bring and how will we adapt to them?

As the saying goes, "forecasting is hazardous, particularly in relation to the future". What we get tends to be a mixture of a gradual evolution of current developments coupled with some completely ground-breaking changes that are triggered by new breakthroughs and insights. The reason that forecasting is so difficult is that it is comparatively easy to extend existing patterns but virtually impossible to predict major innovations. But we have to do the best that we can.

In the future the Internet will be even more central to the way that we work than it is now. The network itself will be expanded and improved with enlarged bandwidth. This will allow faster transmission of information across the system and provide more reliable connections. More people will have access to the Internet; the convergence of technologies will lead to better mobile phones and televisions that can connect to the Internet. As the general population makes greater use of the Internet for commercial transactions and for entertainment purposes, the medium will become less of a novelty and will become completely absorbed into our everyday lives. The hardware and software will be designed so that it requires less specialist expertise to use.

Facilities that we have on the Internet will change their character too. For example, I can imagine that e-mail and telephone calls could both move on from their current simple text and audio transmissions to full sound and vision connections (absorbing video conferencing technology). Then there could be opportunities for both live calls, where both (or all) participants are connected at the same time, and recorded calls, where a message is left for someone who is not currently on-line. This may seem a long way off, but trials of video e-mail systems are already underway.

For those of us in education, improvements in the Internet could have revolutionary consequences. With fast and reliable Internet links lectures (both live and pre-recorded) can come from anywhere in the world. Although personal contact with a tutor and other students at a local level will still be valuable, it may not be necessary to maintain such large faculties when one can draw on the expertise of major figures from around the globe. Pre-recorded material can become interactive and more personalized – on-line quizzes linked to expert systems could ensure that the way in which course material is presented to a user is tailored to his or her own existing knowledge and ways of working.

At a slightly less revolutionary level I think we can anticipate an increasing tendency for software to be accessed on the Internet, rather than from your desktop PC. Just as we have seen the move of software packages from individual hard disks to local servers, once we can be sure of fast and reliable Internet connections it will make sense to keep the software programs on big powerful servers somewhere on the Internet and for users to connect up to them from their remote locations. This will mean that they will always be accessing the latest version of the package and it won't matter what local machine they have – one of the effects of the Internet has been to lessen problems of platform dependency. Already this is possible. Users of the MIMAS service at Manchester can log-in and run many of the main econometrics programs there without the need to have them on their own desktop PCs. At present the service is only suitable for experienced and confident users of computers but over the years complications, such as the need for pre-registration and some familiarity with UNIX, will be removed. We may reach a point where a user is not even aware of where on the Internet the program is running. This process will be assisted if more software developers separate the front-end user interface of their programs from the kernel or engine that does all the work. Already it is possible to work with Mathematica with the kernel on a remote computer and the front end on your local machine. Jurgen Doornik's initiative in separating the front-end part of PcGive (GiveWin) so that it can be used with a number of modules and even programs produced by other software developers also gives a hint of how things might go.

Related to this are moves by some of the big players in the IT and computing industry. Sun Microsystems has a strategy to move us away from the "fat client model" (where you have the software installed on your local machine or network) and towards the "thin client model" (where you access programs from their servers). They offer an alternative to the Microsoft Office Suite of products with their own Star Office Suite, which has a number of components covering all the usual main applications packages (word processing, spreadsheet, database, presentation, graphing, drawing and project planning). For more information go to `http://webevents.broadcast.com/sunmicrosystems/sun0899/`.

Yahoo too has plans to get us to use software on their servers rather than on our own local computers. Already they and many other Internet service providers offer e-mail and project planning services this way. In an interview in *The Guardian* (Online section) on 30 September 1999 the Yahoo CEO Tim Koogle said that he expected other services such as word processing to follow.

Another aspect of these changes will be the increasing tendency for users to personalize the look of their own computer desktop. Windows already allows you to do quite a bit of that, with your own wallpaper, screensavers and arrangement of icons. Yahoo too allows you to select services that are of interest to you and so personalize the screen that you see when you go to their web site. The greater use of "meta data" will be another key to personalizing Internet services. Using cookies and other devices, your own preferences can be stored on your local computer so that when you call up a site on the web you get a version of the service that is specially tailored to your requirements. This could happen with professional economics and econometrics software as it is accessed over the Internet too, so you personalize not only the look of your desktop but also the version of the software or services that you receive. Again this is already happening with data and current awareness services, on-line journal subscriptions etc.

Related developments include the move towards object-oriented programming and reusable chunks of code. On the Internet there are libraries of routines for well-known software packages and Java applets that can be incorporated into your own applications. So whilst on the one hand we have the availability of complete computing environments such as Mathematica and Maple for economists to use, it will also be possible for economists to put together their own tools by combining components from a variety of sources. In fact these need not be contradictory tendencies since Mathematica and the other symbolic algebra packages will have open links via the web to other programs and utilities.

One feature that I think is likely to play a bigger part in the use of computers by economists is an increasing role for computer visualization. Today econometrics software makes much greater, and better, use of graphics than it did ten years ago. One can view regression estimates (and even standard errors) from moving windows of data to help assess their stability across samples, or look at histograms of residuals, cumulative plots against theoretical distributions, spectral densities, etc. One can identify the coordinates for particular places of interest on a graph by pointing the mouse at them. We look at variable response surfaces and dynamic impulse response functions graphically and thereby gain a much better appreciation of what is going on.

With cross-section data too visualization based on computer graphics can reveal patterns in the data, particularly those based on finely defined categories. For example, pockets of high unemployment in particular geographical localities can be revealed through the use of graphics software linked to large databases showing the intensity of unemployment by postcode district through the use of different color or shades to represent different levels of unemployment. This can reveal clusters in small local communities that are much harder to find when working from tables of numbers or summary statistics.

One thing that we haven't mentioned yet that should be of particular interest to economists is the way that we are charged for Internet-based services. A big bone of contention in the UK is the fact that, unlike our US counterparts, we typically don't get Internet access at *free* local telephone rates. This means that some services will be slower to take off than in America. In universities, of course, we have direct access via JANET, based on a subscription charge, although for some services there may be more direct pay as you use charges. Many commercial sites recover their costs through advertising banners, that way keeping the service free to users. As economists we should be interested in the effect of different charging policies, the way that scarce resources are allocated and signals are given to encourage the development of new products and services. Hal Varian is one of the economists who has taken an interest in these matters and if it also interests you, locate his home page and take a look at some of the papers he has written about it.

Another key development is voice-recognition by computers. Already you can get software to enable you to dictate your document to the computer (provided that you also have the necessary hardware). The computer is trained to recognize a user's voice and the words that he or she uses frequently. There are still problems in applying this approach to documents involving equations and quantitative material, but no doubt a solution will be found and computers will break through another barrier in user-friendliness.

Whatever the future brings it is important that you keep your computing (and other) skills up to date. (That should be easier as you will be able to sign up for on-line courses on the latest developments both in the subject and in the tools we use rather than have to take time out for a top-up course.) You need to be flexible – able to transfer ideas from one setting to another and see how they fit in. Don't just train yourself in the use of a particular package but try to understand the concepts and methods that it uses. Then the transition to a new version of the software, or even a different package of the same type, can be as smooth as possible.

# Summary

This chapter has indicated to you three directions in which you could go to extend your computing skills as an economist: develop further expertise with the software tools covered in this book, find out how to use other software tools used by economists in their work and keep up to date with new developments.

Don't forget to visit the book's web site for news, information and ideas about how to develop your computing skills as an economist.

# Exercises and mini-projects

1. Review what you have learned from working with this book. What, if anything, did you want to find out about that was not covered in this book? E-mail your review to me.

2. Produce a brief critique of the computing set-up at your own university or college, or the way that the department uses computing and Internet facilities in its teaching. What could be done to improve your access to software, data and other services? If you think that your report contains some important points that your institution needs to address, ask your lecturer or computer manager if he/she would like to see it.

# References and further reading

Bacon, L.M. (1997) *Getting Started with PowerPoint 7.0 for Windows 95*. John Wiley & Sons, New York.

Baghestani, H. (1991) Cointegration analysis of the advertising–sales relationship. *Journal of Industrial Economics*, **XXXIX**, 671–681.

Begg, D.K.H., Fisher, S. and Dornbusch, R. (1994) *Economics*. Fourth Edition. McGraw-Hill, Maidenhead, UK.

Beharrell, A., Church, K., Paine, J. and Stark, G. (1999) The Virtual Economy. *Computers in Higher Education Economics Review*, **13**(1), 32–34.

Belsley, D.A. (1999) Mathematica as an environment for doing economics and econometrics. *Computational Economics*, **14**(1–2), 69–87.

Blake, D. (1990) *Financial Market Analysis*. McGraw-Hill, Maidenhead, UK.

Booth, A.L. and Burton, J. (1999) *The Position of Women in UK Academic Economics*. Working Paper 99-17. Institute for Social and Economic Research, University of Essex.

Bush, V. (1945) As we may think. *Atlantic Monthly*, **176**, 101–108.

Cameron, S. and Collins, A. (1998) Cigarette consumption in Turkey: Tansel's spurious regression. *Applied Economics Letters*, **5**, 351–353.

Cobb, C. and Douglas, P.H. (1928) A theory of production. *American Economic Review*, **18**(Suppl), 139–165.

Davidson, J., Hendry, D.F., Srba, F. and Yeo, S. (1978) Econometric modelling of the time series relationship between consumers' expenditure and income in the United Kingdom. *The Economic Journal*, **88**, 661–692.

Dickey, D.A. and Fuller, W.A. (1979) Distributions of the estimators for autoregressive time series with a unit root. *Journal of the American Statistical Association*, **74**, 427–431.

Diller, A. (1999) *LATEX Line by Line*. Second Edition. John Wiley & Sons, Chichester.

Doornik, J.A. (1996) *Object-oriented Matrix Programming Using Ox*. International Thomson Business Press, London.

Enders, W. (1996) *RATS Handbook for Econometric Time Series*. John Wiley & Sons, New York.

Engle, R.F. and Granger, C.W.J. (1987) Cointegration and error correction: representation, estimation and testing. *Econometrica*, **55**, 251–276.

Gerrard, W.J. and Godfrey, L. (1998) Diagnostic checks for single-equation error-correction and autoregressive distributed lag models. *The Manchester School*, **66**, 222–237.

Goffe, W.L. and Parks, R.P. (1997) The future information infrastructure in economics. *Journal of Economic Perspectives*, **11**, 75–94.

Granger, C.W.J. (1981) Some properties of time series data and their use in econometric model specification. *Journal of Econometrics*, **28**, 121–130.

Granger, C.W.J. (1986) Developments in the study of cointegrated economic variables. *Oxford Bulletin of Economics and Statistics*, **48**, 213–228.

Granger, C.W.J. and Newbold, P. (1974) Spurious regressions in economics. *Journal of Econometrics*, **35**, 143–159.

Gujarati, D.N. (1995) *Basic Econometrics*. Third Edition. McGraw-Hill, New York.

Hall, B.H. and Cummins, C. (1997) *Time Series Processor Version 4.4 Guide*. TSP International, Palo Alto, CA.

Harris, R.I.D. (1995) *Using Cointegration Analysis in Econometric Modelling*. Prentice Hall/ Harvester-Wheatsheaf, Hemel Hempstead, UK.

Hendry, D.F. (1995) *Dynamic Econometrics*. Oxford University Press, Oxford.

Hendry, D.F. and Doornik, J.A. (1996) *Empirical Econometric Modelling Using PcGive 9.0 for Windows*. International Thomson Business Press, London.

Judge, G. (1990) *Quantitative Analysis for Economics and Business: Using Lotus 1-2-3*. Harvester-Wheatsheaf, Hemel Hempstead.

Judge, G. (1991) Hypertext: A potential teaching tool for economics. *Computer Applications in Business and the Social Sciences*, **2**, 33–55.

Knuth, D. (1986a) *The TEXbook*. Addison-Wesley, Wokingham, UK.

Knuth, D. (1986b) *TEX: The Program*. Addison-Wesley, Wokingham, UK.

Koop, G. (2000) *Analysis of Economic Data*. John Wiley & Sons, Chichester.

Krichel, T. (1997) About NetEc, with special reference to WoPEc. *Computers in Higher Education Economics Review*, **11**(1), 19–24.

Kronstadt, B. (1997) *Getting Started with Microsoft Excel 7.0 for Windows 95*. John Wiley & Sons, New York.

Leuthold, J.H. (1998) Building a home page for your economics class. *Journal of Economic Education*, Summer, Vol. 29, No. 30, 247–261.

Lianos, T. and Katranidis, S. (1993) Modelling the beef market of the Greek economy. *European Review of Agricultural Economics*, **20**, 49–63.

Lipsey, R.G. and Crystal, K.A. (1995) *An Introduction to Positive Economics*. Eighth Edition. Oxford University Press, Oxford.

McAleese, R. (1989) *Hypertext: Theory into Practice*. Blackwell Scientific Publications, Oxford.

McCloskey, D. (1985) Economical writing. *Economic Inquiry* **XXIII** (no 2, April), 187–222.

McKnight, L.W. and Bailey, J.P. (eds) (1998) *Internet Economics*. MIT Press, Cambridge, MA.

Murphy, B. (1996) Scientific Workplace 2.5: a review. *Computers in Higher Economics Review*, **10**(2), 24–27.

Nelson, T. (1981) *Literary Machines*. San Antonio, Texas.

Nelson, T. (1990) On the Xanadu Project. *Byte*, September, 298–299.

Parkin, M., Powell, M. and Matthews, K. (1997) *Economics*. Third Edition. Addison Wesley Longman Higher Education, Wokingham, UK.

Russakoff, S. (1997) *Getting Started with Microsoft Word 7.0 for Windows 95.* John Wiley & Sons, New York.

Russakoff, S. and Bacon, L.M. (1997) *Getting Started with Windows 95.* John Wiley & Sons, New York.

Shaw, C. (1998) IBSS Online: a specialist bibliography for social scientists. *Computers in Higher Education Economics Review*, **12**(2), 28–29.

Shone, R. (1995) Scientific Word and Scientific Workplace. *The Economic Journal*, **105**, 1688–1693.

Shone, R. (1997) *Economic Dynamics. Phase Diagrams and their Economic Application.* Cambridge University Press, Cambridge.

Shone, R. (1999) TK Solver. *The Economic Journal*, **109**, F202–F210.

Sloman, J. (1998) *Economics.* Third Edition. Prentice Hall Europe, Hemel Hempstead, UK.

Soper, J. (1999) *Mathematics for Economics and Business.* Blackwell Publishers, Oxford.

Stavrinos, V. (1987) The effects of an anti-smoking campaign on cigarette consumption: empirical evidence from Greece. *Applied Economics*, **19**, 323–329.

Stein, S. (1999) *Learning, Teaching and Researching on the Internet: A Practical Guide for Social Scientists.* Addison Wesley Longman, Harlow, UK.

Stock, J.H. (1987) Asymptotic properties of least squares estimators of cointegrating vectors. *Econometrica*, **55**, 1035–1056.

Summers, A. and Heston, R. (1991) The Penn World Table (Mark 5): An Expanded Set of International Comparisons, 1958–1988. *Quarterly Journal of Economics*, May, 327–368.

Tansel, A. (1993) Cigarette demand, health scares and education in Turkey. *Applied Economics*, **25**, 521–529.

Thomas, R.L. (1989) *Using Mathematics in Economics.* Longman, London.

Whigham, D. (1998) *Quantitative Business Methods Using Excel.* Oxford University Press, Oxford.

Whitmarsh, D. (1991) A spreadsheet model of renewable resource exploitation. *Computers in Higher Education Economics Review*, **13**, 23–30.

Wickens, M. and Breusch, T. (1988) Dynamic specification, the long-run and the estimation of transformed regression models. *The Economic Journal*, **98**, 189–205.

Zanias, G. (1994) The long-run, causality, and forecasting in the advertising–sales relationship. *Journal of Forecasting*, **13**, 601–610.

# Index